Privileges and Immunities

Recent Titles in Reference Guides to the United States Constitution
Jack Stark, Series Editor

The Right to the Assistance of Counsel
James J. Tomkovicz

Prohibited Government Acts
Jack Stark

State Sovereign Immunity
Melvyn R. Durchslag

Constitutional Remedies
Michael L. Wells and Thomas A. Eaton

Privileges and Immunities

A Reference Guide to the United States Constitution

David Skillen Bogen

Foreword by Chief Judge Robert M. Bell

REFERENCE GUIDES TO THE
UNITED STATES CONSTITUTION, NUMBER 5
Jack Stark, *Series Editor*

PRAEGER

Westport, Connecticut
London

Library of Congress Cataloging-in-Publication Data

Bogen, David S., 1941-
Privileges and immunities : a reference guide to the United States Constitution / David Skillen Bogen ; foreword by Robert M. Bell.
p. cm.—(Reference guides to the United States Constitution, ISSN 1539-8986; no. 5)
Includes bibliographical references and index.
ISBN 0-313-31347-4 (alk. paper)
1. Privileges and immunities—United States—States. I. Title. II. Series
KF4605 .B64 2003
342.73'085—dc21 2002030734

British Library Cataloguing in Publication Data is available.

Library of Congress Catalog Card Number: 2002030734
ISBN: 0-313-31347-4
ISSN: 1539-8986

First published in 2003

Praeger Publishers, 88 Post Road West, Westport, CT 06881
An imprint of Greenwood Publishing Group, Inc.
www.praeger.com

Printed in the United States of America

The paper used in this book complies with the Permanent Paper Standard issued by the National Information Standards Organization (Z39.48–1984)

10 9 8 7 6 5 4 3 2 1

Contents

Series Foreword *by Jack Stark* ix

Foreword *by Chief Judge Robert M. Bell* xiii

Acknowledgments xv

Introduction xvii

Part I A History of Privileges and Immunities of Citizenship from Colonization to the Fourteenth Amendment **1**

The English Heritage: Subjects of the King 1

Charter Guarantees 1

The Evolution of a Phrase: From the Colonies to Independence 4

The Evolution of Privileges and Immunities in England 6

The Rhetoric of Revolution: Principles of the English Constitution and Natural Law 9

The Articles of Confederation: Article IV—Replacing the King 11

The Privileges and Immunities of Free Citizens 12

Free Ingress and Regress to Other States 14

The Privileges of Trade and Commerce and the Regulation of Property Proviso 14

Effect of the Article 16

The Constitution: Article IV, Section 2—Citizens in the Several States 16
Adoption and Ratification 17
Privileges and Immunities of Citizens in America Before the Civil War 21
U.S. Constitution: Amendment XIV—Citizens of the United States 36
The Thirteenth Amendment and the Civil Rights Act of 1866 38
The Fourteenth Amendment 44
Post-Enactment Congressional Debate on the Meaning of the Clause 53
Notes 58

Part II Analysis of the Protection of Privileges and Immunities 67
Article IV: Privileges and Immunities 67
Paul v. Virginia: Privileges No Greater Than a State Decides to Give Its Own Citizens 68
Community Membership: Privileges and Immunities Do Not Include Politics or Public Funding 74
Justifications: Equalization, Procedural Distinctions, and Lack of Forum Connection 86
Right to Travel 99
Amendment XIV: Privileges or Immunities 100
The *Slaughter-House Cases*: The Rejection of Fundamental Rights 101
The Rejection of Incorporation and the Move to the Due Process Clause 107
Federal Privileges and Immunities 123
The Future of Privileges and Immunities 138
Notes 142

Part III Conclusion 147

Bibliographic Essay 149

Primary Source Materials 149
Secondary Source Material 150
Article IV History 150
Fourteenth Amendment History 151
Controversy Over the *Slaughter-House Cases* and Incorporation 154
Article IV Analysis 155
Fourteenth Amendment Analysis 156

Table of Cases **159**

Index **163**

Series Foreword

JACK STARK

One can conceive of the United States Constitution in many ways. For example, noting the reverence in which it has been held, one can think of it as equivalent to a sacred text. Unfortunately, most of its devotees have had less knowledge and even less understanding of the document than they have had reverence for it. Sometimes it is treated as primarily a political document and on that basis has been subjected to analysis, such as Charles Beard's *An Economic Interpretation of the Constitution of the United States*. One can plausibly argue that the Constitution seems most astounding when seen in light of the intellectual effort that has been associated with it. Three brief but highly intense bursts of intellectual energy produced, and established as organic law, most of the Constitution as it now exists. Two of those efforts, sustained over a long period of time, have enabled us to better understand the document.

The first burst of energy occurred at the Constitutional Convention. Although some of the delegates' business, such as the struggle between populous and nonpopulous states about their representation in Congress, was political, much of it was about fundamental issues of political theory. A few of the delegates had or later achieved international eminence for their intellects. Among them were Benjamin Franklin, Alexander Hamilton, and James Madison. Others, although less well known, had first-rate minds. That group includes George Mason and George Wythe. Many of the delegates contributed intelligently. Although the Convention's records are less than satisfactory, they indicate clearly enough that the delegates worked mightily to constitute not merely a polity but a rational polity—one that would rise to the standards envisioned by the delegates' intellectual ancestors. Their product, though brief, is amazing. William Gladstone called it "the most wonderful work ever struck off."

Despite the delegates' eminence and the Constitution's excellence as seen from our place in history, its ratification was far from certain. That state of affairs necessitated the second burst of intellectual energy associated with that document: the debate over ratification. Soon after the convention adjourned, articles and speeches—some supporting the Constitution and some attacking it—began to proliferate. A national debate commenced—not only about the document itself but also about the nature of the polity that ought to exist in this country. Both sides included many writers and speakers who were verbally adroit and steeped in the relevant political and philosophical literature. The result was an accumulation of material that is remarkable for both its quantity and its quality. At its apex is the *Federalist Papers*, a production of Alexander Hamilton, James Madison, and John Jay that deserves a place among the great books of Western culture.

Another burst, although not as impressive as the first two but highly respectable, occurred when the Bill of Rights was proposed. Some delegates to the Constitutional Convention had vigorously asserted that such guarantees should be included in the original document. George Mason, the principal drafter of the Virginia Declaration of Rights, so held, and he walked out of the convention when he failed to achieve his purpose. Even those who had argued that the rights in question were implicit recognized the value of adding protection of them to the Constitution. The debate was thus focused on the rights that were to be explicitly granted, not on whether any rights ought to be explicitly granted. Again many writers and speakers entered the fray, and again the debate was solidly grounded in theory and was conducted on a high intellectual level.

Thus, within a few years a statement of organic law and a vital coda to it had been produced. However, the meaning and effect of many of that document's provisions were far from certain; the debates on ratification of the Constitution and the Bill of Rights had demonstrated that. In addition, the document existed in a vacuum, because statutes and actions had not been assessed by its standards. The attempt to resolve these problems began after Chief Justice John Marshall, in Marbury v. Madison, asserted the right of the U.S. Supreme Court to interpret and apply the Constitution. Judicial interpretation and application of the Constitution, beginning with the first constitutional case and persisting until the most recent, is one of the sustained exertions of intellectual energy associated with the Constitution. The framers would be surprised by some of the results of these activities. References in the document to "due process," which seems to refer only to procedures, have been held also to have a substantive dimension. A right to privacy has been found lurking among the penumbras of various parts of the text. A requirement that states grant the same "privileges and immunities" to citizens of other states that they granted to their own citizens, which seemed to guarantee important rights, was not held to be particularly important. The corpus of judicial interpretations of the Constitution is now as voluminous as that document is terse.

As judicial interpretations multiplied, another layer—interpretations of interpretations—appeared, and also multiplied. This layer, the other sustained intellectual effort associated with the Constitution, consists of articles, most of them published in law reviews, and books on the Constitution. This material varies in quality and significance. Some of these works of scholarship result from meticulous examination and incisive thought. Others repeat earlier work, or apply a fine-tooth comb to matters that are too minute even for such a comb. Somewhere in that welter of tertiary material is the answer to almost every question that one could ask about constitutional law. The problem is finding the answer that one wants. The difficulty of locating useful guidance is exacerbated by the bifurcation of most constitutional scholarship into two kinds. In "Two Styles of Social Science Research," C. Wright Mills delineates macroscopic and molecular research. The former deals with huge issues, the latter with tiny issues. Virtually all of the scholarship on the Constitution is of one of those two types. Little of it is macroscopic, but that category does include some first-rate syntheses such as Jack Rakove's *Original Meanings*. Most constitutional scholarship is molecular and, again, some fine work is included in that category.

In his essay, Mills bemoans the inability of social scientists to combine the two kinds of research that he describes to create a third category that will be more generally useful. This series of books is an attempt to do for constitutional law the intellectual work that Mills proposed for social science. The author of each book has dealt carefully and at reasonable length with a topic that lies in the middle range of generality. Upon completion, this series will consist of thirty-seven books, each on a constitutional law topic. Some of the books, such as the book on freedom of the press, explicate one portion of the Constitution's text. Others, such as the volume on federalism, treat a topic that has several anchors in the Constitution. The books, on constitutional history and constitutional interpretation range over the entire document, but each does so from a single perspective. Except for a very few of the books the special circumstances of which dictate minor changes in format, each book includes the same components—a brief history of the topic, a lengthy and sophisticated analysis of the current state of the law on that topic, a bibliographical essay that organizes and evaluates scholarly material in order to facilitate further research, a table of cases, and an index. The books are intellectually rigorous—in fact, authorities have written them—but, due to their clarity and to brief definitions of terms that are unfamiliar to laypersons, each is comprehensible and useful to a wide audience, one that ranges from other experts on the book's subject to intelligent non-lawyers.

In short, this series provides an extremely valuable service to the legal community and to others who are interested in constitutional law, as every citizen should be. Each book is a map of part of the U.S. Constitution. When this series is complete, each book will be a third kind of scholarly work that combines the macroscopic and the molecular. Together they will explicate all of the important constitutional topics. Anyone who wants assistance in understanding either a topic in constitutional law or the Constitution as a whole can easily find it in these books.

Foreword

CHIEF JUDGE ROBERT M. BELL

What is citizenship? More particularly, what does it mean to be a citizen of the United States? Or of one of the states? These are pertinent questions at any time, but they take on particular significance during times of national stress, when people may be attacked simply because they are not citizens, or when individuals with certain physical characteristics, citizens or not, are seized and held without the benefit of constitutional protections.

Citizenship is a key element in the United States Constitution. Under Article I, citizenship, albeit not by birth, is a prerequisite for election to Congress. Article II also requires the President to be a citizen. By excluding all persons "except a natural born Citizen, or a Citizen of the United States, at the time of the Adoption of this Constitution," it expressly recognizes that there may be distinctions drawn even among citizens. Although Article III, which grants federal judicial power, does not mention citizenship as a qualification for appointment, it refers to state citizenship several times and in several contexts. The Fourteenth Amendment to the Constitution provides, "[a]ll persons born or naturalized in the United States, and subject to the jurisdiction thereof, are citizens of the United States and of the State wherein they reside." This language takes account of, and remedies, the decision of the United States Supreme Court in Dred Scott v. Sandford, 60 U.S. (19 How.) 393, 15 L.Ed. 691 (1856), in which the Court held that African-Americans were not citizens and, in fact, "that they had no rights which the white man was bound to respect."

Two constitutional provisions, one an amendment to the document, speak of the "privileges and immunities" of citizenship. Article IV provides that "the Citizens of each State shall be entitled to the Privileges and Immunities of Citizens in the several States." Although it refers to the "privileges and immunities" of citizens in terms of a state or of the several states, read in context, this clause actually and effectively conferred on each citizen a form of national citizenship: it prohibits a citizen of one state from being treated as an alien in another state of the Union. This became, and remains, one of the cornerstones of our national identity. To be sure, Patrick Henry was a Virginian and could refer to himself as such wherever he might be; however, he was also an American, whether in Virginia or Massachusetts or any of the other several states. But if we were all to be bound together by our common citizenship, there was still a great wound to be healed. A nation riven by slavery was seriously flawed, and needed mending. The Fourteenth Amendment responded to the evils of slavery and racism by providing that "[a]ll persons born or naturalized in the United States, and subject to the jurisdiction thereof" are included in the definition of citizens of the United States. It also mandated that "no state shall abridge the privileges or immunities of citizens of the United States." The Fourteenth Amendment, on its face, thus promised substantive guarantees that would protect all citizens from abuses by the states.

The promise of the Fourteenth Amendment's privileges or immunities clause has never been fulfilled. While its equal protection and due process clauses have become the source for substantive guarantees, the Supreme Court has said that the privileges or immunities of citizens of the United States are rights that have their source in the treaties and laws of the United States and in the other clauses of the Constitution. No new rights, the Court has indicated, were added by the privileges or immunities clause of the Fourteenth Amendment.

In this book, Professor Bogen reviews the history of the two privileges and immunities clauses and explores their current interpretation—what they mean today and how they came to have that meaning. This is, for Professor Bogen, no mere academic exercise, it is an exploration of the very essence of our constitutional government. It is in an earnest effort objectively to understand how it is that a promise so clearly made has never been fulfilled or, more important, fully acknowledged. He proposes no revolution in constitutional law, only changes that could clarify some of the murkiness and restore meaning to our most basic heritage.

I commend this book to your reading. If we are to understand, or even consider more deeply, what it means to be a citizen of the United States, I know of no better resource for the task.

Acknowledgments

To all my friends, colleagues, and student assistants, most recently Brian Kobil of the University of Maryland School of Law and Ruth Burns of the University of Denver College of Law, who have helped me with this book and the articles that preceded it. To T. Carroll Brown for his unwavering support of scholarship and education at the University of Maryland School of Law. To Dean Karen Rothenberg of the University of Maryland School of Law who supported the writing of this book with summer grants and a sabbatical from the University of Maryland Law School. To Bryan Fitzgerald and the Southern Cross University Faculty of Law, Kathleen McEvoy, Linda Kirk and the University of Adelaide Faculty of Law, George Williams and the University of New South Wales Faculty of Law, and Ralph Simmonds and Murdoch University Faculty of Law for providing friendship and facilities for the writing of the book during my sabbatical stay in Australia, to Mary Ricketson and the Denver College of Law faculty for their support of my work during the spring of 2002, and to my wife, Patricia, for putting up with me while I was writing it. Finally, to Chief Judge Robert M. Bell, whose humor, seemingly inexhaustible energy, and passion for justice as the head of our judicial system make it a privilege to be a citizen of Maryland.

Introduction

The concept of *privileges and immunities* has been a part of English and American history from feudal England to modern America. Whether as English subjects, as citizens of a state, or as citizens of a nation, people have always claimed that their status entitled them to "privileges and immunities."

The English crown encouraged settlement in the new world by promising colonists all privileges and immunities as if they had been abiding and born within this our realm of England. The colonists justified the American Revolution on the grounds that their privileges and immunities had been denied. After the Revolution, the Articles of Confederation declared in Article IV that the free inhabitants of the states shall be entitled to "all privileges and immunities of free citizens in the several States." When the U.S. Constitution was adopted a few years later, Article IV, Section 2, provided that, "The citizens of each state shall be entitled to all privileges and immunities of citizens in the several states." After the Civil War, the Fourteenth Amendment again embedded privileges and immunities in the fundamental document with the statement, "No state shall make or enforce any law which shall abridge the privileges or immunities of citizens of the United States." The consistent use of the phrase suggests a consistent meaning, but that has not been its history. Instead, it evolved to serve new purposes as the context for its invocation shifted. Ultimately, the privileges and immunities of an Englishman, a free inhabitant of a state, a citizen of a state, and a citizen of the United States are varied.

The reference to privileges and immunities in colonial charters promised that the King would not overuse his power or treat colonists as aliens. The colonists came to identify privileges and immunities with both local law and basic English principles of government. When the Revolution ended the colonists' ties to the King, they inserted a guarantee of the privileges and immunities of citizenship in the Articles of Confederation to maintain a common bond. The Constitution imported the clause with some changes only a few years later. Article IV secured citizens of one state from discrimination by other states on the basis of residence. Courts attempted to limit the scope of the protection by confining it to *fundamental rights*. In this respect, the words became identified with basic civil rights such as the ability to contract, own property, and sue and be sued.

Slavery was a denial of all such rights, and the Civil War Amendments were designed to stop it. The Fourteenth Amendment forbade states from making or enforcing any law that would abridge the privileges or immunities of citizens. The amendment's framers believed the clause would secure fundamental rights against racial discrimination by the state and would give citizens rights against the state that had previously applied only against the federal government. The U.S. Supreme Court, fearful of expanding federal power through natural rights jurisprudence, gutted the clause of any significance for more than a century by interpreting it to apply only to rights derived from other sources, including the federal structure of government. Today, it is the textual source for new residents' rights to equal treatment as other state citizens, and the Court could possibly revive the clause's importance.

Part I of this text recounts the development of privileges and immunities as successive generations provide new meaning to the concept. Its development shows the power of orators and judges, experience and logic, and dreams and current reality.

Part II discusses the application of the constitutional provisions. Article IV requires that states afford citizens of other states the rights it gives to its own citizens unless the difference can be justified. Thus most of the statutory and common law of each of the fifty states is a privilege or immunity of citizenship in that state that can be claimed by citizens of other states. Part II analyzes the basis for determining whether a particular right of a citizen is a privilege or immunity to which citizens of other states are entitled and the justifications for treating those citizens differently.

Although Article IV has helped preserve the nature of the union, the Court has held that the Fourteenth Amendment adds nothing to the existing privileges of citizens of the United States, which consist of their rights under federal laws and treaties and other provisions of the Constitution. Part II discusses the cases that rejected attempts to give the amendment a substantive role, and examines those privileges or immunities that do exist. Only a small number of privileges of U.S. citizenship, primarily the right to travel and migrate to another state, are inherent in the nature of the Union and not expressly set forth. Nevertheless, the clause retains the potential for significant development in the future.

Part I

A History of Privileges and Immunities of Citizenship from Colonization to the Fourteenth Amendment

THE ENGLISH HERITAGE: SUBJECTS OF THE KING

Little controversy existed over the privileges and immunities clause in Article IV of the Articles of Confederation and Article IV of the Constitution because the provisions were based on a familiar principle. Even before the Revolution, individuals had rights in colonies other than their own—rights rooted in fundamental documents and everyday life. The colonists had a common political tie to the King of England, charters that expressly guaranteed them rights in other colonies, and the practical experience of movement and trade across colonial boundaries.

Charter Guarantees

English voyagers sought reassurance and some connection to the land they left behind. The Crown supplied it with promises that their families would never be treated as aliens. They would have all the privileges, liberties, franchises, and immunities of Englishmen.

The Virginia Company charter provided that all the Crown's subjects in the colony and their children born there "shall have and enjoy all Liberties, Franchises, and Immunities, within any of our other Dominions, to all Intents and Purposes, as if they had been abiding and born, within this our Realm of *England*, or any other of our said Dominions." Maryland's proprietary grant secured "all privileges, franchises and liberties of this our kingdom of England . . . in the same manner as our liege-men born, or to be born within our said kingdom of England." Rhode Island and Connecticut both secured all subjects born in the province "all Liberties and Immunities of free and natural subjects within any the dominions of us . . . as if they . . . were born within the realm of England." North Carolina's charter referred to "all liberties, franchises and privileges."[1]

The charter guarantees prefigured the form of Article IV of both the Articles of Confederation and the Constitution. Both the charters and Article IV protect persons who lived in a defined territory (colony or state) and who owe allegiance to the authority of that territory. Both provide a specific entitlement—*privileges and immunities* in the Constitution and the Articles of Confederation; *privileges, liberties, franchises,* and *immunities* as alternatively phrased in different charters. Both identify the standard for entitlement in terms of the most protected class within the political framework (natives of England under English rule, *free citizens* under the Articles, and *citizens* under the Constitution). Finally, both secure the rights wherever the individual may be within the authority of the granting document (the charters secure the rights "within any of our dominions," the Articles secured them "in the respective states," and the Constitution secured them "in the several states"). The parallel structure and linguistic similarity between charter guarantees and Article IV demonstrate the charters' influence on the framers. The syntax indicates that colonial experience under the charters had particular relevance to Article IV.

The charter formula assured colonists that they and their children would not lose their rights under English law by leaving England. They would receive all the rights that an Englishman had in England with respect to activities in the mother country. For example, one of an Englishman's most important rights was the ability to own land. Under English law, aliens could not own real property in England. When King James of Scotland ascended the English throne as James I, it created questions for the status under English law of persons born in Scotland. Although England and Scotland had a common king, each had a separate parliament. On the eve of colonization, English judges, led by Lord Edward Coke, the chief justice of the Court of Common Pleas, decided that a person born in Scotland after James became king of England could inherit English land. In *Calvin's Case* (1608), Coke said, "whosoever at his birth cannot be an alien to the king of England, cannot be an alien to any of his subjects of England."[2]

Calvin's Case did not limit the discretion of the King or Parliament to treat subjects differently depending on the country in which they lived. However, in the context of that case, the charter guarantees of the privileges of persons born in England promised that the King would not impair the colonists' right to own and inherit land in England. By extension, power over property generally and the ability to exercise that power through suit in court were privileges of Englishmen.

The full scope of privileges and immunities remains murky; the term was never neatly defined. Many royal documents granted *privileges*, but the term usually referred to the powers of a political entity rather than an individual. Thus one early legal reference work defined privileges as "liberties and franchises granted to an office, place, towne, or mannor, by the King's great charter, letters patent, or Act of Parliament: as toll, sake, socke, infangtheefe, outfangtheefe, turne or delfe, and divers such likes."[3] In other words, the King granted communities certain powers to raise revenues and exercise jurisdiction over wrongdoers. Privilege was used in the sense of a capacity to exercise power in several documents of the late sixteenth century, such as the "jurisdictions, *privileges*, authorities, immunities" belonging to the King as head of the church, or the East India Corporation's charter making it "capable in law to have . . . and retain lands, rents, *privileges*, liberties, jurisdictions, franchises and hereditaments."[4]

More generally, a privilege is "a right, advantage, or immunity granted to or enjoyed by a person, or a body or class of persons, beyond the common advantages of others; an exemption in a particular case from certain burdens or liabilities."[5] The Latin root of the word may shed further light. *Priviligium* under Roman law was the right of Roman citizens to the civil law of marriage, wills, and commerce. The Roman citizen was distinguished from the slave who lacked rights and the alien who could only claim rights under the *jus gentium* or law of persons. The Roman citizen claimed rights under the *jus civile*.[6] By analogy, the privileges of persons born in England involved their capacity to exercise legal rights under the common law and statutes of England and to be immune from restrictions placed on aliens.

Although the colonists and their children might return to England with rights unimpaired, succeeding generations were more concerned with their rights in the colonies. The charters did not promise them every legal right and remedy in the colonies that English subjects enjoyed at home. The charters promised them only those privileges and immunities that an Englishman would have in their colony or that an Englishman or native of another colony would have in that other colony. This left the door open for differing views on the content of those rights.

Almost every governing document granted to the proprietor, corporation, governor, or council the power to make laws to govern the settlers "so always as the said statutes, ordinances, and proceedings, as near as conveniently may be, be agreeable to the laws, statutes, government and policy of this our realm of England."[7] This formula controlled the local lawmaking body. As a restriction imposed by the Crown on others, it did not limit royal power. Nevertheless, it provided some basis for colonists to claim that their *privileges and immunities* were to have laws in the colonies "agreeable to the laws, statutes, government and policy of England." *As near as conveniently may be* recognized that the colonial situation justified differences from the law prevailing in England and also suggested that privileges and immunities might be general concepts adjusted to specific conditions.

Privilege referred to rights against the government and legal rights against others, such as the parliamentary *privilege* against arrest and the privilege against self-incrimination. However, which rights the charters secured against the government was debatable. The King could contend that his extensive power over foreign affairs made restrictions on his prerogative within England inapplicable abroad, but colonists could claim that the Magna Carta applied to Englishmen everywhere, and therefore it applied to them.

The charters guaranteed colonists the same legal capacity to contract, hold property, and sue as persons born in England and may have assured certain rights like due process and habeas corpus that protected against arbitrary government action. Yet the privileges were only promised insofar as they were within the King's power. As a grant from the King, the charter did not limit Parliament. Discrimination against colonists—even discrimination proposed by the King—would not violate colonial charters if Parliament enacted it. Further, privileges, immunities, franchises, and liberties did not at that time have any impact on political rights because other charter provisions granted lawmaking power to specific individuals or groups. Even in England, only a small group of people could exercise political power.

The charters did not define privileges, liberties, immunities, and franchises, and they promised the colonist no more than any other English subject possessed. *Privileges*, *liberties*, and *immunities* referred to rights in actual practice in English law, not some theory of rights that ought to exist. Further, local circumstances could justify departures from English law. Because the Crown controlled administration in England, colonists appeared to be in a poor position to determine the content of privileges and immunities. Thus charter guarantees did not seem much of a threat to the King's discretion in controlling the colonies and none at all to royal control when he acted with Parliament. However, the vagueness that enabled the Crown to consider the promises as offering little restraint also enabled the phrases to take on broader and deeper meaning during more than 150 years of British colonial rule.

The Evolution of a Phrase: From the Colonies to Independence

The meaning of privileges and immunities evolved throughout the colonial period, although it never attained a clear definition. Three factors had a major effect on the colonial understanding of *privileges and immunities*: (1) the treatment that colonists received in other colonies, (2) the expansion of individual rights against government in England and its connection to developments in political theory, and (3) the rhetoric of the American Revolution.

Intercolonial Movement

Charter guarantees were secured, not only in the province for which the charter was given but also in "any of our dominions." Consequently, colonists relied on the experience of intercolonial recognition of British nationality to give content to their rights. British subjects had the ability to travel to other colonies, visit or trade there without discrimination against residence, and become a member of the community. Colonial restrictions did not destroy the sense of entitlement that developed into an assertion of a privilege or immunity of intercolonial movement. Those restrictions, however, became relevant in cases involving the later constitutional provisions on privileges and immunities.

Throughout the colonial period, nonslave immigrants came largely from England and other English colonies. The common allegiance to the King meant that the colonist could travel to England or other colonies as freely as the English subject who lived in England. The right to travel was an established English liberty since the Magna Carta.[8] On the other hand, the subject's right to travel was restricted by concerns for religion, protection of creditors, and provision of welfare. During early English settlement, a religious oath requirement restricted emigration from England. Within the colonies, individuals not conforming to the dominant religion might be refused settlement rights and driven from the area. Various "pass laws" restricted travel in order to prevent servants from escaping service and to enable masters to enforce the indenture term.[9] Even if free to leave an area, an indigent might be prevented from staying in a new town. Colonies adopted settlement laws for local jurisdictions that excluded nonresidents in order to prevent welfare claims.[10]

Although *poor laws* and religious intolerance kept some people out, colonial laws did little to prevent people from leaving. With so much unsettled territory, a continued stream of migration flowed from one colony to another, especially to the West. The Rhode Island charter in 1663 entitled inhabitants of Rhode Island towns to free movement for lawful purposes through any other of the king's dominions.[11] Even without specific charter assurances, freedom of movement was common in practice.[12] Colonial law did not keep individuals in their home area unless fleeing from a service obligation. Although the unemployed and unpropertied migrant might be excluded from living in new areas, the exclusion related to the economic conditions of each area and was not usually colonywide.

For commercial purposes, colonists experienced a great deal of equality in treatment as they moved through the colonies. Alexander Hamilton cited colonial free trade in *The Federalist Papers* to buttress his argument on the need for a single nation. States in isolation would pursue different commercial policies, he said, and cause:

> . . . distinctions, preferences, and exclusions, which would beget discontent. The habits of intercourse, on the basis of equal privileges, to which we have been accustomed since the earliest settlement of the country, would give a keener edge to those causes of discontent than they would naturally have independent of this circumstance.[13]

Equal privileges did not mean that laws could not distinguish between residents and nonresidents; it meant only that the distinctions related to problems posed by nonresidency, such as the possibility that a nonresident would not remain in the colony. A variety of regulations on attachment, suit, and acknowledgment of conveyances were directed at locating and asserting jurisdiction over the nonresident and did not reflect antagonism toward the nonresident status.[14]

When colonists moved to other colonies, they could acquire all the rights of natives of that community. They were not becoming new citizens—just new residents. To England, the colonies were dependent governments. A Virginia colonist was not a citizen of an independent state but an English subject inhabiting Virginia. Local assemblies exercised delegated authority to promulgate local community rules, but community membership was a consequence of living there.

Although the Englishman could become a member of a community by moving there, some communities required a period of residence before full acceptance. A number of provinces established voting residence requirements, contrary to the English practice.[15] Concerned that outsiders would come to the colony to reap its profits without becoming part of its life, colonists imposed durational residency requirements for holding public offices. Local ordinances excluded newcomers from offices except by immediate commission from the Crown.[16] The *poor law* concept of settlement could create durational residency requirements for the exercise of other rights. Until a community accepted an individual, real residence was not established. Because support obligations were local, community acceptance was a local issue rather than for the colony as a whole. One achieving settlement in an area was entitled to civil and political rights available to long-time residents.

Aside from these restrictions, colonial concerns focused on inclusion rather than exclusion. Colonies encouraged immigration by assuring foreigners of property and contract rights. They held out the promise of naturalization, but England was reluctant to accept colonial naturalization as equivalent to parliamentary naturalization. Under English law, an alien naturalized under Massachusetts law was an alien and treated as one throughout English dominions unless parliament approved the colony's process. Indeed, one of the charges against King George in the Declaration of Independence was that, "He has endeavored to prevent the population of these states; for that purpose obstructing the laws for naturalization of foreigners; refusing to pass others to encourage their migrations hither & raising the conditions of new appropriations of lands."[17]

England was concerned only with attempts to naturalize foreigners. Individuals born in England or a colony were already English subjects, and they needed no naturalization procedures to obtain the rights held by natives of a colony. The Crown wanted to facilitate their acceptance. If colonies had restricted English immigration, England would have disallowed their laws. Indeed, English authorities did disallow several colonial laws that were designed to prevent the transportation of convicts or paupers to the colonies.[18] Thus, in practice, a Virginian became a New Yorker simply by moving there and waiting to become a full community member.

In short, wherever the colonists went, whether passing through or moving permanently, they could claim substantial equality with the residents of that colony because they were all English subjects entitled to the rights of Englishmen.

The Evolution of Privileges and Immunities in England

The rights of Englishmen received a more solid foundation and clearer exposition in the seventeenth century. Early in the century, King James I invoked the divine right of kings, but the century ended with more concern for the rights of the individual.[19] Sir Edward Coke, England's leading jurist and scholar, tried to limit the monarch by appealing to the *ancient constitution* with the claim that the basic principles of government and the law declared by the courts as the law common to the whole kingdom of England proceeded from time immemorial.[20] Coke commented at length on the Magna Carta as an embodiment of those ancient principles.[21] Although many parts of the document reflected outmoded feudal concerns, others grew in relevance and importance as it was revised and reiterated over the centuries. For example, Coke discussed Chapter 29 of the Magna Carta in some detail, expounding on the ancient lineage of *due process* and *law of the land*, although he gave new content to the terms. Trial by ordeal may have been part of the law of the land and due process for King John in the twelfth century, but only a jury sufficed for Coke in the seventeenth.

The Magna Carta symbolized the limitations on royal power, but the Crown often exceeded those bounds. Other statutes of Parliament played a significant role in keeping Magna Carta provisions applicable, extending their scope and entrenching them in the English heart. Thus the Petition of Right of 1628 insisted that no person should be compelled to pay taxes except by the common consent of Parliament, that no freeman may be imprisoned "but by the lawful judgment of his peers or by the law of the land," and that no man should be taken without being brought to answer "by due process of law."[22] This document reasserted the claim to the rule of law by pointing to the reiterations of Magna Carta.

The seventeenth century saw spectacular changes in English politics: the beheading of a king, an interregnum without a king, the restoration of the monarchy, and the joint rule of William and Mary after the forced resignation of James II in the Glorious Revolution of 1688. These events led to another fundamental English document. The Bill of Rights of 1689 contained a litany of claimed violations of rights by James II, including suspension of the laws, maintaining a standing army without consent of Parliament, breaching of the privileges of Parliament, requiring excessive bail, imposing excessive fines, inflicting illegal and cruel punishments, levying money for the Crown without the consent of Parliament, and imposing fines or forfeitures before conviction or judgment.[23] Most of these rights could trace their lineage to the Magna Carta. This claim of rights and the ensuing limitation of the King could not help but generally affect the understanding of the rights of Englishmen. When the English ruling class claimed their rights in universal language, the colonist could hear the echo and apply it to himself.

Coke expounded on historical rights, and Parliament enacted new ones, but John Locke changed the way people thought about rights.[24] Locke wrote *Two Treatises of Civil Government* while in exile from James II, seeking ways to oust him. Decades later, colonists studied Locke and cited his ideas in justifying their own revolution, chastising the British government for its failure to afford them their natural rights.

A long tradition of natural law theorists had believed that principles of social organization could be derived from the nature of man, including ancient Rome's great orator Cicero and the medieval Italian theologian St. Thomas Aquinas. Similarly, others had used social contract theory to analyze government, positing a state of nature in which humans agree with each other to surrender their natural liberties to the community—the social contract. For example, in *The Leviathan*, Thomas Hobbes used social contract theory to justify the power of the ruler, undermining Coke's reliance on custom to curb the King, but Locke's *Two Treatises of Civil Government* fused natural law and social contract theory in a way that could justify revolution. Locke reasoned from the nature of man to the relationship of individuals to government. He argued that individuals in a state of nature have natural rights and that they surrender some of those natural rights to form civil society in exchange for government's commitment to protect their lives, liberty, and property. However, they surrender only those rights necessary for government to fulfill its functions. If government violates those rights, it breaches its trust and can be replaced.

Locke did not publish his work until 1690, after the ascension of William and Mary. The new King and Queen had come to power after the forced resignation of James II with the approbation of Parliament, and they were bound to the Bill of Rights of 1689. In this context, Locke's work implicitly justified the new regime rather than appearing to urge radical revolution. Thus tamed, Locke's writings could be freely disseminated because they provided a source of legitimacy for government. The rights of individuals under the statutes and the common law fulfilled government's obligation under natural law.

Blackstone's *Commentaries on the Laws of England* (1765–1769) reflected this view of privileges and immunities. The purpose of the *Commentaries* was to present a comprehensive and organized view of English law. Blackstone began with Locke, but he repudiated any right of revolution and affirmed the absolute power of Parliament. In this sense, he was totally incompatible with revolutionary ideas. Nevertheless, his articulation of English law as the embodiment of the proper balance between natural rights and government struck a chord. Generations of Americans who sought to understand the law used his work. It both influenced and reflected popular thought. Volume I described the privileges and immunities of the people of England, which Blackstone said were the rights of all mankind; of course, in Blackstone's view, England preserved them, and other countries did not.

After listing the various English documents declaring rights and liberties, such as the Magna Carta, the Petition of Right, and the Bill of Rights of 1689, Blackstone wrote:

> The rights themselves thus defined by these several statutes, consist in a number of private *immunities*; which will appear, from what has been premised, to be indeed no other, than either that residuum of natural liberty, which is not required by the laws of society to be

> sacrificed to public convenience; or else those civil *privileges*, which society hath engaged to provide, in lieu of the natural liberties so given up by individuals.[25] (Emphasis supplied)

This passage linked *privileges* and *immunities* to Locke's social contract and to the particulars of existing English laws. Blackstone then offered a general categorization of privileges and immunities that continued to echo in subsequent discussions of the term:

> [T]hese may be reduced to three principal or primary articles; the right of personal security, the right of personal liberty, and the right of private property: because as there is no other known method of compulsion, or of abridging man's natural free will, but by an infringement or diminution of one or other of these important rights, the preservation of these, inviolate, may justly be said to include the preservation of our civil *immunities* in their largest and most extensive sense.[26] (Emphasis supplied)

Blackstone did not spell out in detail the specific privileges "which society hath engaged to provide, in lieu of the natural liberties so given up." He did describe property rights as "some of those civil advantages, in exchange for which every individual has resigned a part of his natural liberty." Elsewhere, he referred to trial by jury as "the most transcendent privilege which any subject can enjoy."[27] However, Blackstone was elaborating on the law of England and was not defining privileges or immunities. He discussed the law of abortion, self-defense, welfare provisions, assault, defamation, due process, habeas corpus, and property law as examples of the rights provided by the law of England. The remainder of the Commentaries go into still more detail on English law. This leaves the reader with the impression that immunities and privileges refer to the specific legal rights of individuals in England rather than any notion of fundamental rights divorced from existing laws. Blackstone did not blindly extol every aspect of English law. He questioned the policy of a number of laws, including the current operations of the poor law, but he distinguished laws that reflect natural law, such as the prohibition against murder or assault, and those that are just matters of policy, such as trade tariffs.

It was not Blackstone's originality but the degree to which he reflected common understanding that made him important to the meaning of privileges and immunities. The eighteenth century had integrated Locke's ideas into the status quo by limiting natural rights and identifying existing laws as either based on natural law or not within its scope. However, no fully developed and universally accepted understanding of the parameters of natural law existed.

The Rhetoric of Revolution: Principles of the English Constitution and Natural Law

The American colonists did not spend much time battling for English laws because they soon gained control over making their own. Government required cooperation by the populace, particularly to support taxation. Local assemblies gained legislative power by insisting that no tax for the operation of local government could be raised without their consent. By the end of the seventeenth century, local assemblies made law in most colonies.[28] The Crown's power to control domestic colonial law was effectively reduced to the same veto power it retained over acts of Parliament. Although local legislatures enacted local laws, the British government still controlled laws of trade and foreign relations and could impose specific laws when it thought necessary. What colonists wanted were the limits on government power they identified in the structure of English law.

England acknowledged that the colonists should be treated as British subjects, and British subjects had a right to have parliamentary law apply through proper procedures. Colonists responded that local assemblies in the colonies were the equivalent of Parliament. Having identified charter guarantees with English law, the colonists contended that the charters required conformity with the principles of English government. Those principles, in turn, reflected natural law, and they included the right not to have property taken without consent. The colonists claimed that English subjects had a right to be governed by their own representatives, that Americans had no representation in Parliament, and that consequently, laws made by Parliament for the colonies violated their rights. Thus, on May 30, 1765, the Virginia House of Burgesses claimed that the Stamp Act violated the rights of Englishmen—rights both inherent in subjects of the King and granted specifically by charter.[29] The rights claimed were limits on government, such as no taxation without representation. The colonist's representation argument changed *privileges and immunities* from limits on the King's prerogative to limits on the exercise of power by any sector of English government.

On October 14, 1774, the First Continental Congress issued a Declaration and Resolves that stated an even broader view of the rights of Americans, claiming rights "by the immutable laws of nature, the principles of the English constitution, and the several charters and compacts." Article VII asserted their rights to "all the immunities and privileges granted and confirmed to them by royal charters, or secured by their several codes of provincial laws."[30]

While they were still subjects of the King, the colonists rested their claims primarily on rights identified within the existing English legal system, such as the common law, the English statute, and the charter provision or provincial code. They wanted what Englishmen had, although they defined the applicable law at a somewhat abstract level. England argued that the privilege or immunity was not to be taxed without the consent of Parliament, but the colonists defined the rights of Englishmen as not to be taxed without the consent of one's representatives. Natural law reasoning looked for the general principle behind the specific instance to describe the right at stake. Thus it supported the claim that a desired *privilege or immunity* was in the existing legal structure.

On the eve of the American Revolution, the *liberties, franchises, privileges*, and *immunities* in colonial charters had developed new meanings. Their content expanded as the rights of the individual expanded. The phrases were identified with the basic principles the colonists found in English government—privileges of protection by government of life, liberty, and property through the civil and criminal law and immunities from government found in documents like the Magna Carta. At every step, privileges and immunities were identified through existing law, but the colonists would generalize from the applicable law in order to take different situations into account. The invocation of natural law to justify the existing legal structure created the possibility that some persons would come to view privileges and immunities as dependent on natural law.

THE ARTICLES OF CONFEDERATION: ARTICLE IV—REPLACING THE KING

Before declaring independence, each colony regarded itself as a separate dominion headed by a common King. Under the various charters, the King had promised colonial subjects entitlement to the same liberties, privileges, franchises, and immunities in every other colony as if born in England or that colony. As British subjects, colonists had rights to travel; to become members of another colony by moving there; and to be free of discrimination in trade, property ownership, and other legal rights in other colonies. Colonial governments had to recognize their common link with other colonies through the King.

Independence broke the link with the King and ended the requirement that persons from other colonies be treated as common subjects and not aliens. Unless some provision was made, each state could discriminate freely against persons from other states. The need to restore the common nationality and intercolonial rights that existed before independence led to the privileges and immunities clause of the Articles of Confederation.

The states took a number of years before reaching consensus on a framework for government. The Continental Congress was a coordinating body in which each state had one vote. In November 1777, it approved the Articles of Confederation for circulation to the states. Although no record exists of the discussions that produced either the draft or the final form of the Articles, several forms of the proposed committee article on privileges and immunities have survived.[31] Congress made a number of changes to the form reported by the committee, and the committee on style made two minor alterations.[32] After the Articles were circulated, a number of state representatives offered amendments that were heard, considered, and rejected. Congress then adopted the Articles, and the last state ratified them in 1781.

Article IV of the Articles of Confederation had five major clauses. The first secured the privileges and immunities of free citizens in the several states. The second protected a right to travel. The remaining clauses fit together as a structure for the regulation of property, assuring nonresidents equality with residents in trade and commerce, giving them a right to remove property brought into the state, and providing intergovernmental immunity from state taxes.

The changes between drafts to the final product reveal much about the drafters' intention, and even the later rejected proposals shed some light. However, they also permit disagreement, sowing both confusion and understanding. The meaning of Article IV in the Articles of Confederation is important because it was the source for the Constitutional provision. It is therefore relevant to whether the framers of the Constitution intended free African-Americans to have constitutional rights, whether privileges and immunities referred to fundamental rights, whether they applied to voting, and whether they included a right to travel.

The Privileges and Immunities of Free Citizens

The committee draft of the first clause stated, "the Inhabitants of every State [Paupers Vagabonds and fugitives from Justice excepted] going to reside in another state shall be entitled to all the rights and priviledges of the natural born free Citizens of the State to which they go to reside."

The Continental Congress added *free* before *inhabitants*. Thus, a person bound to labor in one state would not receive the rights of a *free citizen* in another. The distinction between *inhabitants* and *free inhabitants* suggests that they considered the problem of slavery, carefully excluding slaves from the rights of free citizens. On the other hand, the Continental Congress rejected South Carolina's attempt to restrict the benefits by inserting *white* between *free* and *inhabitants*.[33] That amendment's defeat is subject to several interpretations; it might have reflected a desire to prevent discrimination against free African-Americans, an agreement to disagree on whether African-Americans came within the historic understanding of *inhabitants*, or just a rush to finish with the Articles and avoid changes that would have required each state to reconsider the Articles de novo. Nevertheless, the Continental Congress and the individual states knew that race was an issue when they approved the Articles, and they made no racial distinctions in the text.

The Articles of Confederation excluded paupers, vagabonds, and fugitives from justice from the protections of Article IV. This reflected the colonial laws that forced such persons to return to their place of origin. If they could be expelled, they could not claim the privileges and immunities of free citizens. The Maryland delegates proposed to strike *paupers* from the clause, but to add, "that one state shall not be burthened with the maintenance of the poor who may remove into it from any of the others in the Union."[34] This proposal would have protected the social welfare structure while recognizing that persons who happen to be paupers should be treated as citizens. However, the Continental Congress rejected this proposal, as it did all amendments proposed after the Articles were sent to the states.

Before sending the Articles to the states, however, the Continental Congress had made significant alterations to the committee's proposed text. The committee draft had secured citizenship rights for persons going to a state to reside and also prohibited states from interfering with persons and property crossing state lines. However, the inhabitant of one state who inherited property in another fit neither category. He was not going to reside in the state where his property was located, his property did not move across state lines, and it would not even be his property if the state barred inheritance by noncitizens. The right to inherit property in another of the King's dominions was one of the oldest of all intercolonial rights, traceable to *Calvin's Case*. The Continental Congress secured inheritance rights by extending the protection of the privileges and immunities of citizens to free inhabitants "in the respective states" or, as amended by the committee on style, "in the several states," and not just in a state where they go to reside:

> And the better to secure and perpetuate mutual friendship and intercourse among the people of the different states in this union, the free inhabitants of each of these states, paupers, vagabonds, and fugitives from justice excepted, shall be entitled to all privileges and immunities of free citizens in the several states. . . . (Articles of Confederation, Article IV)

The new language of Article IV created a textual ambiguity with respect to the standard of entitlement. *In the several states* could refer either to the place where free inhabitants get rights (i.e., when in the several states) or to the place for measuring the rights that they receive (i.e., those of the citizens that live in the several states). In other words, were the "privileges and immunities of free citizens" the abstract fundamental natural law rights of free citizens located anywhere, or were they the specific rights of citizens residing in the several states? Privileges and immunities had been identified with existing rights up to that time and had not been given a natural law meaning. Colonial charters and earlier Article IV drafts specified privileges and immunities by reference to the legal entitlement of specific persons. It seems unlikely that the Continental Congress intended to untie privileges and immunities from their mooring in the rights of a specific existing group. On the other hand, the privileges and immunities of Englishmen had been filtered through a natural law lens that abstracted principles from the specific rule to fit the different context of the colonies.

Delegates to the Continental Congress were cautious about imposing obligations on their states. They specified that the free inhabitants receive all "privileges and immunities of free citizens" rather than all "rights and privileges of natural born free citizens," which was the language of the committee report. One committee draft assured persons moving to another state the *rights and privileges* of citizens of that state, but a provision in another draft said persons visiting other states were only entitled to *privileges and immunities* there.[35] This suggests that Congress intended to narrow the conferred protection when it chose *immunities* instead of *rights* in conjunction with *privileges*. *Rights* of citizens might be total, including voting or welfare benefits inappropriate to visitors. *Immunities* have the narrower sense of freedom from particular obligations.

Privileges, the word used in both committee drafts and the final form, remained a broad and undefined term. Its vagueness led at least one contemporary to mistakenly apply it to voting. Thomas Burke, a North Carolina delegate who was not present when the privileges and immunities clause was being considered, accused the clause of giving nonresidents the power to vote in a state's elections, "which would be a political absurdity."[36] Eliminating the voting residence requirement would have offended a number of states, but none suggested changing Article IV. Thus Burke must have misunderstood the scope of the privileges and immunities clause. Either voting was not a *privilege or immunity*, or the nature of the privilege was to vote for *one's own* representative, which would only apply to the representative of the state of residence. If the clause embodied colonial rights, discrimination permitted under the charters would not violate it. Thus the privileges and immunities of free citizens in Article IV would include privileges such as property ownership and capacity to sue and immunities such as freedom from discriminatory regulation, but they would not afford nonresidents any rights to vote or hold political office.

Free Ingress and Regress to Other States

The committee draft provided the people of each state free ingress and egress "for their persons and property to and from every other state without hindrance, molestation or imposition of any kind."[37] If taken literally, this language prohibited states from using their police power to exclude diseased or other undesirable property. The only property regulation permitted was the imposition of nondiscriminatory imposts and duties.

The Continental Congress changed the committee draft by separating the right of personal movement from the movement of property and then treating the two issues differently. The revised article allowed greater regulation of the movement of property but retained the absolute bar on hindering interstate movement of persons. The second clause of Article IV forbade states from interference with the travel of its own persons and prohibiting any exclusion of citizens from other states. It stated that "the people of each state shall have free ingress and regress to and from any other State."

The Privileges of Trade and Commerce and the Regulation of Property Proviso

The congressional revision also permitted states to regulate nonresidents engaging in trade and commerce to the same extent that it regulated its own inhabitants. The language permitted trade barriers and prohibitions based on the goods nature or origin but not if the barrier was based on the residence of the person importing the goods. According to the final version of Article IV, persons going to a state:

> . . . shall enjoy therein all the privileges of trade and commerce, subject to the same duties, impositions and restrictions as the inhabitants thereof respectively; provided that such

restriction shall not extend so far as to prevent the removal of property imported into any State to any other State of which the owner is an inhabitant; provided, also, that no imposition, duties, or restriction, shall be laid by any State on the property of the United States, or either of them.

James Madison was perplexed over the need to have a separate clause for the privileges of trade. Writing in *The Federalist Papers*, he contrasted the proposed new constitution with the infirmities of the Articles of Confederation. "[W]hat was meant by super-adding to 'all privileges and immunities of free citizens,' 'all the privileges of trade and commerce,' cannot be readily determined."[38]

The answer to Madison's conundrum lies in the drafting history. The privileges of trade and commerce were the other half of the clause on interstate travel. Privileges and immunities "in the respective states" referred to rights *within* a state. Separate clauses dealt with interstate movement. When the Continental Congress deleted property from the interstate travel clause, it decided to detail how the interstate movement of property could be regulated. The "privileges of trade and commerce" clause made it clear that states retained power over property entering their borders so long as their regulations applied equally to residents. On the other hand, the state's power to subject nonresidents to the same laws as residents was modified by a limited guarantee for nonresidents to remove property from the state despite any state restriction on its own citizens.

The Continental Congress thought the special protection for nonresident property was needed to deal with the state's power to prevent exports. A policy of nondiscrimination was only adequate with respect to problems with importation. A law forbidding removal of any property brought into the state would affect state residents differently than those who reside elsewhere. If a state could forbid the removal of property brought into the state by a nonresident, the nonresident might be discouraged from entering the state with property to trade. Thus Article IV prevented restrictions on "the removal of property, imported into any State, to any other state of which the owner is an inhabitant." The new clause may have also protected the slaveowner traveling to another state. Slavery was not yet illegal in any of the states, but abolition was being discussed.

The *proviso* did not deprive states of any power to prevent imports or exports that might injure them, despite some misguided private expressions of concern by Thomas Burke in his letters. The proviso was an exception to a state's power to enact nondiscriminatory restrictions over the trade and commerce of persons of another state. It did not apply to state power over its own inhabitants. On its face, the proviso only prevented states from barring nonresidents from taking home any property that was brought into the state from elsewhere. A prohibition on natural resource exportation would be valid because natural resources were not imported from another state. Similarly, a prohibition on the importation of any specific goods would be valid, because the proviso only protects nonresident exports.

The revision of the article to expand state power on imports may have led Congress to consider its impact on interstate relations when applied to the property of other states or the United States. The regulation and taxation of a sovereign entity would have been a source of friction. The revised article eliminated the problem by granting governmental property immunity.

Effect of the Article

When the Articles of Confederation were finally ratified by all the states, a committee was appointed to report on their effect. The committee responded that an exposition of the Articles would be voluminous and any omissions might be taken as denying power, so it would be better to await the exercise of power and deal with it then. The committee did say "that the Confederation requires execution in the following manner . . . 2. By describing the privileges and immunities to which the citizens of one State are entitled in another."[39]

Despite the committee's urging, the Continental Congress never defined the privileges and immunities to which citizens of one state were entitled in another. The Articles of Confederation failed to create a viable enforcement mechanism. No federal court existed to interpret the document, and the ambiguities in Article IV remained unresolved.

Despite uncertainty, one function of Article IV of the Articles of Confederation remained clear: it prohibited states from imposing restrictions on nonresidents engaged in trade or commerce that were not applicable to their own citizens. Without federal enforcement, however, states breached this command with impunity during the pre-Constitution period.

THE CONSTITUTION: ARTICLE IV, SECTION 2—CITIZENS IN THE SEVERAL STATES

Section 2. The citizens of each state shall be entitled to all privileges and immunities of citizens in the several states.[40]

When the state delegates convened and proposed a new Constitution, they considered the problem of the Article IV violations occurring without redress. Madison noted in his Preface to Debates in the Convention of 1787 that:

> The same want of a general power over Commerce, led to an exercise of the power separately, by the States, which not only proved abortive, but engendered rival, conflicting and angry regulations. . . . In sundry instances as of N.Y., N.J., [Pennsylvania] & [Maryland] the navigation laws treated the Citizens of other States as aliens.[41]

The solution for the weaknesses of the Articles was the creation of a national government. The Constitutional Convention did not even consider the privileges and immunities clause until the national character of the new government had been established. Under the Articles of Confederation, each person was a citizen only of the state of permanent residence. States had obligations to citizens of other states and to the other states themselves, but the state was always a mediating body between the individual and Congress. The Constitution changed this relationship. It gave Congress direct power to legislate over individuals. The direct relationship between individual and national government transformed citizenship in the United States. Article I gave Congress the power to "establish [a] uniform Rule of Naturalization,"[42] which made citizenship a federal matter, at least with respect to aliens. Qualifications for the federal legislature required that the legislator be a "citizen of the United States."[43] The new national government now performed the role once played by the King in uniting the colonies under a single citizenship.

Adoption and Ratification

The Virginia delegation opened the convention by presenting a set of resolutions stating principles for an essentially national government, with representation based on population. After some weeks of discussing the Virginia plan principles, William Paterson of New Jersey presented an alternative proposal more closely conforming to the Articles of Confederation, with representation based on states. Madison opposed the New Jersey plan on June 19, 1787, and raised the issue of the Confederation's impotency to enforce its provisions. He argued that the New Jersey plan suffered from the same infirmity:

> Will it prevent trespasses of the States on each other? Of these enough has been already seen. He instanced Acts of [Virginia] & Maryland which give a preference to their own Citizens in cases where the Citizens of other States are entitled to equality of privileges by the Articles of Confederation.[44]

The conflict between large and small states, reflected in the rival plans at the convention, was resolved by a compromise that left the states with two votes each in the Senate and House representation based on population. With some basic principles resolved, the convention referred comprehensive document drafting to a committee of detail. The committee was to bring together the principles adopted by the convention and articles not in dispute. The committee draft of August 1787 introduced the following privileges and immunities clause to the Convention:

> The free (inhabs) Citizens of each State shall be entitled to all Privileges & Immunities of free Citizens in the sevl States.[45]

In its report, the Committee on Detail dropped *(inhabs)* and omitted *free* as a modifier of citizen. Madison subsequently argued in *The Federalist Papers* that *inhabitants* in the privileges and immunities clause of the Articles of Confederation suggested that an alien resident of one state could achieve the rights of a citizen in other states. The use of *citizens* instead of *inhabitants* prevented this. Madison also pointed out that the Articles permitted a state to naturalize as its citizens foreigners who would be unacceptable in other states. The new Constitution conferred on Congress the uniform power of naturalization. Madison thought this resolved the problem.[46] Thus the Committee of Detail report specified that *citizens* of each state be entitled to the privileges and immunities of citizens.

The change had other effects that Madison did not discuss. In the Articles of Confederation, *free* modified *inhabitants* to prevent slaves from being given rights. This was unnecessary when *citizen* was used, because slaves were not citizens. The Committee of Detail report also eliminated *free* in the measure of rights afforded to citizens of a state. Nothing in the convention debates indicates that thought was given to the status of free African-Americans and whether the change of the protected class from *free inhabitant* to *citizen* would affect their rights.

Thirty years after the convention, Charles Pinckney of South Carolina claimed that free African-Americans were not citizens, because he did not consider them citizens when he wrote Article IV.[47] This intimated that the change from *free inhabitant* to *citizen* had a racial significance. Pinckney's claim to authorship of Article IV was based on his submission at the Constitutional Convention of a plan that slightly altered the Articles of Confederation and included a proposal based on Article IV of the Articles of Confederation. [48] However, his plan was referred to the Committee of Detail with all other proposals and was never discussed on the convention floor.[49] Pinckney was not on the Committee on Detail, which produced the final form of Article IV of the Constitution and considered whether to use *inhabitants* or *citizens*.[50] Nothing indicates that Pinckney even engaged in any discussion at the convention over the meaning of the Article. His views on African-American citizenship three decades later should have little, if any, relevance to the understanding of the convention or the ratifying conventions. Madison's contemporary public explanation for the use of *citizen* remains the best evidence of the reason for the change. This indicates that the new language had no effect on whether free African-Americans were entitled to privileges and immunities.

Other changes from the form of Article IV in the Articles of Confederation were necessary to fit the structure of government created by the Constitution, which conferred new authority on Congress. As a result of the grant of power to regulate commerce among the several states,[51] Congress now supervised the interstate movement of property. This removed the need to discuss state regulation of interstate movement of goods, and the Committee of Detail therefore omitted the Articles of Confederation provision on privileges of trade and commerce, as well as the proviso on nonresident property.

The elimination of the clause providing for "free ingress and egress to and from any other state" is more difficult to explain. As Professor Zecharaiah Chafee wrote, "[T]he reason for not expressly giving 'free ingress and regress' across state lines must be that it is in the Constitution, somewhere else. But where?"[52] The express reference in the Articles of Confederation was designed to distinguish the movement of persons from the movement of property, but the Constitution did not need that distinction because it did not have the same clause on property. The Committee of Detail and the rest of the Convention probably thought that personal interstate movement was implicit in Article IV, because it provides that "the citizens of each state shall be entitled to all privileges and immunities of citizens in the several states." Interference with interstate travel, whether by a state of origin or destination, would deprive citizens of this constitutional entitlement by preventing them from traveling to another state to receive it.

Finally, the Committee of Detail report omitted the exception for paupers, vagabonds, and fugitives from justice that was contained in Article IV of the Articles of Confederation. The exception for fugitives was redundant because both the Constitution and the Articles provided for the extradition of fugitives to the state charging them with a crime. The Constitution extended the extradition clause to persons charged with any crime, not just treason, felony, or high misdemeanors. Thus fugitives could never claim all privileges and immunities of citizens under the Constitution because they were always subject to extradition.

Paupers and vagabonds raised a unique set of questions. The national citizenship established by the Constitution broke down part of the reluctance to acknowledge paupers moving into the state as citizens. Further, the obligation of support for the poor was local; therefore both persons within and without the state might be denied permission to settle in a particular local area to avoid the imposition of a community burden. Article IV may have protected the right to cross state borders, but it did not necessarily protect the right to reside in a particular community. Thus the members of the Convention may have believed that no exception for paupers and vagabonds was necessary to preserve the states' right to deal with the problems they posed.

The Committee of Detail proposed the privileges and immunities clause in its report to the Convention as a separate article, numbered XIV: "The Citizens of each State shall be entitled to all privileges and immunities of citizens in the several states."[53]

The clause received little debate at the Convention. It was raised indirectly during consideration of a proposal to require a period of citizenship before individuals would be eligible to serve in the national legislature. Pennsylvania delegate James Wilson objected that the proposal conflicted with his state's constitution, which granted foreigners all the rights of citizens after two years' residence. He argued that citizenship in Pennsylvania required treatment as a citizen everywhere under Article IV of the Articles of Confederation, so Pennsylvania's grant of citizenship promised foreigners that they would be treated as citizens throughout the United States. The adoption of a restriction on their eligibility for federal office would be a breach of faith. The only response recorded to this concern was that discrimination on the basis of place of birth was no more objectionable than an age limit.[54]

The notes of the debates do not show any discussion of the Article IV problem Wilson raised, but that could simply reflect its irrelevance. Pennsylvania remained free to grant all the rights of citizens to aliens within its borders but could not impose obligations on other states by doing so. Those aliens who had already become citizens of Pennsylvania would continue to be afforded the privileges and immunities of citizenship in other states that had been secured by the Articles. There could be no vested right to an office in a body (Congress under the new Constitution) that did not previously exist, so the privileges and immunities clause posed no real problem to Pennsylvania's constitutional commitment.

The only recorded direct discussion of the clause in the Convention occurred on August 28, 1787, when the Convention considered the privileges and immunities clause, numbered Article XIV. Madison's notes stated: "General PINKNEY was not satisfied with it. He seemed to wish some provision should be included in favor of property in slaves."[55]

South Carolina sent two Charles Pinckneys to the Convention. The first had proposed an Article IV based on the Articles, but it was the other Pinckney that objected to the clause that came from the committee. Madison's notes are unclear about General Charles Cotesworth Pinckney's thoughts on amending the clause. He may have sought assurances that slaveowners could bring their slaves into other states without risking loss. This might have been done by including the phrase in the Articles of Confederation allowing nonresidents to remove any property that they brought into a state. There is no clarification of Pinckney's remarks nor is there a notice of a reply to them in the records of the Convention, but Virginia delegate George Mason, did note on his draft copy of the Constitution:[56]

> Section 2nd, Article 4th—The citizens of one State having an estate in another, have not secured to them the right of removing their property as in the 4th Article of the Confederation—amend by adding the following clause: and every citizen having an estate in two or more States shall have a right to remove his property from one State to another. (not proposed)

Whether Mason was reflecting Pinckney's objections or pondering whether to make his own proposal, his note indicates no formal proposed amendment to the clause was made and he did not make this omission grounds for his later opposition to the Constitution.

The Convention referred the Constitution to the Committee of Style, which reported it out on September 12, 1787. The Committee renumbered the privileges and immunities clause but made no other changes:

> IV . . . Sect. 2. The citizens of each state shall be entitled to all privileges and immunities of citizens in the several states.[57]

On September 15, 1787, the Convention voted to adopt the Constitution as amended, and on September 17, it voted to adopt it as enrolled.[58]

The privileges and immunities clause was not seriously debated during the Constitutional Convention or during the ratification process because it was a familiar provision that was generally satisfactory. As the Supreme Court noted in Austin v. New Hampshire (1975), "the provision was carried over into the comity article of the Constitution in briefer form but with no change of substance or intent, unless it was to strengthen the force of the Clause in fashioning a single nation."

Madison argued in *The Federalist Papers* Number 42 that the new language improved on the Articles of Confederation by eliminating unnecessary duplication and using *citizens* rather than *free inhabitants*, but he did not elaborate further on the clause.[59] Alexander Hamilton, wrote in *The Federalist Papers* Number 80: "It may be esteemed the basis of the Union that 'the citizens of each State shall be entitled to all the privileges and immunities of citizens of the several States.'"[60] Rather than discuss the substance of the clause, however, Hamilton focused on the procedure for enforcing it, because his purpose was to justify the grant of federal jurisdiction in diversity of citizenship cases. In short, the clause engendered no controversy that might lead to a discussion illuminating its scope until long after its adoption.

Privileges and Immunities of Citizens in America Before the Civil War

The zealous concern for state sovereignty manifested in the Articles of Confederation and the continuing anxiety over the independence of the states under the Constitution made it unlikely that the Constitutional Convention intended for the privileges and immunities clause to destroy all distinctions between citizens of a state and citizens of other states. Neither Congress nor the prior discussions of the clause offered details as to which rights must be the same. The courts were left to hammer out an interpretation of privileges and immunities that would preserve the union without encroaching on state sovereignty.

Corfield v. Coryell and the Fundamental Rights Limit

Privileges and immunities conceivably could have encompassed every right a citizen has, but courts quickly attempted to narrow the scope of the phrase. In one of the earliest decisions under Article IV, Pennsylvania financier Robert Morris challenged the Maryland law that permitted attachment of real property in the state in order to compel a defendant's appearance. Maryland citizens who remained within the state were exempt from the statute because they could be forced to appear by personal process, and Morris claimed that the distinction violated the privileges and immunities clause. The judges in the state courts upheld the law at every stage, using two narrowing definitional techniques (Campbell v. Morris, Md. 1797). In the General Court decision, Judge Jeremiah Townley Chase said:

> It seems agreed, from the manner of expounding, or defining the words immunities and privileges, by the counsel on both sides, that a particular and limited operation is to be given to these words, and not a full and comprehensive one. It is agreed it does not mean the right of election, the right of holding offices, the right of being elected.

Because everyone agreed that nonresidents could be excluded from the franchise, Judge Chase's definition of privileges and immunities focused on property rights and excluded political rights:

> The Court are of opinion it means that the citizens of all the States shall have the peculiar advantage of acquiring and holding real as well as personal property, and that such property shall be protected and secured by the laws of the State, in the same manner as the property of the citizens of the State is protected. It means, such property shall not be liable to any taxes, or burdens which the property of the citizens is not subject to. It may also mean, that as creditors, they shall be on the same footing with the State creditor, in the payment of the debts of a deceased debtor. It secures and protects personal rights.

Chase noted that restrictions on property ownership historically had been a major characteristic distinguishing aliens from citizens, and that "one of the great objects [of Article IV, Section 2] . . . was the enabling the citizens of the several states to acquire and hold real property in any of the states. . . ." However, Jeremiah Townley Chase thought procedure was not a privilege or immunity, as long as the citizen of another state had a fair opportunity to vindicate the property rights that were privileges and immunities.

Although Judge Chase upheld the Maryland statute, he vacated the attachment on the grounds that the defendant lacked legal title to the lands attached. Thus his discussion of privileges and immunities was dicta, unnecessary to the decision. Chase's opinion confined Article IV to the prevention of discrimination in rights defined by history and the needs of the union. It offered no hint of natural law reasoning.

The Court of Appeals took a different tack on review. They reversed Judge Chase's decision and upheld the attachment. They agreed with Chase that the state statute was constitutional, but they denied that Article IV was designed to assure equal rights. They thought it was designed instead to assure "the general rights of citizenship." The Court said:

> It does not declare that "the citizens of each state shall be entitled to all privileges and immunities of the citizens of the several states." Had such been the language of the constitution, it might, with more plausibility, have been contended that this act of assembly was in violation of it; but such are not the expressions of the article; it only says that "The citizens

of the several states shall be entitled to all privileges and immunities of citizens in the several states." Thereby designing to give them the rights of citizenship, and not to put all the citizens of the United States upon a level; consequently, the injury, as to the effect of a law of any state, will not be whether it makes a discrimination between citizens of the several states; but whether it infringes upon any civil right, which a man as a member of civil society must enjoy.

Because the Court of Appeals did not define the civil rights "which a man as a member of civil society must enjoy," later judges often cited Judge Chase's opinion for a description of privileges and immunities rather than that of the Maryland Court of Appeals.

Twenty-five years later, Supreme Court Justice Bushrod Washington did describe the privileges and immunities of citizens in the celebrated case of Corfield v. Coryell (1823). The plaintiff Corfield owned a vessel, the Hiram, that was subleased to Keene and Courtney, who used it to dredge for oysters out of season in New Jersey waters. New Jersey law prohibited nonresidents from gathering oysters in the state and penalties included the forfeit of the boat they used. Defendant Coryell and others seized the Hiram, and New Jersey magistrates declared it forfeit. Corfield brought an action in trespass to recover the value of the boat.

Justice Washington, a nephew of the first president, presided over the trial in his capacity as Circuit Court justice. Before the creation of the Circuit Courts of Appeal, Supreme Court justices spent more time hearing cases in the circuit to which they were assigned than they did in meeting together as the Supreme Court. In this case, Corfield claimed that Coryell acted improperly because, among other things, New Jersey's law violated the privileges and immunities clause. Justice Washington responded that the protections of the clause were limited to fundamental rights:

The inquiry is, what are the privileges and immunities of citizens in the several states? We feel no hesitation in confining these expressions to those privileges and immunities which are in their nature, fundamental; which belong, of right, to the citizens of all free Governments; and which have, at all times, been enjoyed by the citizens of the several states which compose this Union, from the time of their becoming free, independent and sovereign.

Justice Washington described fundamental rights in general terms that echoed Blackstone's rights of personal security, personal liberty, and private property, as well as the Declaration of Independence's reference to life, liberty, and the pursuit of happiness:

What these fundamental principles are, it would perhaps, be more tedious than difficult to enumerate. They may, however, be all comprehended under the following general heads: Protection by the government; the enjoyment of life and liberty, with the right to acquire and possess property of every kind, and to pursue and obtain happiness and safety; subject nevertheless to such restraints as the Government may justly prescribe for the general good of the whole.

Washington then enumerated specific rights included in the general concept of privileges and immunities:

The right of a citizen of one state to pass through, or to reside in any other state, for purposes of trade, agriculture, professional pursuits, or otherwise; to claim the benefit of the writ of habeas corpus; to institute and maintain actions of any kind in the courts of the state; to take, hold and dispose of property, either real or personal; and an exemption from higher taxes or impositions than are paid by the other citizens of the state; may be mentioned as some of the particular privileges and immunities of citizens, which are clearly embraced by the general description of privileges deemed to be fundamental:

The specific right to travel and nondiscrimination in imposts came directly from Article IV of the Articles of Confederation, and the right to habeas corpus came from both fundamental documents in England and the Constitution. Thus Washington's view of fundamental rights had deep roots in American history. He went on, however, to add a much more controversial item to his list of fundamental rights—"to which may be added the elective franchise, as regulated and established by the laws or constitution of the state in which it is to be exercised."

The franchise was a basic right that echoed new democratic ideals. Washington probably inserted the reference to regulation by the state to indicate that states could properly restrict the vote to residents even though it was a privilege. The franchise was, however, an awkward fit with all the other rights he had mentioned because citizens of other states could claim them. Thus later judges did not follow this aspect of Washington's opinion; they believed instead that political rights were not privileges under Article IV.

Justice Washington's list of privileges was open-ended, and the mechanism for enforcing them was not entirely clear. At the end of his examples, he said:

These, and many others which might be mentioned, are, strictly speaking, privileges and immunities, and the enjoyment of them by the citizens of each state, in every other state, was manifestly calculated (to use the expressions of the preamble of the corresponding provision in the old articles of confederation) "the better to secure and perpetuate mutual friendship and intercourse among the people of the different states of the Union."

Washington was using fundamentality as a mechanism to limit the state's obligations to nonresidents. Thus he probably meant that a state was obligated to give citizens of other states only those fundamental rights provided to its own citizens; however, the opinion was ambiguous. It could require that a state afford all fundamental rights to citizens of other states, regardless of what the state provides its own citizens. It could also be interpreted to require that a state provide fundamental rights to its own citizens. Washington did not make clear which of these three interpretations he intended because he believed it would make no difference. He assumed that states would secure fundamental rights to their own citizens, and he asserted the states had in fact done so. Oyster dredging was not that kind of privilege or immunity.

Justice Washington found that the privileges and immunities clause did not require the state to extend to nonresidents rights in the common property of the state. Thus in *Corfield*, nonresidents could be prohibited from dredging for oysters. Oysters in state waters, Washington said, are the common property of the citizens of the state, and "it would, in our opinion, be going quite too far to construe the grant of privileges and immunities of citizens, as amounting to a grant of a cotenancy in the common property of the state to the citizens of all the other states."

Washington's opinion was not a model of clarity. When he contended that the privileges and immunities clause could not be used to diminish the rights of citizens of the state, he appeared to analyze the common ownership of natural resources in the state in terms of the proprietary rights of individuals. He left open whether the right to commonly owned natural resources was outside the definition of privileges and immunities or whether it was a privilege, like the electoral franchise, that could appropriately be defined solely in terms of citizens who are residents of the state. Later courts tended to view Corfield v. Coryell (1823) as deciding that rights to public goods were not privileges and immunities.

Washington's discussion of privileges and immunities was not only murky, it was also dicta. He decided the case on procedural grounds and did not need to comment on the privileges and immunities issue. He held that Corfield brought the wrong form of action when he sued in trespass, because the seizure disrupted his lessee's possession and not his own. Nevertheless, Washington's description of privileges and immunities became the reference point for courts and congress for almost a century.

There were many reasons for the prominence and long life of the dicta in *Corfield.* It was the first discussion of privileges and immunities at any length by a justice of the Supreme Court. It resonated with the traditions of fundamental rights, and it functioned reasonably well to protect national citizenship while allowing states to make distinctions that did not threaten federalism.

Natural law was one of the bases for American claims during the revolutionary war. Courts thereafter were generally willing to use natural law language, as the Maryland Court of Appeals had done in *Campbell.* Although Judge Chase seemed to look to history, another Maryland Chase was one of natural law's strongest advocates. In Calder v. Bull (1798), Supreme Court Justice Samuel Chase asserted that the people did not give their state or federal government power to violate natural law. Justice James Iredell responded that natural law was a debatable subject "and all that the Court could properly say in such an event, would be, that the Legislature (possessed of an equal right of opinion) had passed an act which, in the opinion of the judges, was inconsistent with the abstract principles of natural justice." Despite Iredell's persuasiveness, judges in the post-revolutionary period sometimes referred to natural law in support of opinions that could have rested on particular clauses of the Constitution. For example, Chief Justice Marshall invoked natural law in a case that also rested on the contract clause (Fletcher v. Peck, 1810). Thus Bushrod Washington had reason to look to natural law sources when the vague language of the clause invited it.

Washington's opinion would not have lasted unless it was also a practical model for judicial decisions on Article IV. Indeed, his fundamental rights make some sense as rights that must be equal to maintain common citizenship and prevent federalism from disruption. Thus in Baldwin v. Fish and Game Commission of Montana (1978), Justice Harry Blackmun spoke of Washington as using "the term 'fundamental' in the modern as well as the 'natural right' sense." Washington argued that the standard of "all privileges and immunities of citizens" in Article IV did not refer to the specific privileges and immunities of citizens of a state but to privileges that are inherent in the concept of citizenship. It was only with respect to those general privileges that Article IV required the state to treat citizens of other states equally.

Washington included virtually all restrictions on natural liberties when he described privileges and immunities involving freedom from burdens: "the enjoyment of life and liberty . . . and to pursue and obtain happiness and safety," along with the right to pass through or reside in any other state and have exemption from higher taxes. The individual could do all these things if no government existed. To that extent the privilege or immunity was from government interference.

The other privileges Washington mentioned were benefits the government was expected to provide, such as protection of the person and property, rights to acquire and possess property of every kind, and the institutions for the enforcement of the rights created, including procedures like habeas corpus to assure the law has been appropriately applied. Most of these public benefits are products of the state's regulation of private relationships and are ancillary to that regulation. Nonresidents should be treated equally in all these areas. Equal does not mean the same because different circumstances may require different rules to produce equivalent results.

Washington's list of fundamental privileges and immunities did not extend to all the resources a state government conferred on individuals. It did not mention the provision of goods or services by the government beyond the types of traditional services stated. Thus later courts could use his description of fundamental rights to find that governments could appropriately limit special benefits created for their own residents.

Although Justice Washington did not specifically mention the first ten amendments to the Constitution (the Bill of Rights), they fit within his framework because they involve the enjoyment of liberty or are protections of person or property. He did mention habeas corpus as a fundamental right, but his opinion was unclear on whether states must afford fundamental rights to their own citizens. Courts and litigants understood that Article IV protected interstate concerns, and *Corfield* focused on the denial of privileges and immunities to citizens of other states. Washington said that Article IV secured the enjoyment of fundamental rights by citizens of each state "in every *other* state" (emphasis supplied). Habeas must be afforded to nonresidents if it was a remedy available to citizens of the state but not necessarily if it was denied to everyone. Thus *Corfield* was consistent with the understanding that Article IV privileges and immunities included the rights mentioned in the Bill of Rights but that citizens of other states were only guaranteed those privileges and immunities that the state decided to afford its own citizens.

Within a decade, the Supreme Court held that states were not bound by the Bill of Rights (Barron v. Baltimore, 1833). In *Barron*, Chief Justice Marshall wrote, "Had Congress engaged in the extraordinary occupation of improving the constitutions of the several states, by affording the people additional protection from the exercise of power by their own governments, in matters which concerned themselves alone, they would have declared this purpose in plain and intelligible language." By that reasoning, Article IV would not secure rights for a state's own citizens.

Corfield could, in theory, be used to argue that Article IV did secure rights for a state's own citizens because Justice Washington's opinion pointed to natural law and was vague about the mechanics of its application. Nevertheless, in practice, courts did not regard that decision as significantly different from the positive law approach of Judge Jeremiah Townley Chase's opinion in *Campbell.* Justice Washington wrote in *Corfield* that fundamental rights were "subject to such restraints as the government may justly prescribe for the general good of the whole." Thus the specific laws enacted by each state government became part of his definition of privileges and immunities.

Both Chase and Washington used *privileges and immunities* as a term of art to limit the scope of claims that a nonresident could assert. Not every state law conferred a privilege or immunity of citizenship. That perspective encouraged courts to find further justifications for upholding state laws that distinguished between residents and citizens of other states. A different law for nonresidents could be justified under Article IV if, in effect, it merely established an equality of rights between citizens and nonresidents. The nonresident could not be denied the right to own property in a state (a property right or fundamental right), but his property rights could be subject to special rules (e.g., attachment) when the rules produced effective equality with the state's own citizens (e.g., amenability to suit).

Although orators and courts spoke of the importance of Article IV in creating a national identity, courts rarely invalidated differential treatment between citizens of a state and citizens of other states. As a source for judicial protection of an economic common market, the privileges and immunities clause was far less important than the grant of power over interstate and foreign commerce and the prohibition against taxing imports or exports in Article I.[61]

Antebellum Decisions and Political Debate

Roughly a quarter of all privileges and immunities decisions in appellate courts before the Civil War involved issues of slavery. The law of many northern states declared that slaves who came there with their masters were entitled to freedom. Slaveowners unsuccessfully argued that they were entitled to the privileges of the law of their home state when traveling into another state. They found a better argument in *Corfield*'s reference to fundamental rights, arguing that protection of property was a fundamental right. Northern states could prohibit their own citizens from holding slaves, because Article IV did not apply to citizens in their state of residence; however, the nonresident slaveowner claimed that the failure to recognize his property rights in the slave constituted a denial of the privileges and immunities of citizens in the northern state. Not surprisingly, northern courts rejected these arguments. Property in another person is the antithesis of a fundamental right. Thus Massachusetts Chief Justice Lemuel Shaw wrote in Commonwealth v. Aves (1836):

> Though by the laws of a foreign state . . . a person may acquire property in a slave, such acquisition, being contrary to natural right, and effected by the local law, is dependent upon such local law for its existence and efficacy, and being contrary to the fundamental laws of this State, such general right of property cannot be exercised or recognized here.

State courts did not have to argue natural law to find that the privileges and immunities clause did not protect the slaveowner who sought to travel in the north with a slave. Courts like those of New York could insist that the clause dealt only with discrimination against nonresidents and gave no additional substantive rights (Lemmon v. People, 1860).

Southern laws posed a different problem. Fearful that free blacks might instigate slave insurrections, many slave states, as well as a number of free states, either prohibited the immigration of free blacks or discriminated against them. Parties challenged these laws as barriers to commerce and abridgments of the privileges and immunities of citizenship. The state courts sustained the laws against commerce clause objections, finding they were proper exercises of the police power. Even the U.S. Supreme Court seemed to agree. When the Court invalidated statutes of New York and Boston that restricted landing of immigrants, Justice James Wayne's majority opinion specifically noted in dicta that states retained their police powers to turn away persons who threatened the state: "[T]he States where slaves are have a constitutional right to exclude all such as are, from a common ancestry and country, of the same class of men" (*Passenger Cases,* 1849). State courts upheld racially discriminatory laws because the discrimination was not based on state citizenship, or sometimes on the grounds that free Negroes were not citizens and thus were not entitled to the protection of Article IV (Pendleton v. State, Ark., 1846; Amy v. Smith, Ky., 1822; State v. Newsome, N.C., 1844; State v. Claiborne, Tenn., 1838).

State courts, where most Article IV litigation occurred, usually did not distinguish between the reasoning of Chase and Washington. *Corfield*'s language created problems only if the state court were to find that the state's domestic legislation was valid under the state constitution yet that it violated the fundamental rights of citizens. State courts were understandably reluctant to find either that their state constitution failed to protect fundamental rights or that their state government had denied anyone a fundamental right. Because fundamental rights refer to a natural law moral concept and to a potentially enforceable legal right, disclaiming legal effect for fundamental rights would not, of course, avoid the moral responsibility to afford such rights. However, state courts had little incentive to announce that the state was not legally bound to afford citizens the fundamental rights of citizenship, especially when it was so easy to assert that the state did not violate these rights. Even if a state totally failed in its obligation to protect property, a court would necessarily be reluctant to supply the missing protection. Without some positive law protecting the property of some group, a court would have no basis for determining what specific protection would be appropriate. Thus Washington's fundamental rights definition of privileges and immunities did not help a litigant get any rights that did not already exist under positive law for the citizen of a state.

In any event, state court decisions could not conclusively determine the meaning of Article IV, and the few federal decisions on privileges and immunities were inconclusive as well. These early decisions of state and federal courts often took the form of a reference to *Campbell* or *Corfield* (if any precedent was discussed) for a description of *privileges and immunities,* followed by a few words exalting the importance of these rights and a decision that the state law in question was valid. The few early cases decided by the Court either applied the clause narrowly or discussed it in dicta that was not necessary for the decision.

For example, the Court stated that the privileges and immunities clause did not apply to corporations but held in favor of the corporation on other grounds (Bank of Augusta v. Earle, 1839). Chief Justice Roger Taney reasoned that corporations were considered citizens for purposes of Article III, which provides federal jurisdiction in cases between citizens of different states only insofar as the court looked to the people who carried on the business in the corporate name. If the corporation claimed Article IV privileges in the name of its shareholders and officers, the individuals should also take on the liabilities. Taney asserted that the clause gave citizens from other states no more rights than citizens of the state retained:

> The clause of the Constitution referred to certainly never intended to give to the citizens of each state the privileges of citizens in the several states, and at the same time to exempt them from the liabilities which the exercise of such privileges would bring upon individuals who were citizens of the state. This would give the citizens of other states far higher and greater privileges than are enjoyed by the citizens of the state itself. (Bank of Augusta v. Earle, 1839)

Imposing liability on shareholders would, however, defeat the whole nature of a corporation. Therefore Taney concluded, corporations were not citizens for purposes of the privileges and immunities clause of Article IV. Nevertheless, he held that a Georgia bank suing in federal court on the basis of diversity of citizenship could recover on a bill of exchange it purchased in Alabama because the Court presumed that Alabama would recognize the validity of the contract under principles of interstate comity (*Bank of Augusta* 1839).

When the Court discussion was not dicta, it was narrow. The Court, in an opinion by Justice Benjamin Curtis, said that a claim under Article IV could be raised only where the state law discriminated on the basis of state citizenship and not where it classified on some other basis (Conner v. Elliot, 1856). He eschewed any general definition of privileges and immunities, leaving it to a case-by-case approach.

> We do not deem it needful to attempt to define the meaning of the word privileges in this clause of the constitution. It is safer, and more in accordance with the duty of a judicial tribunal, to leave its meaning to be determined, in each case, upon a view of the particular rights asserted and denied therein. And especially is this true, when we are dealing with so broad a provision, involving matters not only of great delicacy and importance, but which are of such a character, that any merely abstract definition could scarcely be correct; and a failure to make it so would certainly produce mischief. (Conner v. Elliot 1856)

Although Curtis said that a failure to make a correct definition of privileges would produce mischief, his refusal to define it also created difficulties.

The failure of the courts to articulate a clear theory of the privileges and immunities of Article IV left the door open to arguments that it embodied natural law principles of fundamental rights. Judicial dicta on natural law together with Justice Washington's reference to fundamental rights in Article IV reinforced the idea that the Constitution in some fashion incorporated natural law principles. Although the Court never accepted natural law as an independent principle of decision and its application to privileges and immunities remained in judicial confusion, the doctrine retained significant power in political rhetoric.

Natural law was an important theme in opposition to slavery. As the Civil War neared, issues surrounding the enforcement of the fugitive slave clause (U.S. Const. Art. IV, § 2, Cl. 3) and the possible extension of slavery to the territories sparked discussion. Southern states insisted on the government's constitutional obligation to protect the institution of slavery. Speakers relied primarily on the fugitive slave clause along with policy considerations and appeals to a fundamental right of *self-determination* for the territories. Some even argued that the Fifth Amendment prohibited the federal government from eliminating slavery in areas under its control because that would deprive slaveowners of property in violation of the provision that "no person shall be . . . deprived of life, liberty or property without due process of law, nor shall private property be taken for public use, without just compensation." (U.S. Const., Amend. V). Most northerners, despite significant racial prejudice, believed slavery immoral and found these arguments preposterous. Nevertheless, many were willing to compromise if necessary to preserve the Union, and although they resented southern suppression of abolitionist speech, many also disapproved of abolitionist agitation.[62]

Abolitionists could be divided into three groups, each with different views on the obligations of government. They all agreed that slavery violated natural law. The largest group believed that, although slavery was contrary to natural law, principles of federalism embedded in the Constitution precluded interference with slavery within the southern states. They embraced the Constitution, however, because they thought that it was a source of power for isolating the hated institution and ultimately choking it to extinction. They believed the commerce clause gave the federal government power to abolish the interstate slave trade, and congressional power over the District of Columbia and the territories supported proposals for laws abolishing slavery there.[63] Another group thought that the Constitution, especially the fugitive slave clause, required the protection of slavery. They therefore denounced the Constitution as a pact with the devil that violated natural law.

Only a handful of abolitionists contended that natural law was legally binding. This third group of abolitionists, the *antislavery constitutionalists,* was important despite its small size, because their ideas influenced the drafting of the Fourteenth Amendment. They did not rely on Article IV because it did not assist citizens who remained in their home state; however, the antislavery constitutionalists used the idea of fundamental rights of citizenship that had been developed within the context of that clause. A number of antislavery constitutionalists argued that the due process clause of the Fifth Amendment had a substantive dimension that precluded Congress from taking from any man his property in himself. Among them, Alvin Stewart even argued that the Fifth Amendment was binding on the states, despite the *Barron* decision. Joel Tiffany and Lysander Spooner insisted that all persons born in the United States were citizens of the United States. Tiffany and Spooner said that citizens were entitled to fundamental rights by virtue of their citizenship, relying on the Preamble to the Constitution and the Declaration of Independence to bolster their arguments.[64] The speeches and writings of these men marked out a path for using substantive due process and natural law privileges and immunities of citizenship to further minority freedom. The desire to use the Constitution in that cause made such arguments attractive at the end of the Civil War.

During the antebellum period, however, the courts, like the general population, paid scant attention to antislavery constitutionalists. The mainstream abolitionist position was a moral and philosophical position on citizenship, not a legal constitutional claim. Legally, a slave was the personal property of his owner. An item of property could not be considered a member of society. Most abolitionists denounced this situation as a moral outrage but acknowledged that it was legally accurate. If slaves, although native-born persons, were not citizens, it followed that citizenship did not depend on place of birth alone. What then determined citizenship, and what rights did citizenship entail? The naturalized alien could demonstrate citizenship by a document obtained in a legal proceeding. The native-born person had no such document. Citizens were entitled to some rights under the Constitution, but by 1857 the Supreme Court had not yet settled what those rights were nor had it figured out how the citizenship of native-born persons should be determined.

Dred Scott and the Significance of Citizenship

Citizenship was crucial to the infamous *Dred Scott* decision (Dred Scott v. Sandford, 1857), where Chief Justice Taney said that African-Americans were not citizens. Congressmen consistently invoked *Dred Scott* as the exemplar of what the Civil War Amendments were intended to overrule. Thus it is necessary to examine that case to understand these later enactments, as well as to appreciate its discussion of privileges and immunities.

Dred Scott was born a slave. He resided for most of his life in Missouri. He accompanied his master, Dr. Emerson, a U.S. Army surgeon, on a tour of duty in Illinois, a state where slavery had been abolished. They later moved to a post in the upper Louisiana Territory, where slavery was prohibited by the terms of the Missouri Compromise. After returning to Missouri with Scott, Dr. Emerson died. Scott brought a petition for freedom against Emerson's widow in state court, claiming that his previous residence in a free state and a free territory had made him a free man. The Missouri court held that Scott, having voluntarily returned with his master to the slave state of Missouri after temporary residence elsewhere, was a slave under Missouri law. Subsequently, Mrs. Emerson moved to Massachusetts and remarried, leaving the administration of her former husband's estate with her brother, John Sanford of New York. Dred Scott then sued for his freedom in federal circuit court, asserting that the federal court had diversity of citizenship jurisdiction under Article III of the Constitution. Dred Scott said he was a citizen of Missouri and defendant Sanford was a citizen of New York. Sanford filed a plea in abatement (a pleading to stop the proceedings for procedural reasons), claiming that the court had no jurisdiction because Scott could not be a citizen for purposes of diversity jurisdiction. The Circuit Court accepted jurisdiction, but it directed a verdict on the merits for the defendant. Scott appealed to the Supreme Court.[65]

The Court held that Scott's suit should be dismissed for lack of jurisdiction. Although each justice wrote separately, Chief Justice Taney's opinion was denominated the opinion of the Court. He set forth three basic propositions: (1) that a Negro was not a citizen for purposes of diversity of citizenship jurisdiction, (2) that the free or slave status of a black man was dependent on state law, and (3) that the federal government could not prohibit slavery in its territories. The privileges and immunities clause of Article IV was not an issue in the case, but a number of justices thought it relevant to the issue of citizenship.

Four justices discussed the preliminary jurisdictional question whether, assuming Scott could prove he was free, he would be a citizen of a state for purposes of diversity jurisdiction. All four agreed that individuals must be citizens of the United States to be a citizen of a state for purposes of Article III. Justice Curtis's dissent contended that the states retained power to determine which of their own native-born inhabitants were citizens of the state and thus the United States because the federal power of naturalization extended only to aliens. Curtis noted that free African-Americans were considered citizens by a number of states, including various northern states, at the time of the adoption of the Constitution. Therefore if Scott was a citizen by the laws of the state of his birth, he was a citizen of the United States and was entitled to sue under diversity jurisdiction. Because the plea in abatement did not disclose the state of his birth or his status under its laws, nothing in the pleadings was inconsistent with his being a citizen, and the plea was therefore properly overruled.

Justice Curtis suggested that free African-American citizenship posed no problems for slave states under Article IV, Section 2 because a state would not violate the section if it denied nonresident African-Americans the same privileges that were denied resident free African-Americans. Curtis repeated his stance from *Conner*, insisting in his dissent in *Dred Scott* that the privileges and immunities clause requires only that no discrimination occurs on the basis of citizenship in applicable laws:

> [T]his clause of the Constitution does not confer on the citizens of one State, in all other States, specific and enumerated privileges and immunities. They are entitled to such as belong to citizenship, but not such as belong to particular citizens attended by other qualifications. Privileges and immunities which belong to citizens of a State, by reason of the operation of causes other than mere citizenship, are not conferred. . . . It rests with the States themselves so to frame their Constitutions and laws as not to attach a particular privilege or immunity to mere naked citizenship. (Dred Scott v. Sandford, 1857, Curtis. J. dissenting)

In other words, discrimination on the basis of race would not violate Article IV because it would not be discrimination on the basis of citizenship.

Chief Justice Taney and his concurring colleagues insisted that states could not determine citizenship for purposes of the federal constitution. The power of naturalization was given to Congress to prevent states from being able to make citizens of undesirable aliens and impose them on other states through Article IV. The same policy concerns applied to allowing the states power to determine which native born inhabitants were citizens. Chief Justice Taney, and Justices James Wayne and Peter Daniel, contended that the Constitution determined citizenship of native-born inhabitants. Because the document made no express statement on the issue, these justices argued that citizenship depended on the understanding of the framers and ratifiers when the Constitution was adopted.

With respect to the adoption of the Constitution, Justice Curtis' dissent had pointed out that Negro voters participated in its ratification in several northern states. Chief Justice Taney rejoined that citizenship was a uniform national concept and that the behavior of a few isolated states where few African-Americans lived did not determine the meaning of citizenship for the whole nation. States could create rights within their boundaries for African-Americans or aliens. Before the Constitution, states could make anyone a citizen of the state. Nevertheless, possessing rights of citizenship within a state did not make an individual a citizen of a state for national purposes. After all, only Congress had power to naturalize aliens.

Chief Justice Taney stressed that slavery existed in every state of the Union at the date of the adoption of the Constitution, and this demonstrated a disregard for African-Americans:

> They had for more than a century before been regarded as beings of an inferior order, and altogether unfit to associate with the white race, either in social or political relations; and so far inferior, that they had no rights which the white man was bound to respect; and that the negro might justly and lawfully be reduced to slavery for his benefit. (Dred Scott v. Sandford, 1857)

Taney cited extensive evidence that free African-Americans were regarded as inferior and subject to discrimination throughout the United States, but that did not compel his conclusion that African-Americans were not citizens. Second-class citizens are citizens. Women were subject to discrimination, yet no one doubted their citizenship.

Chief Justice Taney's conclusion that Negroes were not citizens rested on the consequences he attributed to citizenship. The lynchpin of his argument was the privileges and immunities clause. A citizen could sue under diversity jurisdiction in federal court to receive the privileges and immunities of citizens when in other states, and states could not bar citizens of other states from entrance. Chief Justice Taney was committed to the latter proposition by his dissent in the *Passenger Cases* (1849), where he noted in dicta that he would have struck down any restrictions on citizen movements:

> For all the great purposes for which the Federal government was formed, we are one people, with one common country. We are all citizens of the United States; and as members of the same community, must have the right to pass and repass through every part of it without interruption, as freely as in our own States. (*Passenger Cases,* 1849, Taney, J. dissenting)

Thus if an African-American from Massachusetts were a citizen for constitutional purposes, he would be entitled to enter Maryland and receive the privileges and immunities of a citizen there. In *Dred Scott*, Chief Justice Taney said this would be an impossible result: "It cannot be believed that the large slaveholding States regarded them as included in the word citizens, or would have consented to a Constitution which might compel them to receive them in that character from another State."

Chief Justice Taney could not conceive that African-Americans could be citizens under the Constitution, because the privileges and immunities of citizenship included freedom of movement, freedom of speech, freedom of assembly, and the right to bear arms. Chief Justice Taney said that if African-Americans could claim the privileges and immunities of citizens under Article IV:

> . . . it would exempt them from the operation of the special laws and from the police regulations which they considered to be necessary for their own safety. It would give to persons of the negro race, who were recognized as citizens in any one State of the Union, the right to enter every other State whenever they pleased, singly or in companies, without pass or passport, and without obstruction, to sojourn there as long as they pleased, to go where they pleased at every hour of the day or night without molestation, unless they committed some violation of law for which a white man would be punished; and it would give them the full liberty of speech in public and in private upon all subjects upon which its own citizens might speak; to hold public meetings upon political affairs, and to keep and carry arms wherever they went. And all of this would be done in the face of the subject race of the same color, both free and slaves, inevitably producing discontent and insubordination among them, and endangering the peace and safety of the State. (Dred Scott v. Sandford, 1857)

Chief Justice Taney's home state of Maryland had no compunction about prohibiting African-Americans from immigrating, requiring free African-Americans to carry certificates attesting to their free status, restricting meetings of free African-Americans, and requiring special licenses for African-Americans to own weapons. Unlike the slave, the free African-American in Maryland had rights (to sue, be sued, and own property) but these rights were weakened in practice by a prohibition on African-American testimony against whites. Moreover, the dominant powers in the state generally believed that these rights existed only so long as the white state legislature chose to acknowledge them, and that the legislature could constitutionally abolish all such rights and re-enslave free African-Americans because they were not citizens.[66]

Chief Justice Taney gave privileges and immunities a different content than did Justice Curtis. Chief Justice Taney saw greater problems because he thought the privileges and immunities clause required more than protection against disadvantages based on nonresidence. He assumed that the privileges and immunities of citizenship recognized in Article IV referred to fundamental obligations of the state. Chief Justice Taney understood that the Constitution did not intervene between the state and its own inhabitants, but he believed that the privileges and immunities clause required the state to treat citizens of other states as it treated those residents to whom it afforded the fundamental rights of citizens.

Although Chief Justice Taney said the Constitution gave each citizen rights outside his home state, in that it "placed him in every other State upon a perfect equality with its own citizens as to rights of person and rights of property," he argued that a state that does not protect the person and property of some of its inhabitants is not treating them as citizens. If a citizen of a state migrates to another state, Chief Justice Taney wrote, he is no longer a citizen of the first state, "[a]nd the State in which he resides may then, unquestionably, determine his status or condition, and place him among the class of persons who are not recognized as citizens, but belong to an inferior and subject race; and may deny him the privileges and immunities enjoyed by its citizens." In other words, "citizen of a state," for purposes of standing to raise a claim under Article III or IV of the Constitution, referred to a national citizenship that was uniformly determined. The Article IV claim of the nationally defined citizen of a state was to equality in privileges and immunities in another state with those residents the state (rather than the Constitution or national government) deemed its citizens. The out-of-state citizen did not get more rights than the citizen of the state, but the same rights that the state gave those persons it considered citizens. Additionally, one can determine whether a state recognizes a class of persons as citizens by the treatment that the state affords them—that is, whether the state provides them the fundamental rights of citizenship.

Chief Justice Taney probably did not expect his interpretation of the privileges and immunities clause to change radically the judicial role in reviewing Article IV claims. As a practical matter, only African-Americans had been drastically denied the fundamental rights ensured by Article IV. After they were excluded from the reach of Article IV, other state laws would almost certainly comply with its vague commands unless they discriminated against nonresidents. In essence, Chief Justice Taney used natural law reasoning to preserve what he saw as the status quo.

Taney also used natural law notions to give substance to the Fifth Amendment's due process clause, holding that the federal government could not prohibit slavery in the territories. That holding drew the most immediate fire because it undermined a major plank of the Republican Party platform. The political response was to condemn the portion of the opinion that invalidated the Missouri Compromise as poorly reasoned dicta, not binding on future legislation. This tactic diverted attention from the merits of his citizenship decision.

After the Civil War, the Thirteenth Amendment abolished slavery, and the discussion of *Dred Scott* focused on Taney's comments. Taney had insisted that citizenship carried important rights but excluded African-Americans. Reversing his decision by a constitutional amendment forced Congress and the courts to confront an issue left unresolved by *Dred Scott*: What were the privileges and immunities of citizenship?

U.S. CONSTITUTION: AMENDMENT XIV—CITIZENS OF THE UNITED STATES

The Fourteenth Amendment declared that all persons born in the United States were citizens of the United States and of the state where they reside, thus overturning by constitutional amendment Chief Justice Taney's *Dred Scott* opinion. The amendment also declared that no state shall abridge the privileges or immunities of citizens of the United States, taking its cue from that same opinion. The Civil

War amendments reflected agreement on the proposition that African-Americans were entitled to the fundamental rights of citizens, but they did not reflect a similar agreement on the exact definition of those rights or the mechanism for their enforcement.

The history of the Fourteenth Amendment has been canvassed thoroughly, but it continues to provide fodder for controversy because scholars from Michael Curtis to Raoul Berger claim that it resolves important issues of interpretation. Much of the dispute focuses on the meaning that the drafters and ratifiers of the amendment gave to *privileges and immunities*. Scholars agree that the framers intended the words to refer to the fundamental rights of citizens, but they disagree widely on what that meant.

Professor Michael Curtis has been a leading spokesman for incorporation. Curtis contends that *privileges and immunities* in the Fourteenth Amendment is a shorthand phrase that incorporates the first eight amendments.[67] He relies heavily on the statements of Representative John Bingham, the amendment's drafter, as well as the remarks of Senator Jacob Howard, who introduced it in the Senate, to demonstrate that the clause made the provisions of the first eight amendments to the Constitution applicable to the states.

Opponents of incorporation argue that Bingham never clearly articulated the proposition that the Bill of Rights was incorporated during the debates and insist that he was a confused and muddled thinker. They dismiss Howard as a last minute substitute for the ill committee chair. They argue that, if the states believed the clause made the amendments applicable to them, they would not have ratified the clause without discussing its impact on their own laws because several state statutes conflicted with the first eight amendments. Raoul Berger espoused the narrowest version of the privileges and immunities clause.[68] He confined it to the protection of property and person exemplified by the Civil Rights Act of 1866, not including any of the individual rights amendments.

Berger relied on statements that the amendment codified the Civil Rights Act and comments in the statutory debate that congressional power to enact the law came from its power to assure the rights of citizens to former slaves. However, the amendment uses general language that does not seem so limited. Congressmen referred to the individual rights of free speech and rights to assemble and petition for redress of grievances as rights of citizenship that had been abridged. They cited *Corfield* to define fundamental rights of citizens, which were more extensive than those in the Civil Rights Act, and they deleted references to *civil rights and immunities* from that statute because it might cover too much. This suggests that privileges and immunities include some rights that are found in the first eight amendments to the Constitution.

Professor Akil Amar has offered a controversial new approach to the privileges and immunities clause and the issue of incorporation, or *refined incorporation*.[69] Amar argued that the original Bill of Rights was significantly concerned with institutional relationships rather than individual rights, designed to protect the central role of the states and the majority of the population from the corruption of a government losing touch with the "people." He contended that *privileges and immunities* incorporated the constitutional provisions that were personal rights, while not affecting those concerned with federalism. On the other hand, Amar said that social changes altered the common understanding of the original provisions so that some originally designed for federalism became personal rights by the time of Reconstruction.

A host of other authors have canvassed the same debates and taken a variety of positions on the meaning that the framers gave the clauses; some suggest that the participants in the amendment process did not realize that their views were inconsistent, whereas others insist the enterprise is futile because the vague term meant different things to different people and no single original meaning ever existed.

Any attempt to make sense of the dispute requires an examination of debates that preceded the final form of the Fourteenth Amendment. The discussion of the Fourteenth Amendment made constant reference to the Civil Rights Act of 1866, which involved discussions of citizenship, definitions of civil rights and immunities, and reflected on the meaning of the Thirteenth Amendment with respect to these issues. Bingham's critical comments were made during discussions of a proposed amendment before passage of the Civil Rights Act of 1866.

The Thirteenth and Fourteenth amendments were intended to end the denial of the fundamental rights of citizenship to African-Americans. To effectuate this intention, the Fourteenth Amendment's framers adopted the general language of the Constitution regarding the privileges and immunities of citizenship. As a result, the amendment suffered from the vagueness that had afflicted the privileges and immunities clause of Article IV, Section 2. Rights could be defined—if at all—only in an infinite series of concrete cases. At the time, this vagueness was, to some extent, appealing. The general language concealed serious conflicts between persons involved in the amendment adoption process. It also hid the contradictory intentions often held by individual framers who wanted to "have their cake and eat it too," that is, to secure fundamental rights without discrimination yet preserve state sovereignty. The rebel states were to be reconstructed by heavy federal intervention, whereas the loyal states were to be beyond federal power—and this was to be accomplished by a single uniform constitutional command. After the amendment was adopted, congressional debates on its meaning reiterated earlier discussions of fundamental rights, but for the first time they also suggested a distinction between the privileges and immunities of citizens of a state and those of the United States that would largely negate the impact of the privileges and immunities clause.

The Thirteenth Amendment and the Civil Rights Act of 1866

After the Civil War the institution of slavery bore the blame for every denial of fundamental rights found in America. As the abolitionists had argued, slavery violated natural law, by depriving slaves of their natural rights. Further, slaveowners violated the natural rights of free citizens to maintain the institution. Northerners believed the institution had corrupted southern society, leading to suppression of all dissent over the morality of slavery and eventually to rebellion against the Union itself. Slavery also led the southern states to inflict their restrictive laws on northerners who entered slave states. Thus during the debate on the Thirteenth Amendment, Senator Henry Wilson of Massachusetts said:

> Twenty million free men in the free States were practically reduced to the condition of semi-citizens of the United States; for the enjoyment of their rights, privileges and immunities as citizens depended upon a perpetual residence north of Mason and Dixon's line. South of that line, the rights which I have mentioned [freedom of speech, of religion, and the right to peaceably assemble and petition for redress of grievances], and many more which I might mention could be enjoyed only when debased to the uses of slavery.[70]

The Thirteenth Amendment, which abolished slavery, was widely viewed as a cure for the ills of antebellum America; however, the debates leading to the adoption of the amendment were not very illuminating on how the medicine would work. For example, Senator Wilson and Representatives John Kasson of Iowa and Green Smith of Kentucky argued for the amendment by stressing the loss of free speech that had occurred in the slave states.[71] The abolition of slavery would presumably end prosecutions for abolitionist speech, but it was not readily apparent how the amendment would secure freedom of speech on other topics. Not surprisingly, the abolition of slavery did not eliminate oppression.

Many southern states responded to abolition by enacting black codes, discriminating against African-Americans in basic rights and forcing them to remain on the plantations. Senator Lyman Trumbull of Illinois introduced a bill in the Senate to deal with this issue. Congressional reaction to the black codes and Trumbull's bill evoked the first real debate over the Thirteenth Amendment's scope. This debate is by no means an accurate guide to the intentions of the amendment's framers. Each side sought to characterize the amendment to advance their immediate goal: the support or defeat of a civil rights bill that prohibited racial discrimination in certain matters, a context the amendment's drafters had not envisioned.

The Republican majority argued that African-Americans were citizens or at least that Congress could assure their citizenship. This led them to discuss the fundamental rights of citizenship in relationship to the proposed bill. As a result the debate on the Civil Rights bill is crucial to understand the views of congressmen on the meaning of the phrase "privileges or immunities of citizens of the United States" when they adopted the Fourteenth Amendment only a few months later.

Opponents of the civil rights bill articulated a narrow view that denied citizenship to African-Americans. Democrats argued that the abolition of slavery did not empower Congress to legislate against racial discrimination. According to Chief

Justice Taney in *Dred Scott*, free African-Americans were not citizens of the United States, and neither Congress nor the individual states could alter that status. Only a constitutional amendment could confer citizenship on African-Americans born within the United States. Under this view, the abolition of slavery simply meant that all African-Americans would have the same status that free African-Americans had before the Civil War, which in many states involved pervasive discrimination. This restrictive interpretation was voiced by Democrats, including Senators who had voted for the Thirteenth Amendment, like Reverdy Johnson of Maryland and Peter Van Winkle of West Virginia, and by nominal Republicans like Senator Edgar Cowan of Pennsylvania. "It was intended," said Senator Cowan, "to give to the negro the privilege of the habeas corpus; that is, if anybody persisted in the face of the constitutional amendment in holding him as a slave, that he should have an appropriate remedy to be delivered. That is all."[72]

Senator Trumbull, the sponsor of the civil rights bill, took a very different view. The Thirteenth Amendment altered Taney's fundamental assumption, because it placed African-Americans beyond state power to enslave. Thus it removed the major ground for deciding that they were not citizens. Radical Republicans could now argue forcefully that African-Americans, like all other citizens, were entitled to the fundamental rights of citizens in a free society. Trumbull contended that the Thirteenth Amendment of its own force forbade racial discrimination with respect to contract rights and property ownership. When Democratic Senator Thomas Hendricks argued that "no new rights are conferred upon the freedman" by the Thirteenth Amendment,[73] Senator Trumbull responded:

> With the destruction of slavery necessarily follows the destruction of the incidents to slavery. When slavery was abolished, slave codes in its support were abolished also.
>
> Those laws that prevented the colored man going from home, that did not allow him to buy or to sell, or to make contracts; that did not allow him to own property; that did not allow him to enforce rights; that did not allow him to be educated, were all badges of servitude made in the interest of slavery and as a part of slavery.[74]

Subsequently, Trumbull said, "[A]ny statute which is not equal to all, and which deprives any citizen of civil rights which are secured to other citizens, is an unjust encroachment upon his liberty; and is, in fact, a badge of servitude which, by the Constitution, is prohibited."[75] He cited both *Campbell*[76] and *Corfield*[77] as descriptive of the civil rights of citizens. Antebellum restrictions on free African-Americans did not prove that discrimination was separate from slavery; instead, they were part of the heritage of slavery. Thus Trumbull argued that the Thirteenth Amendment abolished racial discrimination in all laws involving the protection of life, liberty, and property.[78]

Most Republicans, whatever their own views, realized that others might read Section 1 of the amendment to do no more than forbid the existence of slavery.

They relied instead on Section 2, which provided that Congress should have power to enforce the amendment, as the constitutional basis for the statute. For example, when the House considered the bill, Representative James Wilson of Iowa said, "A man who enjoys the civil rights mentioned in this bill cannot be reduced to slavery. Anything which protects him in the possession of these rights insures him against reduction to slavery. This settles the appropriateness of this measure, and that settles its constitutionality."[79]

The Senate passed a bill, which began by contradicting the views on citizenship found in Chief Justice Taney's *Dred Scott* opinion. It stated, "That all persons in the United States and not subject to any foreign Power, excluding Indians not taxed, are hereby declared to be citizens of the United States without distinction of color."

The second clause in the bill set forth a general prohibition on racial discrimination: "And there shall be no discrimination in civil rights or immunities among the inhabitants of any State or Territory of the United States on account of race, color or previous condition of slavery."

Finally, the bill specified which rights should the same for inhabitants of the United States:

> . . . the inhabitants of every race and color . . . shall have the same right to make and enforce contracts, to sue, be parties, and give evidence, to inherit, purchase, lease, sell, hold and convey real and personal property, and to full and equal benefit of all laws and proceedings for the security of person and property, and shall be subject to like punishment, pains and penalties, and to none other, any law, statute, ordinance, regulation or custom to the contrary notwithstanding.[80]

When the House took up the bill, the House Judiciary Committee proposed to change all references to *inhabitants* to refer to *citizens*, and to add that all citizens shall have the same right "as is enjoyed by white citizens."[81] Limitation to citizens satisfied constitutional objections over the power of Congress to require equal treatment of noncitizens. The qualification that the "same right" be the right "enjoyed by white citizens" demonstrated that the law did not break down all legal distinctions but only prohibited racial discrimination.[82] The Committee's work did not quell all doubts; the phrase "civil rights or immunities" in the bill still troubled members of the House and gave rise to a debate that examined the term in greater detail.

Speaking for the committee, Representative Wilson explained that the language of "no discrimination in civil rights or immunities" did not apply to voting, jury service, or presence in schools. In his view, civil rights were only the rights of personal security, personal liberty, and the right to acquire and enjoy property, including the rights of contract and access to courts essential to secure property. Civil rights did not apply to the establishment, support, or management of government.

Immunities were designed only to create equality in the exemptions from operations of law.[83]

Representative John Broomall of Pennsylvania thought that *rights and immunities* referred to personal liberties like speech and movement. He argued that the bill was necessary because southern states denied personal liberties:

> . . . for thirty years prior to 1860 everybody knows that the rights and immunities of citizens were habitually and systematically denied in certain States to the citizens of other States: the right of speech, the right of transit, the right of domicil, the right to sue, the writ of *habeas corpus*, and the right of petition.[84]

Democrats seeking to defeat the bill articulated their own views on what rights the bill would reach. Columbus Delano of Ohio inquired whether the bill gave African-Americans the right to be jurors but did not seem reassured when Wilson replied that it did not. Delano objected to equality in testimony, inheritance, and schools. Michael Kerr of Indiana argued that the language of "civil rights and immunities" was vague and might possibly apply to schools.[85] Yet broad views of the term were not confined to obstructionist Democrats. Republican John Bingham of Ohio complained that the language prohibiting discrimination in civil rights would extend to political rights and moved to delete it. Bingham also argued that the penal provisions of the act were not constitutional because:

> . . . the enforcement of the bill of rights, touching the life, liberty, and property of every citizen of the Republic within every organized State of the Union, is of the reserved powers of the States, to be enforced by State tribunals and by State officials acting under the solemn obligations of an oath imposed upon them by the Constitution of the United States. . . . The Constitution does not delegate to the United States the power to punish offenses against the life, liberty, or property of the citizen in the States, nor does it prohibit that power to the States, but leaves it as the reserved power of the States, to be by them exercised. . . .[86]

The bill was returned to the committee, which struck out the prohibition on discrimination in civil rights and immunities. Wilson explained that this was done to make clear that the bill did not cover the franchise. He contended that the deletion did not change the bill's effect because the other sections dealt with everything that was a civil right or immunity.[87] The amended bill defined citizenship of the United States without regard to color; specified that all citizens have the same rights as white citizens to contract, sue, testify, and acquire property, and to full and equal benefit of all laws for the security of person and property; and that they shall be subject to like punishment. Congress passed the bill, but President Andrew Johnson vetoed it.

Senator Trumbull responded to the veto message by affirming that abolition secured African-Americans citizenship and enabled Congress to assure they obtain the rights of citizens:

> To be a citizen of the United States carries with it some rights; and what are they? They are those inherent, fundamental rights which belong to free citizens or free men in all countries, such as the rights enumerated in this bill, and they belong to them in all the States of the Union.[88]

In the House, Representative William Lawrence of Ohio argued that the privileges and immunities clause of Article IV gave Congress power to protect the fundamental rights of citizens.[89] He claimed that fundamental rights of citizens are anterior to and independent of the Constitution, but that Article IV recognizes them and "by implication affirms [them] to exist among citizens of the same State."[90] Lawrence defined privileges and immunities as simply the rights to life and personal security and the right to acquire and enjoy property.[91] Lawrence's view of congressional power under Article IV had no judicial support and was inconsistent with the language and history of that clause. He took Justice Washington's view that privileges and immunities were fundamental rights of all citizens, but he ignored the way courts had limited its impact to proscribing discrimination on the basis of residence. Instead, Lawrence adopted the antislavery constitutionalist argument that the federal government could protect all the rights of citizens.

Congress overrode Johnson's veto, and the Civil Rights Act of 1866 became law. According to its supporters, the power to pass the Civil Rights Act came from the Thirteenth Amendment, which, by giving Congress power to enforce the abolition of slavery, meant that Congress could secure for the class of persons formerly subjected to slavery all the privileges and immunities that "belong of right to citizens of all free governments." Whether the act included all such privileges and immunities, however, is questionable.[92] Even Trumbull had stated that the rights in the bill were only examples of inherent fundamental rights. The Civil Rights Act of 1866 had dealt with the most egregious examples of racial discrimination under state law, and the omission of comprehensive language in the statute made precise definition of the words *civil rights* or *immunities* irrelevant. Congress recognized the continuing racial prejudice in the North and South, and it made no attempt to end discrimination in political rights.

The defects of the Thirteenth Amendment as a vehicle for dealing with racial discrimination were apparent. Its authority as the basis for the abolition of the black codes was uncertain. Despite strong arguments that it authorized congressional action against any racial discrimination in civil rights, many had doubts about the reception such arguments would receive in the courts. Even if the courts deferred to congressional power under Section 2 of the amendment, a later Congress could repeal civil rights legislation. Thus Congress recognized the need for an amendment to the Constitution that would place the constitutionality of federal legislative efforts to abolish racial discrimination beyond question and would secure those rights in the Constitution itself.

The Fourteenth Amendment

When the Thirty-Ninth Congress opened in December of 1865, the House and Senate established a Joint Committee on Reconstruction to formulate a plan to deal with the aftermath of the Civil War, including conditions for readmission of states that had been in rebellion. In February of 1866, after the Civil Rights bill had passed the Senate but before the House discussed it, the joint committee proposed a new constitutional amendment:

> The Congress shall have power to make all laws which shall be necessary and proper to secure to the citizens of each State all privileges and immunities of citizens in the several States, and to all persons in the several States equal protection in the rights of life, liberty, and property.[93]

The proposal came from Congressman John Bingham of Ohio, who a few days later opposed the Civil Rights bill as beyond the power of Congress under the Thirteenth Amendment. Thus Bingham believed a constitutional amendment was needed to enable Congress to deal with the problems of reconstruction. Bingham's views are critical to the ultimate form of the amendment but are not easy to appreciate.

Bingham copied the privileges and immunities clause directly from Article IV, but he had an unusual understanding of its meaning. Bingham believed that the rights claimed by citizens of a state in Article IV were the privileges and immunities "of citizens of the United States." For example, in 1859, debating the admission of Oregon as a state, Bingham said, "There is an ellipsis in the language employed in the Constitution, but its meaning is self-evident that it is 'the privileges and immunities of citizens of the United States in the several States' that it guaranties." According to Bingham, those privileges included "the rights of life and liberty and property, and their due protection in the enjoyment thereof by law." He argued that Oregon's Constitution denied persons of color these protected rights, including habeas corpus, trial by jury, property ownership, contract, and the ability to maintain suits.[94] Similarly, debating a bill on the District of Columbia in 1862, Bingham said:

> "All privileges and immunities of citizens of the United States in the several States," is what is guarantied by the Constitution, as gentlemen doubtless know, which must be supplied to express clearly its meaning. The great privilege and immunity of an American citizen to be respected everywhere in this land, and specially in this District, is that they shall not be deprived of life, liberty, or property without due process of law.[95]

Thus Bingham believed that the privileges and immunities of citizens of the United States were fundamental rights including ones like due process and trial by jury that were specified among the amendments to the Constitution.

Bingham's fundamental rights version of privileges and immunities was paired with his belief that Congress had no power to enforce those rights. States had an obligation by Article IV to secure all fundamental rights to citizens, and they took an oath to the Constitution that required them to do so. However, Article IV was not a grant of power, and Congress had been given no power to enforce this clause. Bingham's position may be traced to the antislavery argument on the fugitive slave act that Congress could not enforce the fugitive slave provisions of Article IV because they were not in the form of a grant of power.[96] Bingham drafted the amendment to give Congress power to enforce these fundamental rights.

The grant of power drew strong objection. Representative Robert Hale, a moderate Republican from New York, argued that Bingham's proposal violated the basic principles of the Constitution, by granting power rather than limiting it to protect against abuses of individual rights. Hale pointed to the due process clause as an example of the way limitations properly worked. He suggested that the proposal gave Congress power to legislate on life, liberty, and property, subject to the condition that the federal legislation be uniform.[97] Bingham responded that the amendment would not authorize such legislation but was needed to make state officials act properly. Bingham challenged Hale to give him a case in which the Constitution protected a citizen's rights against the state. Another representative then challenged Bingham to name a case where the Constitution was insufficient. When it was his turn to talk the next day, Bingham responded:

> A gentleman on the other side interrupted me and wanted to know if I could cite a decision showing that the power of the Federal Government to enforce in the United States courts the bill of rights under the articles of amendment to the Constitution had been denied. I answered that I was prepared to introduce such decisions; and that is exactly what makes plain the necessity of adopting this amendment.[98]

Bingham then cited Barron v. Baltimore (1833), which held that the first eight amendments did not apply to the states. Believing that states were bound by the privileges and immunities clause to afford all their citizens fundamental rights including the first eight amendments, Bingham thought the case simply precluded federal enforcement of those rights.

In proposing this new amendment, Bingham said that its language came from Article IV, Section 2 and from the Fifth Amendment:

> The proposition pending before the House is simply a proposition to arm the Congress . . . with the power to enforce the bill of rights as it stands in the Constitution today. . . .

> Gentlemen admit the force of the provisions in the bill of rights, that the citizens of the United States shall be entitled to all the privileges and immunities of citizens of the United States in the several States, and that no person shall be deprived of life, liberty, or property without due process of law; but they say "We are opposed to its enforcement by act of Congress under an amended Constitution, as proposed."[99]

In this passage, Bingham did not use "bill of rights" to refer specifically to the amendments to the Constitution. He said he was referring to the privileges and immunities clause of Article IV, Section 2 and the due process clause of the Fifth Amendment. However, Bingham believed that the privileges of Article IV included rights specifically stated in the amendments to the Constitution. Because he had made clear in his colloquy with Hale that the amendment was needed to deal with state violations of those rights, Congressmen knew that Bingham intended the words "privileges and immunities of citizens in the several states" in his proposed amendment to include the rights contained in the first eight amendments.

Bingham also claimed in presenting his proposed amendment that the Constitution already declared "all men are equal in the rights of life and liberty before the majesty of American law."[100] Apparently he reasoned that rights to life, liberty, and property are protected by due process, and that process is the same for all men. Although that is the easiest manner of reading constitutional language to expressly secure equality, he might also have considered equality in privileges and immunities to be the result of the privileges and immunities clause of Article IV.

Opponents of the proposed amendment, understanding the impact that a broad interpretation of the phrase *privileges and immunities* could have, protested that the proposal would convert the privileges and immunities clause from a prohibition of discrimination against nonresidents into a general charter for federal legislation. Democratic Congressman Andrew Rogers of New Jersey objected that, under the proposed amendment, all rights would become federal. He referred to the listing of privileges and immunities made by Justice Bushrod Washington in *Corfield*. Rogers noted that the list included the exercise of the franchise, and he argued that the proposed amendment would enable Congress to determine the qualifications for voting.[101]

A moderate Republican from New York, Giles Hotchkiss, like Hale, objected that the amendment appeared to authorize Congress to pass uniform laws protecting life, liberty, and property in the states. He argued that the destruction of state power over municipal legislation was inadvisable.[102] Bingham protested this construction, but Hotchkiss replied that, at best, the language was unclear. He added that the proposal was also defective because it only granted power to Congress, and therefore Congress could refuse to prohibit discrimination and could repeal any law it had passed. Hotchkiss suggested that the amendment should be changed to say that no state shall discriminate against any class of citizens.

Action on the committee's proposal was then postponed indefinitely, and it was never passed. In the Senate, Senator William Stewart of Nevada noted that this proposed amendment did not accomplish its framer's intention but was a general grant of power.[103]

The debates on this early proposal and its ultimate rejection provide the basis for the argument that the Thirty-Ninth Congress did not intend to shift power to the federal government to enact the type of legislation that was previously the exclusive province of the states. They demonstrate that Representative Bingham used *privileges and immunities* to include the first eight amendments to the Constitution; however, Congress did not pass the version of the Fourteenth Amendment to which his remarks were directed.

After the passage of the Civil Rights Act, the House took up a new bill proposing an amendment to the Constitution. This bill contained the language of the present Fourteenth Amendment's Section 1, without the first sentence on citizenship:

> No State shall make or enforce any law which shall abridge the privilege or immunities of citizens of the United States; nor shall any State deprive any person of life, liberty, or property without due process of law; nor deny to any person within its jurisdiction the equal protection of the laws.[104]

The form had been changed from a grant of power to secure privileges and immunities to a prohibition on state abridgment of them, with a power merely to enforce the prohibition. Unlike Bingham's first proposed amendment, the privileges and immunities were specified to be those of citizens of the United States. The specification was significant to Bingham, whose position that *privileges and immunities* included the first eight amendments depended on the privileges being those of citizens of the United States. Five years after the Fourteenth Amendment was adopted, Bingham explained that he had mistakenly believed the supremacy clause made the Bill of Rights binding on the states when he made his first proposal. He then realized that *Barron* held the rights did not apply to the states at all. Thus when Bingham came forth with a new proposal several months later, he attempted to make sure that they did apply. Looking back in 1871, he insisted that "the privileges and immunities of citizens of the United States, as contradistinguished from the citizens of a State, are chiefly defined in the first eight amendments to the Constitution of the United States."[105] However, Bingham did not mention incorporation of the Bill of Rights in the floor debate on the new proposal. His remarks there made only a veiled allusion:

> It is the power in the people, the whole people of the United States, by express authority of the Constitution to do that by congressional enactment which hitherto they have not had the power to do, and have never even attempted to do; that is, to protect by national law

> the privileges and immunities of all the citizens of the Republic and the inborn rights of every person within its jurisdiction whenever the same shall be abridged or denied by the unconstitutional acts of any State.
>
> Allow me, Mr. Speaker, in passing, to say that this amendment takes from no State any right that ever pertained to it. No State ever had the right, under the forms of law or otherwise, to deny to any freeman the equal protection of the laws or to abridge the privileges or immunities of any citizen of the Republic although many of them have assumed and exercised the power, and that without remedy.[106]

Congressmen familiar with Bingham's previously expressed views should have understood his reference to privileges and immunities included the Bill of Rights, but at face value Bingham's remarks were consistent with a generalized reference to fundamental rights.

The change of phrasing from "citizens in the several states" to "citizens of the United States" bore little significance to anyone other than Bingham, because no clear distinction had been articulated between the privileges and immunities of citizens of a state and those of citizens of the United States. Speakers discussed the new proposed amendment as though the privileges and immunities of United States citizens that it mentioned were identical to the privileges and immunities of the citizen of a state referred to in Article IV. For example, Representative Farnsworth of Illinois said, "There is but one clause in [Section 1 of the proposed amendment] which is not already in the Constitution, and it might as well in my opinion read, 'No State shall deny to any person within its jurisdiction the equal protection of the laws.'"[107] The leading radical, Thaddeus Stevens of Pennsylvania, while introducing the new proposal, said that the provisions of Section 1:

> . . . are all asserted, in some form or other, in our DECLARATION or organic law. But the Constitution limits only the action of Congress, and is not a limitation on the States. This amendment supplies that defect, and allows Congress to correct the unjust legislation of the States, so far that the law which operates upon one man shall operate equally upon all. . . . Some answer, "Your civil rights bill secures the same things." That is partly true, but a law is repealable by a majority.[108]

Stevens's opening phrase stated fairly clearly that the language of Section 1 comes from Article IV, just as equal protection was derived from the Declaration of Independence assertion that all men are created equal and the due process clause came from the Fifth Amendment. Congress could correct racial discrimination in privileges and immunities because of the new clause and the equal protection guaranty, and the new due process clause now limited the states explicitly. Stevens's remark was opaque on whether any other amendments now applied to the states. No one else in the House discussed whether they applied to the states.

Some opponents of the amendment argued that its language allowed too broad a federal power. Democrats objected to the vagueness of the term, and said the federal government would use it to secure the vote. Representatives Benjamin Boyer[109] and Samuel Randall of Pennsylvania complained this would happen.[110] Andrew Rogers of New Jersey thought the privileges and immunities clause could be understood to involve "all the rights we have under the laws of the country"—that is, the right to vote, to marry, to contract, to be a judge or a juror.[111]

Supporters denied this construction, specifically focusing on the thorny issue of voting rights. Bingham noted, "The amendment does not give, as the second section shows, the power to Congress of regulating suffrage in the several States."[112] Others sadly admitted that the people would surely reject any attempt to grant suffrage to blacks.[113]

Whatever their views of its scope, representatives on both sides of the aisle agreed that the measure corresponded to the Civil Rights Act of 1866. John Broomall of Pennsylvania noted that those who were to vote on the proposed constitutional amendment "voted for this proposition in another shape, in the civil rights bill."[114] Henry Raymond said he voted against the civil rights bill because he thought it unconstitutional, "[b]ut now it comes before us in the form of an amendment to the Constitution, which proposes to give Congress the power to attain this precise result," and he supported the amendment.[115]

The measure passed in the House, and in May 1866 the Senate took up consideration of the proposed amendment. When the amendment was introduced, the committee chairman, Senator William Fessenden of Maine, was ill, and Senator Jacob Howard of Michigan introduced the amendment giving "so far as I understand [the] views and motives [of the committee which drafted the amendment]."[116]

Howard first addressed the privileges and immunities clause. "[W]e may gather some intimation of what probably will be the opinion of the judiciary by referring to a case adjudged many years ago in one of the circuit courts of the United States by Judge Washington," he said, speaking of *Corfield*.[117] Howard stated that this case correctly characterized the privileges and immunities in the second section of Article IV.

The identification of the Fourteenth Amendment privileges and immunities with both *Corfield* and the Civil Rights Act raises the question of their relationship. Trumbull cited *Corfield* when he proposed the Civil Rights Act, and Representative Wilson had claimed that the act contained all the civil rights and immunities basic to citizens. Justice Washington in *Corfield* had listed protection by the government, the right to institute and maintain actions in court, and the right to hold and dispose of property as fundamental privileges and immunities. The Civil Rights Act included these fundamental rights. It conferred on African-Americans the same rights as white citizens "to sue, be parties and give evidence, to inherit, purchase, lease, sell, hold and convey real and personal property, and to the full and equal benefit of all laws and proceedings for the security of person and property."[118]

Other privileges and immunities discussed in *Corfield* were indirectly secured. *Corfield* mentioned the right to "pass through or to reside in any other state, for purposes of trade, agriculture, professional pursuits, or otherwise," and the benefit of habeas corpus. These were not expressly mentioned in the Civil Rights Act of 1866, but the act's declaration of citizenship secured the right to travel and change residence through the privileges and immunities clause of Article IV and the nature of the federal government. The act secured habeas corpus to the extent it was available to white citizens, because it is a proceeding for the security of the person. Freedom to pursue an occupation was within both the general and specific headings of privileges of *Corfield*, yet it was protected by the 1866 act only by the provision on the right to contract.

In *Corfield*, Justice Washington left the listing of privileges and immunities open —"these and many others which might be mentioned." Representative Broomall's list of rights and immunities during the initial stages of debate on the Civil Rights Act emphasized rights not mentioned by Washington—the right of free speech and the right to petition. It was, of course, this open-textured nature of *rights and immunities* that led the House to omit it from the statute in favor of a specific enumeration. Congress dropped the general language of *civil rights and immunities* to avoid any implication that the statute might apply to another privilege mentioned by Washington in *Corfield*—the elective franchise. In sum, congressmen agreed that the matters specified by the statute were privileges and immunities of citizenship, but believed there were privileges and immunities not covered by the act, although they reached no consensus on the full coverage of that term.

Senator Howard certainly viewed the listing of *Corfield* and its reflection in the Civil Rights Act as only a part of the items protected. "To these privileges and immunities, whatever they may be—for they are not and cannot be fully defined in their entire extent and precise nature—to these should be added the personal rights guaranteed and secured by the first eight amendments of the Constitution. . . ."[119] Howard said that these rights "are secured to the citizen solely as a citizen of the United States and as a party in their courts."[120] He acknowledged that these rights did not currently restrict state legislatures, nor did the Constitution empower Congress to give them effect against the states. "The great object of the first section of this amendment is, therefore, to restrain the power of the States and compel them at all times to respect these great fundamental guarantees."[121]

Howard, like all the other supporters of the amendment, insisted that the amendment did not apply to political rights: "the first section of the proposed amendment does not give to either of these classes the right of voting. The right of suffrage is not, in law, one of the privileges or immunities thus secured by the Constitution. It is merely the creature of law.[122]

The rest of Howard's speech and the discussion that followed focused on the other sections of the proposed amendment. Several days later, Howard proposed the present first sentence of the amendment dealing with citizenship: "All persons born or naturalized in the United States, and subject to the jurisdiction thereof, are citizens of the United States and of the state wherein they reside."[123] This was the language that had been inserted in the Civil Rights Act. No one, however, suggested that the clause defining U.S. citizenship had any bearing on the content of the privileges and immunities clause. Indeed, Republican Senator John Henderson of Missouri, discussing the new clause on citizenship, referred to Chief Justice Taney's *Dred Scott* opinion. He said that Chief Justice Taney conceded to members of the community "all the personal rights, privileges, and immunities guaranteed to citizens of this 'new Government.'"[124] Chief Justice Taney had discussed the privileges of citizenship under Article IV in terms of their application to citizens of the United States. Henderson's speech indicated agreement with Chief Justice Taney's views on privileges and immunities of citizenship, but, of course, condemned him for excluding African-Americans from citizenship.

At the beginning of June, the Republicans held a closed party caucus. They agreed on the language of the Fourteenth Amendment, including some changes in Sections 2 through 4 that dealt with immediate postwar issues, and agreed to stand behind the result without splintering on the merits of particular clauses or proposed alterations. This meant that proponents did not engage in much later discussion on the meaning of particular clauses. Howard's statement that *privileges and immunities* include the first eight amendments was never repeated. After the caucus, Republican Senator Luke Poland of Vermont said that the privileges and immunities clause "secures nothing beyond what was intended by the original provision of the Constitution, that 'the citizens of each State shall be entitled to all privileges and immunities of citizens in the several States.'"[125] Senator John Henderson of Missouri referred to the Freedman's Bureau Bill and the Civil Rights Act as affording "[t]hose fundamental rights of person and property which cannot be denied to any person without disgracing the Government itself."[126] Democrats, such as Thomas Hendricks of Indiana and Reverdy Johnson of Maryland, objected to the insertion of privileges and immunities in the proposed Fourteenth Amendment because, as Johnson said, "I do not understand what will be the effect of that." [127] Nonetheless, the Senate passed the amendment. The House then passed the Senate version, with virtually no debate other than protestations of sadness at the lack of a guarantee for suffrage.[128]

The debates leave no room for doubt that the privileges or immunities clause of the Fourteenth Amendment referred to the same privileges and immunities as Article IV. Every speaker who touched on the issue stated that the Fourteenth Amendment clause was derived from Article IV.[129] Justice Washington's description in *Corfield* of privileges and immunities under Article IV as the fundamental rights of citizens in a free society was taken as applicable to the new clause in the Fourteenth Amendment, with an exception for the franchise, which was viewed as a political right not subject to either Article IV or the Fourteenth Amendment. Thus, the framers of the Fourteenth Amendment understood that they were placing a guarantee of *fundamental rights* in the document.

Hindsight shows the threat to federalism from placing undefined fundamental rights in the Constitution, and some contemporaries pointed it out as well.[130] At the time, however, most framers apparently hoped to ensure such rights to African-Americans, while preserving state sovereignty in its then current form. The general language they adopted masked the potential conflict between these goals.

State and federal courts, construing the privileges and immunities of Article IV, had never given it a precise definition. They had insisted on leaving it for a case-by-case determination, so that they could find it applicable to any law when discrimination against nonresidents would threaten the functioning of the nation. They did not want to foreclose decision on any law that had not been considered individually in a concrete case for this purpose.[131] Congress understood, as Howard said, that it would be similarly up to the courts to construe the privileges and immunities clause of the new amendment on a case-by-case basis. The courts would decide whether a particular right was fundamental and therefore whether a law on that matter must be equal as to all.[132] Congress overrode objections to the vagueness of the term *privileges and immunities* because no one thought the insertion of the clause in the Constitution would result in interference with laws they believed proper.

Experience with judicial decisions under Article IV suggested there was no cause for alarm. Under Article IV the privileges and immunities guaranteed to a nonresident were defined primarily by the laws applicable to residents of the state that he entered. In Justice Washington's terms, privileges and immunities were the fundamental rights of a citizen subject to "such restraints as the Government may justly prescribe for the general good of the whole." Thus their content was identified in the context of existing laws. Similarly, the state laws applicable to white citizens defined the rights of black citizens under the Civil Rights Act of 1866. Instead of a vast expansion of rights, the framers of the Fourteenth Amendment saw privileges and immunities as a limiting concept. It selected only some of the existing laws of a state as basic rights of citizenship that must be applied to all. Members of the Republican majority asserted that states under their own constitutions already afforded their citizens all fundamental privileges and immunities, except for those states that previously had slavery and were then enacting black codes.[133]

The fear of vagueness in the term *civil rights and immunities*, which led Congress to drop it in favor of a specific enumeration of rights in the Civil Rights Act of 1866, produced less terror in the case of the privileges and immunities clause in the Fourteenth Amendment. Section 2 of the amendment provided strong textual evidence that the privileges and immunities of citizens of the United States did not include political rights.[134] A statement of principle was more appropriate in a constitution than in a statute. To some extent, the vagueness of the principle actually enhanced its acceptability. It was impossible to oppose the Fourteenth Amendment in the Thirty-Ninth Congress without appearing to oppose fundamental rights.[135]

The essential theme of the series of congressional debates was that slavery was the root cause of all denials of fundamental rights in a democratic society. Thus the abolition of slavery and its incidents by the Thirteenth Amendment, Civil Rights Act, and first section of the Fourteenth Amendment, would automatically result in the assurance of all that was fundamental without greatly altering the federal structure.

The members of the Thirty-Ninth Congress did not want to create a centralized government whose power would include the authority to define the scope of a citizen's rights. They believed that each state would adequately protect the interests of its own white citizens, so that a prohibition on racial discrimination in the fundamental rights of the state legal system would adequately secure those rights to African-Americans. The Civil Rights Act was designed to secure racial equality in what Congress believed to be the most important rights of a citizen in society—rights that the states themselves had already, presumably, defined. The Fourteenth Amendment was to raise nondiscrimination in all these fundamental rights to the level of a constitutional command. The Congress that proposed the Fourteenth Amendment, however, failed to define privileges or immunities and did not see that the distinction between the language of Article IV and that of the Fourteenth Amendment posed problems for achieving the results they sought.

Post-Enactment Congressional Debate on the Meaning of the Clause

Congress debated the meaning of the privileges and immunities clause of the Fourteenth Amendment within a few years of its enactment. The ability of African-Americans to take advantage of their rights was threatened by organized violence, especially the activities of the Ku Klux Klan. Congress responded with the Enforcement Act of 1871.[136] The legislation, as initially proposed, raised fears that Congress, in its attempts to protect black citizens, would usurp state sovereignty. Congressional authority to pass such legislation required application of the Fourteenth Amendment to situations beyond those considered by its framers, and each side interpreted the new amendment according to their desire to enact or block the proposed law. Suddenly, the claims in the Fourteenth Amendment debate that privileges and immunities were nothing new became a contention that the Fourteenth Amendment worked no change.

Section 2 of the proposed new act initially dealt with private conspiracies against private individuals. It took provisions of the local federal criminal law that applied to places like the District of Columbia and the territories, which were within the exclusive jurisdiction of the United States, and expanded them to every state. The proposed Section 2 made it criminal for two or more persons within the limits of any state to:

> . . . band or conspire together to do any act in violation of the rights, privileges, or immunities of another person, which, being committed within a place under the sole and exclusive jurisdiction of the United States, would, under any law of the United States then in force, constitute the crime of either murder, manslaughter, mayhem, robbery, assault and

battery, perjury, subornation of perjury, criminal obstruction of legal process or resistance of officers in discharge of official duty, arson, or larceny. . . .[137]

Representative Shellabarger claimed that this provision was authorized by the Fourteenth Amendment. The power to enforce the amendment "gave Congress power to legislate directly for enforcement of such rights as are fundamental elements of citizenship."[138] Those fundamental rights, he asserted, were those stated by Justice Washington in *Corfield*. Thus Shellabarger contended that Congress could create its own criminal code to protect the life, liberty, and property of U.S. citizens.

Both Republicans and Democrats were alarmed by Shellabarger's reasoning. Republicans were appalled by the Klan's actions and the failure of state governments to convict Klansmen, but many were equally startled by Shellabarger's suggestion of a power to supplant the traditional criminal law of the states by federal laws protecting life, liberty, and property from private injury. They differed in their interpretation of the amendment to avoid that outcome. One view insisted that Section 5 gave Congress power only to redress a state's violations of fundamental rights—that is, its obligation to protect its citizens, give them access to its courts and rights to property, and allow them to pass through or reside in any state.[139]

Some speakers contended that the amendment did not change the Constitution.[140] Republicans who had argued that Article IV and the Thirteenth Amendment enabled Congress to secure rights of citizenship in the Civil Rights Act now argued that the Fourteenth Amendment made no change. Representative Farnsworth repeated his contention that the equal protection clause was the only new provision, citing Senator Poland's remark that the privileges and immunities clause essentially reiterated Article IV.[141] Several speakers took the position that the clause in the Fourteenth Amendment protected only against the same narrowly defined forms of discrimination forbidden by Article IV.[142]

Democrat Michael Kerr of Indiana pointed to the distinction between rights of state citizenship protected by Article IV and rights of U.S. citizenship protected by the Fourteenth Amendment to indicate that the latter were very limited. He did not, however, clearly develop this premise.[143]

In the face of these objections, the bill was redrafted to specify that the criminal act was conspiracy "for the purpose, either directly or indirectly, of depriving any person or any class of persons of the equal protection of the laws, or of equal privileges and immunities under the laws."[144] After the bill was amended, the equal protection clause, not the privileges and immunities clause, of the Fourteenth Amendment was regarded as the constitutional source of power for the statute. Representative Horatio Burchard of Illinois, supporting the amended bill, denied that Washington's statements in *Corfield* of privileges and immunities were correct. Those were the privileges of all men, not just citizens. He noted that if Washington's description applied to the privileges and immunities of U.S. citizenship, the power to protect them "must have been conferred by the original Constitution. If the General Government originally received no such power, this construction of the meaning of those words must be erroneous, and no such power can be claimed from their use in the [fourteenth] amendment."[145]

The same issues of state sovereignty and federal power were raised in the Senate. Senator Lyman Trumbull, who had argued that the Thirteenth Amendment prohibited racially discriminatory laws, insisted that the Fourteenth Amendment provision on privileges and immunities did not change the Constitution.[146] "[T]his national Government was not formed for the purpose of protecting the individual in his rights of person and of property."[147] Senator Matthew Carpenter of Wisconsin protested, "That is what I understand to be the very change wrought by the fourteenth amendment. It is now put in that aspect and does protect them." Trumbull rejoined, "Then it would be an annihilation entirely of the States. Such is not the fourteenth amendment. The States were, and are now, the depositaries of the rights of the individual against encroachment." Carpenter intervened, "And that Constitution forbids them to deny them, and authorizes Congress to legislate so as to carry that prohibition into execution." Trumbull denied this:

> If the Constitution had said that the privileges and immunities of citizens of the United States embraced all the rights of person and property belonging to an individual, then the Senator would be right; but it says no such thing. In my judgment, the fourteenth amendment has not changed an iota of the Constitution, as it was originally framed, in that respect.[148]

Trumbull then stated his view of the privileges and immunities clause in terms that would be echoed by Justice Miller in the Supreme Court within a few years:

> I insist that the privileges and immunities belonging to the citizen of the United States as such are of a national character, and such as the nation is bound to protect, whether the citizen be in foreign lands, or in any of the States of the Union. . . . National citizenship is one thing, and State citizenship another; and before this constitutional amendment was adopted the same obligation, in my judgment, rested upon the Government of the United States to protect citizens of the United States as now.[149]

A number of other senators disputed Trumbull's reading of the clause, insisting, like Carpenter, that it gave Congress the power to protect all the fundamental rights of citizens.[150]

Confronted with conflicting interpretations of the privileges and immunities language, legislators relied instead on the equal protection clause for enforcing power. The major evil Congress hoped to remedy with the Enforcement Act of 1871 was state inaction in the face of Ku Klux Klan outrages. African-Americans were assaulted and murdered, and their property was destroyed, while the state did nothing to protect them. In this context, the prohibition against state denial of equal protection of the laws seemed to offer a more firm basis for federal legislation than did the privileges and immunities clause. The statute depended in large measure on finding either state inaction or some interference with the state's ability to act impartially in the specific case.

Congressional debate on other proposals during January of 1872 revealed continued disagreement over the content of the privileges or immunities clause and further illustrated how a fundamental rights view of the clause could expand federal power to enact legislation in matters traditionally committed to the states. Senator Charles Sumner made repeated attempts to secure passage of a broad civil rights bill requiring equality in inns, common carriers, theatres, schools, churches, and cemeteries, proscribing racial discrimination in jury selection, and striking the word *white* from all legislation.[151] Sumner and his supporters argued that access to all these places were privileges of citizenship.

Senator Lot Morrill of Maine sought to avoid the reach of the privileges and immunities clause to this bill by arguing that public accommodations were not privileges of citizenship. He maintained that the privileges and immunities of citizenship were limited to the rights stated in the Civil Rights Act of 1866 (to contract, hold property, sue, and so on) and did not extend "to the matters of education, worship, amusement, recreation, entertainment, all of which enter so essentially into the private life of the people, into the personal rights of the people, they belong exclusively to the State, of which the Government of the United States has no right to take cognizance."[152]

Senator Matthew Carpenter of Wisconsin took a position between Sumner and Morrill, proposing amendments to make the bill conform to his views. He thought jury membership was not a privilege or immunity of citizenship, because it involved participation in the establishment and management of government. Carpenter also believed that access to businesses or activities was not a privilege or immunity of citizenship unless the state regulated them. The widespread statutory and common law protection for access to inns and common carriers, however, led Carpenter to treat such access as a privilege of citizenship regardless of the law in any particular state. He would have forbidden race discrimination in any public inn, place of public amusement for which a license from a legal authority is required, or means of public carriage.

Democratic Senator Allen Thurman of Ohio conceded that equal access to all places created or regulated by law was a privilege of U.S. citizenship. Nevertheless, Thurman objected to the proposed statute on the grounds that it operated directly on individuals regardless of whether state law provided a remedy for discrimination.[153]

Senator Oliver Morton of Indiana replied that, if equality in privileges afforded by the state was a right of U.S. citizenship, it could be secured directly by federal legislation.[154] In Morton's view, for example, federal legislation could require state-chartered businesses to treat people equally. Thurman responded that if direct legislation on individuals was permitted under the privileges and immunities clause of the Fourteenth Amendment, Congress could supplant all state laws:

> What is that argument? It is that privileges, immunities, life, liberty, property, and the protection of laws in the United States are all taken in charge, and are under the guarantee of the Constitution and the United States, and that thus taken in charge and under its guarantee and protection, Congress has a right to legislate upon any subject whatsoever, according to its own discretion, that relates to the privileges, the immunities, the life, the property, or the liberty of a citizen of the United States. . . . If this is the case, then all local self-government is wiped out in this land. . . .[155]

Senator Carpenter disputed Thurman's view that Congress lacked authority to act directly on individuals under the Fourteenth Amendment. State denials of privileges or immunities could theoretically be struck down on appeal in federal courts. Therefore, Carpenter argued, the framers must have envisioned some more affirmative power when they granted Congress the power to enforce the amendment. In addition, Carpenter said that the authority could be inferred from the distinction between the language of the amendment and that of Article IV. Assuming that the privileges and immunities were identical in both provisions, Carpenter noted that Article IV forbade only discrimination in favor of citizens of the state, whereas the Fourteenth Amendment secured privileges and immunities to every citizen. Because no state could abridge the privileges and immunities of any citizen of the United States, he concluded that the privileges of all citizens must be the same. "[I]f the State does not, by its legislation, put all citizens upon a common footing, Congress may do so."[156] If the object of the amendment was equality before the law in privileges and immunities, Congress was not confined to reiterating the constitutional prohibition but "must be considered as authorized to enforce, by affirmative legislation, the object intended to be secured by this amendment."[157]

In response, Thurman contended that if Congress could assure individuals their privileges and immunities by providing a federal cause of action, Congress could supplant all local laws. Property ownership, and the protection of person and property were all fundamental rights. If they were privileges or immunities of citizenship, Sections 1 and 5 of the Fourteenth Amendment together would produce the same result as Bingham's original proposed amendment to give Congress the power to secure to citizens of each state all privileges and immunities of citizens—a proposal that had been rejected out of fear that it would allow Congress to usurp state power.

Congress did not pass the legislation on public accommodations in 1872, but the debates on federal legislative power in 1871 and 1872 affected the Court's construction of the Constitution. The debates revealed the potential of the Fourteenth Amendment to restructure political authority and outlined the contours for a restrictive interpretation.

Within a year, the Court repudiated the fundamental rights view of the Fourteenth Amendment in the *Slaughter-House Cases* (1873). Privileges and immunities in Article IV referred to fundamental rights, but operated to select which rights of a state's citizens that citizens of another state could claim. It did not require a state to afford a fundamental right if it did not give it to its own citizens. The Court then said that the Fourteenth Amendment did not refer to fundamental rights of citizenship but to the rights of federal citizenship. That only confirmed rights that had always existed, and, as Trumbull insisted, made no change. Within a few years the political powers largely abandoned Reconstruction, and the restrictive view of the Constitution took root. When the Court and the country were ready for a more active protection of fundamental rights, the Court chose a different route to that end, using the due process clause instead.

NOTES

1. Francis Newton Thorpe, ed., *The Federal and State Constitutions, Colonial Charters, and Other Organic Laws of the States, Territories, and Colonies Now or Heretofore Forming the United States of America* (Washington, GPO, 1909) vol. 1, p. 533 (Connecticut); vol. 5, p. 2747 (North Carolina); vol. 6, p. 3220 (Rhode Island); vol. 7, p. 3788 (Virginia); I *Laws of Maryland* 5 (V. Maxcy ed. 1811) (Maryland).

2. William Swindler, *Sources and Documents of United States Constitutions* (D. Musch ed. 1979) p. 68, 90 (annotated reprint of 2 *Wharton's State Trials* p. 607–58).

3. Termes de la Lay quoted in John S. James, *Stroud's Judicial Dictionary of Words and Phrases*, vol. 4 (P-R) (Fifth Edition: London, Sweet & Maxwell Limited, 1986) p. 2025.

4. Supremacy Act (1534) in C. Stephenson & F. Marcham, *Sources of English Constitutional History*, vol. 1 (1972) p. 311–12; Charter to East India Company (1601), *Sources*, p. 402.

5. *Oxford English Dictionary* (2d Edition prepared by J. A. Simpson and E.S.C. Weiner; Clarendon Press, Oxford, 1989) p. 522 (citing a passage from eighteenth century author Edward Gibbon).

6. Douglas G. Smith, "Citizenship and the Fourteenth Amendment," 34 *San Diego Law Review* (1997): 747–752.

7. Thorpe, *Charters*, vol. III, p. 1833 (Massachusetts, Charter of New England); vol. VII, p. 3801 (Virginia). See also vol. III, p. 1680 (Maryland); vol. 5, p. 2746 (North Carolina).

8. A. E. Dick Howard, *The Road from Runnymede: Magna Carta and Constitutionalism in America* (Charlottesville: University Press of Virginia, 1968) p. 214. The Magna Carta guarantee protecting freedom of movement of foreign merchants became a similar guarantee for natives. J. C. Holt, *Magna Carta* (2d Edition, Cambridge: Cambridge University Press, 1992) p.11–12.

9. Abbot Smith, *Colonists in Bondage: White Servitude and Convict Labor in America 1607–1776* (1947) p. 264–70

10. S. Mencher, *Poor Law to Poverty Program* (1967) p. 39–41; W. Trattner, *A History of Social Welfare in America* (3d Ed. 1984) p. 20–23.

11. Thorpe, *Charters*, vol. VI, p. 3212–13.

12. See Paul Finkelman, *An Imperfect Union: Slavery, Federalism and Comity* (Chapel Hill, University of North Carolina Press, 1981) p. 31. (Under British rule American colonists guaranteed freedom of movement by virtue of imperial citizenship.)

13. Clinton Rossiter ed., *The Federalist Papers* (New York: New American Library, 1961), No. 7 (Alexander Hamilton) p. 62–63.

14. E.g. *Maryland Laws*, 1715, ch. 40, § 2–3; 1716, ch. 20; 1776, ch. 14, § 4.

15. R. Dinkin, *Voting in Provincial America: A Study of Elections in the Thirteen Colonies, 1689–1776* (1977) p. 35.

16. See David Jordan, "Political Stability and the Emergence of a Native Elite in Maryland," and Carole Shammas, "English-Born and Creole Elites in Turn-of-the-Century Virginia," in T. Tate and D. Ammerman, eds., *The Chesapeake in the Seventeenth Century: Essays on Anglo-American Society* (1979) p. 243, 271–72 (Maryland laws), 274, 291–92 (similar Virginia laws).

17. *The Declaration of Independence* (U.S. 1776), para. 10. Parliament had approved a procedure for colonial naturalization in 1740 (13 Geo. II, c. 7), but banned local naturalizations that did not conform to the act in 1773 (13 Geo. III, c. 25). James Kettner, *The Development of American Citizenship, 1608–1870* (Chapel Hill: University of North Carolina Press, 1978) p. 74–75, 104–05.

18. Kettner, *American Citizenship*, p. 108–10.

19. James I speech to Parliament, March 21, 1610, James I, *Works* (1616) p. 528–31.

20. Sir Edward Coke, *Institutes of the Laws of England* (1641; reprinted Buffalo, N.Y., William S. Hein Co. 1986). See discussion of Coke and the ancient constitution in J.A. Pocock, *The Ancient Constitution and the Feudal Law: A Reissue with a Retrospect* (Cambridge, England: Cambridge University Press, 1987) p. 30–55.

21. Edward Coke, *Institutes of the Laws of England*, vol. II (1641).

22. *Statutes of the Realm*, Vol. 5, p 23–24.

23. 1 *William and Mary*, Session 2, Chapter 2.

24. John Locke, *Two Treatises of Civil Government* (London, 1690; Everyman library edition, J.M. Dent & Sons Ltd., London, 1924).

25. William Blackstone, *Commentaries on the Laws of England* Book 1 (1765) (Special Edition 1983; The Legal Classics Library) p. 125.

26. Id.

27. Blackstone, *Commentaries*, Book III, ch. 23, p. 379.

28. Michael Kamman, *Deputyes & Liberties: The Origins of Representative Government in Colonial America* (New York: Knopf, 1969) p. 57–58.

29. John Pendleton Kennedy, ed. *Journals of the House of Burgesses of Virginia, 1761–65* (Richmond, 1907), p. 360, cited in Samuel Eliot Morison, ed., *Sources & Documents Illustrating the American Revolution 1764–1788 and the Formation of the Federal Constitution* (2d Edition, Oxford: Clarendon Press, 1929) p. 17–18.

30. Worthington C. Ford, ed., *Journals of the Continental Congress 1774–1789* (Washington, D.C.: GPO, 1904–1936), vol. 1, p. 63–73.

31. *Journals*, vol. 9, p. 888 (footnotes omitted).

32. *Journals*, vol. 9, p. 899–900, 908–09.

33. *Journals*, vol.11, p. 652–53.

34. *Journals*, vol. 11, p. 631.

35. *Journals*, vol. 9, p. 888.

36. Edmund C. Burnett, ed., *Letters of the Members of the Continental Congress* (8 vols. Washington: Carnegie Institution, 1921–36) vol. 2, p. 552.

37. *Journals*, vol. 9, p. 889.

38. *The Federalist Papers* No. 42 (James Madison)

39. *Journals*, vol. 21, p. 894.

40. Adrienne Koch, ed., *Notes of Debates in the Federal Convention of 1787 Reported by James Madison* (1966) p. 625; Max Farrand, ed., *The Records of the Federal Convention of 1787* (4 vols., New Haven and London: Yale University Press, 1966) vol. 2, p. 601.

41. Madison, *Notes of Debates*, p. 14. Superscripted words have been written in full and text conformed to the transcript of the manuscript as indicated in Koch. Pennsylvania established a form for registering resident-owned ships. *1778 Pennsylvania Laws* Ch. LXXX § 7 (*The First Laws of the Commonwealth of Pennsylvania*, J. Cushing ed. 1984). New Jersey did so in its navigation act, *1781 New Jersey Laws* ch. CCXCIII § 6 (*The First Laws of the State of New Jersey*, J. Cushing ed. 1981). Maryland provided for ship registration in *1784 Maryland Laws* Ch. LXXIX (*The First Laws of the State of Maryland*, J. Cushing ed. 1981). Maryland ships were taxed at six pence per ton while all other ships were taxed at one shilling per ton at entrance or clearance. § 21. Taxes were also laid on specified goods with a deduction of one sixth for vessels built and navigated by Maryland residents. Ch. LXXIV, §16.

42. *Constitution of the United States*. Art. I, § 8, Cl. 4.

43. *Constitution*, Art. II, § 2, Cl. 2, § 3, Cl. 3.

44. Madison, *Notes of Debates*, p. 143; Farrand, *Records*, vol. 1, p. 317.

45. Farrand, *Records*, vol. 2, p. 173–74. This clause was in the last of the series of documents found among the Wilson Papers in the Library of the Historical Society of Pennsylvania. Farrand numbered the document IX and noted: "Found among the Wilson Papers, and in Wilson's handwriting, but with emendations in Rutledge's hand. Parts in parentheses were crossed out in the original; italics represent additions by Wilson; emendations by Rutledge are in angle brackets < >." Farrand, *Records*, vol. 2, p. 163 n.17. The section on privileges and immunities was part of a longer section enclosed in angle brackets, written by Rutledge.

46. *The Federalist Papers* No. 42, (James Madison).

47. Farrand, *Records*, vol. 3, Appendix A, CCCXXXVIII, p. 446.

48. "The 4th article . . . is formed exactly upon the principles of the 4th article of the present confederation, except with this difference, that the demand of the Executive of a State for any fugitive criminal offender shall be complied with. It is now confined to treason, felony, or other high misdemeanor." Observations Pinckney prepared as a speech to accompany his draft. Farrand, *Records*, vol. III at 606–07.

49. Madison, *Notes of Debates*, p. 33 n.36.

50. Farrand, *Records*, vol. 2, p. 97–98

51. *Constitution*, Art. I, § 8.

52. Zechariah Chafee, Jr., *Three Human Rights in the Constitution of 1787* (1956) p. 185.

53. Madison, *Notes of Debates*, p. 394; Farrand, *Records*, vol. 2, p.187.

54. Madison, *Notes of Debates*, p. 439, 441; Farrand, *Records*, vol. 2, p. 270, 272.

55. Madison, *Notes of Debates*, p. 545; Farrand, *Records*, vol. 2, p. 443.

56. Farrand, *Records*, vol. 2, p. 636–37.

57. Madison, *Notes of Debates*, p. 625; Farrand, *Records*, vol. 2, p. 601.

58. Madison, *Notes of Debates*, p. 652, 655; Farrand, *Records*, vol. 2, p. 633, 644.

59. *The Federalist* No. 42 (J. Madison).

60. *The Federalist* No. 80 (A. Hamilton).

61. *Constitution*, Art. I, § 8 (commerce clause). See Cooley v. Board of Wardens, 53 U.S. (12 How.) 299 (1851) (upholding local pilot laws in opinion distinguishing types of state regulations affecting interstate commerce which are permissible from those forbidden); Gibbons v. Ogden, 22 U.S. (9 Wheat.) 1 (1824) (invalidating steamship monopoly granted by state). *Constitution*, Art. I, § § 9, 10 (prohibition on taxes of imports and exports). See Low v. Austin, 80 U.S. (13 Wall.) 29 (1871); Brown v. Maryland, 25 U.S. (12 Wheat.) 419 (1827) (invalidating tax on imported goods still in original package).

Nevertheless, Article IV may have prevented state legislatures from considering some forms of discrimination against citizens of other states. There were some decisions that did strike down state laws as violations of Article IV privileges. See, e.g., Wiley v. Parmer, 14 Ala. 627 (1848) (voiding law taxing slaves of nonresidents more than slaves of residents); see also Ward v. Morris, 4 H. & McH. 330, 340–41 (Md. 1799) (privileges and immunities clause used as an aid to construe a state statute). It is impossible to know the extent to which the existence of the clause simply prevented state legislative consideration of particular parochial proposals.

62. On reaction to southern suppression of abolitionist speech, see G. Barnes, *The Anti-Slavery Impulse 1830–1844*, (1933) p. 109–114, and Russell Nye, *Fettered Freedom: Civil Liberties and the Slavery Controversy 1830–1860* (1963) p. 25, 32. On northern distaste for abolitionists, see L. Richards, *Gentlemen of Property and Standing* (1970) and Martin Duberman, "The Northern Response to Slavery," in *The Anti-Slavery Vanguard* (1965) p. 394–413.

63. Declaration of sentiments of the American Anti-Slavery Society, (proceedings of the Anti-Slavery Convention, assembled at Philadelphia, Dec. 4–6, 1833) reprinted in Louis Ruchames, *The Abolitionists* (1963) p. 82.

64. William Wiecek, *The Sources of Antislavery Constitutionalism in America 1760–1848* (Ithaca: Cornell University Press, 1977) p. 249–75; Jacobus TenBroek, *Equal Under Law* (New York: Collier Books, 1965) p. 94–115.

65. See generally Donald Fehrenbacher, *The Dred Scott Case: Its Significance in American Law and Politics* (New York: Oxford University Press, 1978); Walter Ehrlich, *They Have No Rights: Dred Scott's Struggle for Freedom* (Westport: Greenwood Press,1979).

66. For example, Maryland statutes provided that a free Negro who married a white person became a slave for life. Act of June 8, 1717, ch. 13, § 5. Criminal laws throughout the antebellum period of the nineteenth century permitted convicted free blacks in certain contexts to be sold as slaves for a period of years or for life. The specific circumstances varied under successive laws. J. Brackett, *The Negro in Maryland* (1969 reprint) p. 227–32. Under the principles of *Strader v. Graham, 51 U.S. (10 How.) 82 (1851),* a state might also reduce a white man to slavery, but no state ever thought to do so. Perhaps Taney would have believed that states would void such laws under their own constitutions or that the Court would invalidate them, using principles of natural justice.

67. Michael Curtis, *No State Shall Abridge: The Fourteenth Amendment and the Bill of Rights* (Durham, N.C.: Duke University Press, 1986).

68. Raoul Berger, *Government By Judiciary: The Transformation of the Fourteenth Amendment* (Liberty Fund, Indianapolis, Second Edition 1997).

69. Akhil Reed Amar, *The Bill of Rights: Creation and Reconstruction* (Yale University Press: New Haven & London, 1998).

70. *Congressional Globe*, 38th Cong., 1st Sess. 1202 (1864).

71. *Globe, 38th Cong., 1st Sess.* (1864) p. 1202 (remarks of Sen. Wilson); *Globe, 38th Cong., 2d Sess.* (1866) p. 193 (Kasson), p. 237 (Smith).

72. *Globe, 39th Cong., 1st Sess.* (1866) p. 499 (Cowan). See p. 497 (Van Winkle), and p. 505 (Johnson).

73. *Globe, 39th Cong., 1st Sess.* p. 318.

74. *Globe, 39th Cong., 1st Sess.* p. 322.

75. *Globe, 39th Cong., 1st Sess.* p. 474.

76. *Globe, 39th Cong., 1st Sess.* p. 474 (citing *Campbell v. Morris, 3 H. & McH. 535 (Md. 1797)).*

77. *Globe, 39th Cong., 1st Sess.* p. 474 (citing *Corfield v. Coryell, 6 F. Cas 546 (C.C.E.D. Pa. 1823) (No. 3230)).*

78. *Globe, 39th Cong., 1st Sess.* p. 474.

79. *Globe, 39th Cong., 1st Sess.* p. 1118.

80. *S. 61, 39th Cong., 1st Sess.* (1866), discussed in *Globe, 39th Cong., 1st Sess.* p. 606–07.

81. *Globe, 39th Cong., 1st Sess.* p.1115.

82. *Globe, 39th Cong., 1st Sess.* p. 157 app. (Rep. Wilson stated, "[I]t was thought by some persons that unless these qualifying words were incorporated in the bill, those rights might be extended to all citizens, whether male or female, majors or minor.")

83. *Globe, 39th Cong., 1st Sess.* p. 1117.

84. *Globe, 39th Cong., 1st Sess.* p.1263.

85. *Globe, 39th Cong., 1st Sess.* p.156–59 app. (Delano remarks); p.1270–71 (Kerr).

86. *Globe, 39th Cong., 1st Sess.* p. 1291.

87. *Globe, 39th Cong., 1st Sess.* p.1366.

88. *Globe, 39th Cong., 1st Sess.* p.1758.

89. *Globe, 39th Cong., 1st Sess.* p.1835–36.

90. *Globe, 39th Cong., 1st Sess.* p.1835.

91. Lawrence asserted that rights may be destroyed only by prohibition or failure to protect. A prohibition, he said, is a law which states that a race shall not have a particular right. A failure to protect, he explained, would be a law granting a specific protection for whites only. *Globe, 39th Cong., 1st Sess.* p.1832–33.

92. Representative Wilson contended that it did, or at least that it covered all "civil rights" and immunities, but he was trying to protect himself from any charge that he had weakened the bill by eliminating references to "civil rights and immunities." *Globe, 39th Cong., 1st Sess.* p. 1366.

93. *Globe, 39th Cong., 1st Sess.* p. 1034 (proposal of Select Joint Committee on Reconstruction).

94. *Globe, 35th Cong., 2d Sess.* (1859) p. 984.

95. *Globe, 37th Cong. 2d Sess.* (April 11, 1862) H.p. 1639

96. Earl Malz, "Fourteenth Amendment Concepts in the Antebellum Era," 32 *American Journal of Legal History* (1988): 342.

97. *Globe, 39th Cong. 1st Sess.* p. 1063–64.

98. *Globe 39th Cong. 1st Sess.* (Feb. 28, 1866) H.p. 1089.

99. *Globe, 39th Cong., 1st Sess.* p. 1088–89.

100. *Globe, 39th Cong., 1st Sess.* p. 1084–90, 1094.

101. *Globe, 39th Cong. 1st Sess.* p. 134–35 app.

102. *Globe, 39th Cong., 1st Sess.* p. 1095 (Hotchkiss was worried about southerners controlling Congress and passing laws governing all of the states).

103. *Globe, 39th Cong., 1st Sess.* p. 1082.

104. *Globe, 39th Cong., 1st Sess.* p. 2286.

105. *Globe, 42nd Cong.1st Sess.* app. 85 (1871).

106. *Globe, 39th Cong., 1st Sess.* (May 10, 1866) H.p. 2542.

107. *Globe, 39th Cong., 1st Sess.* p. 2539.

108. *Globe, 39th Cong., 1st Sess.* p. 2459.

109. *Globe, 39th Cong., 1st Sess.* p. 2467.

110. *Globe, 39th Cong., 1st Sess.* p. 2530.

111. *Globe, 39th Cong., 1st Sess.* p. 2538.

112. *Globe, 39th Cong., 1st Sess.* p. 2542.

113. *Globe, 39th Cong., 1st Sess.* p. 2505 (Rep. McKee); p. 2532 (Rep. Banks); p. 2539 (Rep. Farnsworth); p. 2462 (Rep. Garfield).

114. *Globe, 39th Cong., 1st Sess.* p. 2498.

115. *Globe, 39th Cong., 1st Sess.* p. 2513.

116. *Globe, 39th Cong., 1st Sess.* p. 2765.

117. *Globe, 39th Cong., 1st Sess.* p. 2765.

118. Civil Rights Act of 1866, ch. 31, § 1, 14 Stat. 27, 27 (1866).

119. *Globe, 39th Cong., 1st Sess.* p. 2765.

120. *Globe, 39th Cong., 1st Sess.* p. 2765.

121. *Globe, 39th Cong., 1st Sess.* p. 2766.

122. *Globe, 39th Cong., 1st Sess.* p.2766.

123. *Constitution*, Amend. XIV, § 1.

124. *Globe, 39th Cong., 1st Sess.* p. 3032–33.

125. *Globe, 39th Cong., 1st Sess.* p. 2961.

126. *Globe, 39th Cong., 1st Sess.* p. 3035.

127. *Globe, 39th Cong., 1st Sess.* p. 3041. For the remarks of Sen. Hendricks, see p. 3039.

128. For example, Representative George Julian of Indiana complained, "Without the ballot in the hands of the freedmen, local law, reinforced by a public opinion more rampant against them than ever before, will render the civil rights bill a dead letter, and in the future, as it has been in the past, the national authority will be set at defiance." *Globe, 39th Cong., 1st Sess.* p. 3210.

129. See *Globe, 39th Congress, 1st Sess.* p. 2539 (Representative Farnsworth); p. 2459 (Representative Stevens); p. 2765 (Senators Howard); p. 2961 (Senator Poland); and p. 3035 (Senator Henderson). Bingham tied these rights to the "privileges and immunities" clause of article IV, saying that such privileges include "among other privileges, the right to bear true allegiance to the Constitution and laws of the United States, and to be protected in life, liberty and property." He concluded, "That great want of the citizen and stranger, protection by national law from unconstitutional State enactments, is supplied by the first section of this amendment. That is the extent that it hath, no more. . . ." *Globe, 39th Cong., 1st Sess.* p. 2542–43.

130. See, e.g., remarks of Rep. Hale, *Globe, 39th Cong., 1st Sess.* p. 1065.

131. See, e.g., *Conner v. Elliot, 59 U.S. (18 How.) 591, 593 (1856).* ("We do not deem it needful to attempt to define the meaning of the word privileges in this clause of the constitution. It is safer, and more in accordance with the duty of a judicial tribunal, to leave its meaning to be determined, in each case, upon a view of the particular rights asserted and denied therein.")

132. See *Globe 39th Cong., 1st Sess.* p. 2765 (Howard statement that the privileges and immunities are not and cannot be fully defined in their entire extent and precise nature).

133. See, e.g., *Globe, 39th Cong., 1st Sess.* p. 219 app. (remarks of Sen. Howe).

134. See *Globe, 39th Cong., 1st Sess.* p. 2542 (Bingham). Section two provided for reduction in the basis of representation in Congress to the extent the right to vote is denied male inhabitants of a state who are twenty-one years old and citizens of the United States. *Constitution* Amend. XIV, § 2.

135. See *Globe, 39th Cong., 1st Sess.* p. 2468–69 (remarks of Rep. Kelley) and p. 256 app. (remarks of Rep. Baker).

136. Act of April 20, 1871, ch. 22, 17 Stat. 13 (1871).

137. *Globe, 42d Cong., 1st Sess.* (1871) p. 68–69 app.

138. *Globe, 42d Cong., 1st Sess.* (1871) p. 69 app.

139. Representative Farnsworth objected: "Thus then the question presents itself . . . whether we shall obliterate State lines and abolish State constitutions and State Legislatures, and centralize all the power of these States of ours into one grand despotic central Government at Washington, or, will we preserve the State Governments, wherein resides, as I think, the chief protection of the rights of the citizen as well as the source of the powers of the General Government." *Cong. Globe, 42nd Cong., 1st Sess.* p. 117 app. Representative Garfield spoke at length on the power of Congress under the Fourteenth Amendment. He pointed to the rejection of Bingham's first proposal to demonstrate that Congress was not given a general power to legislate where states had previously been the source of legislation. He denied Shellabarger's construction of the privileges and immunities clause, insisting that it gave power to Congress to act only in the event of state violations. But Garfield did state that Congress had power to do justice where state laws were equal but "by a systematic maladministration of them, or a neglect or refusal to enforce their provisions, a portion of the people are denied equal protection. . . ." p. 149–54 app. Other Republicans aghast at the implications of Shellabarger's rationale included Representatives Moore (p. 112 app.), Hawley (p. 382), and Willard (p. 187 app.).

140. See *Globe*, 42d Cong., 1st Sess. (1871) p. 86 app. (Democrat Storm) and p. 112 app. (Republican Moore).

141. *Globe, 42d Cong., 1st Sess.* (1871) p. 116 app.

142. *Globe, 42d Cong., 1st Sess.* (1871) p. 116; see also p. 48 app. (Kerr); p. 87 app. (John Storm of Pennsylvania); p. 209 (James Blair of Missouri); p.152 app. (Garfield).

143. *Globe, 42d Cong., 1st Sess.* (1871) p. 47–48 app.

144. *Globe,* 42d Cong., *1st Sess.* (1871) p. 477.

145. *Globe, 42d Cong., 1st Sess.* (1871) p. 314 app. Senator Poland also supported Farnsworth's views and voted for the bill, as amended: "The Constitution originally left to the State the administration of the local law, both civil and criminal; all offenses against person or property were to be punished by the State authorities. I do not agree that the fourteenth amendment or any amendment has changed that, except to this extent; the last clause

of the fourteenth amendment provides that no State shall deny the equal protection of the laws to its citizens." *Globe, 42d Cong., 1st Sess.* (1871) p. 514.

146. "The protection which the Government affords to American citizens under the Constitution as it was originally formed is precisely the protection it affords to American citizens . . . as it now exists. The fourteenth amendment has not extended the rights and privileges of citizenship one iota." *Globe,* 42d Cong., 1st Sess. (1871) p. 576.

147. *Globe, 42d Cong., 1st Sess.* (1871) p. 577.

148. *Globe, 42d Cong., 1st Sess.* (1871) p. 577.

149. *Globe, 42d Cong., 1st Sess.* (1871) p. 577. Democrats such as Bayard also supported this construction of the fourteenth amendment (p. 242 app.), but their opposition to that amendment meant that their interpretation of it would be given little weight.

150. See, e.g., *Globe, 42d Cong., 1st Sess.* (1871) p. 228 app. (Sen. Boreman); p. 696–97 (Sen. Edmunds).

151. His original proposal in 1870 was reported unfavorably by committee and in the beginning of 1871 a renewed attempt was tabled. *Globe, 42d Cong., 1st Sess.* (1871) p. 21. Summer tried again in December of 1871 to attach his bill as a rider to the Amnesty Act. *Globe,* 42d Cong., 2d Sess. (1872) p. 240–44.

152. *Globe, 42d Cong., 2d Sess.* (1872) p. 5 app.

153. "[T]his bill is only to secure privileges and immunities, and in respect to them the constitution is plain that no State shall make or enforce any law to deprive any citizen of them, and it is equally clear that you have no right to interfere until the State has made or enforced such a law." *Globe, 42d Cong., 2d Sess.* (1872) p. 496. This of course was the holding of the Civil Rights Cases, 109 U.S. 1 (1883), with respect to equal protection.

154. *Globe, 42d Cong., 2d Sess.* (1872) p. 524.

155. *Globe, 42d Cong., 2d Sess.* (1872) p. 527.

156. *Globe, 42d Cong., 2d Sess.* (1872) p. 762.

157. *Globe, 42d Cong., 2d Sess.* (1872) p. 762.

Part II

Analysis of the Protection of Privileges and Immunities

The Civil War and its aftermath radically changed society in the United States. The Fourteenth Amendment reversed *Dred Scott* and finally defined who were citizens, both of the state and of the United States: "All persons born or naturalized in the United States, and subject to the jurisdiction thereof, are citizens of the United States and of the State wherein they reside." State citizenship secured the protection of Article IV, but that protection was limited to stopping unjustified discrimination on the basis of residence. The first section of this part examines the justifications that courts have accepted. Citizens of the United States can claim the protection of the Fourteenth Amendment provision that prohibits states from abridging their privileges or immunities, but the Supreme Court rendered the clause a dead letter. The second section of this part explores how the court stripped the clause of any effect, the current meaning of privileges and immunities of U.S. citizens, and the possible future of the clause.

ARTICLE IV: PRIVILEGES AND IMMUNITIES

Article IV protects citizens of a state against discrimination based on their state citizenship, and only natural persons, not corporations, can claim this protection (Paul v. Virginia, 1868). The privileges and immunities clause secures only those rights a state affords its own citizens. The Court announced a two-part test for determining whether different treatment violates the clause: (1) whether the law burdens a privilege or immunity protected by the clause, and (2) if so, whether the different treatment of nonresidents is justified (United Bldg. and Constr. Trades Council of Camden County and Vicinity v. Mayor and Council of City of Camden, 1984). The steps are not so separate in practice. When the court excludes rights from the definition of privileges and immunities, it believes the different treatment of nonresidents is justified. Where the discrimination poses little threat to the interests of the union, however, the Court appears to use a sliding scale that requires less justification.

The Court has said, "[o]nly with respect to those 'privileges' and 'immunities' bearing upon the vitality of the Nation as a single entity must the State treat all citizens, resident and nonresident, equally" (Baldwin v. Fish and Game Commission of Montana, 1978). The protection of the political integrity of the state and the prevention of nonresident free-riding do not threaten the union but preserve the independence of the states. Thus states can restrict membership in the political community to residents, and a state may limit to residents some of the goods and services that it provides from the revenue it raises. However, states cannot prefer their residents when regulating the market, because privileges and immunities of citizenship include access to contract, property, and trade opportunities in other states and an exemption from any greater liability to tax or other burdens.

"The Clause does not preclude discrimination against nonresidents where (i) there is a substantial reason for the difference in treatment; and (ii) the discrimination practiced against nonresidents bears a substantial relationship to the State's objective" (Supreme Court of New Hampshire v. Piper, 1985). The Court will not consider the reason for any discrimination to be substantial "unless there is something to indicate that non-citizens constitute a peculiar source of the evil at which the statute is aimed" (Toomer v. Witsell, 1948; Hicklin v. Orbeck, 1978). Further, the Court said that "[I]n deciding whether the discrimination bears a substantial relation to the State's objectives, we consider, among other things, whether less restrictive means of regulation are available" (Barnard v. Thorsten, 1989). The state may be able to justify different treatment of nonresidents as an attempt to provide equality for differently situated individuals, to compensate for difficulties in asserting jurisdiction over the nonresident. The Court has also upheld statutory differences to prevent fraud, or to reflect the lack of relationship to the forum with respect to activities outside the state. The state must justify any preference for residents in the allocation of natural resources or in its market decisions, but the Court seems to consider the state's interest in public resources a factor that lessens the burden of justification.

Paul v. Virginia: Privileges No Greater Than a State Decides to Give Its Own Citizens

The first Article IV case decided after the Fourteenth Amendment resolved basic questions. The Court's opinion made it clear that the privileges and immunities clause was directed to prohibiting discrimination against citizens of other states; the clause did not require a state to provide fundamental rights to anyone unless it provided them for its own citizens, nor did it require states to give citizens of other states the rights they had in their home states (Paul v. Virginia, 1868).

Paul involved a challenge to a law that required insurance companies incorporated in other states to obtain a license and file a bond to sell insurance in Virginia. Samuel Paul was convicted of selling insurance on behalf of a New York company that had not obtained the license or filed the bond. Paul claimed, among other things, that the discrimination denied New York insurance companies the privileges and immunities that Virginia afforded its own. The Court rejected his claim on the ground that corporations were not citizens for purposes of claiming Article IV rights. In his opinion for the court, Justice Stephen J. Field said that states "may exclude the foreign corporation entirely." If they allow the corporation in, "such assent may be granted upon such terms and conditions as those States may think proper to impose."

Privileges Are Not Universal: The Rejection of Natural Law Rights

According to *Paul*, the central theme of Article IV was equality between the citizens of one state and citizens of other states, not the securing of any specific substantive right, whether derived from natural law or otherwise:

> It was undoubtedly the object of the clause in question to place the citizens of each state upon the same footing with citizens of other states, so far as the advantages resulting from citizenship in those states are concerned. It relieves them from the disabilities of alienage in other states; it inhibits discriminating legislation against them by other states; it gives them the right of free ingress into other states, and egress from them; it insures to them in other states the same freedom possessed by the citizens of those states in the acquisition and enjoyment of property, and in the pursuit of happiness; and it secures to them in other states the equal protection of their laws. (Paul v. Virginia, 1868)

The Court put the theory into practice the following year. It held that a Maryland law violated Article IV because it imposed a higher tax on nonresident traders than on residents (Ward v. Maryland, 1870). The Court said that the Constitution "requires equality of burden, and forbids discrimination in State taxation when the power is applied to the citizens of the other States."

Any possibility that the Court might find the privileges and immunities clause of Article IV also protected substantive rights ended with the Slaughter-House Cases (1873). The Court made it clear that Article IV only applied to prevent discrimination against nonresidents. Justice Samuel Miller said that it did not affect a state government's power over its own citizens. He insisted that the Constitution did not create the privileges and immunities of citizens of the states but simply made reference to them:

Its sole purpose was to declare to the several states, that whatever those rights, as you grant or establish them to your own citizens, or as you limit or qualify, or impose restrictions on their exercise, the same, neither more or less, shall be the measure of the rights of citizens of other states within your jurisdiction. (Slaughter-House Cases, 1873)

Despite the hints of natural law in opinions like *Corfield* and *Dred Scott* and a smattering of academic commentary, the Court correctly held that Article IV is a tool of federalism rather than a guarantor of fundamental rights. Both the text and historical context of the clause support the Court's view. If fundamental rights are guaranteed, the Fourteenth Amendment and not Article IV should bear that burden.

The stated purpose of the privileges and immunities clause in the Articles of Confederation was "the better to secure and perpetuate mutual friendship and intercourse among the people of the different states in this Union." Preventing parochialism was more important than individual rights. Article IV was the only provision in the Articles of Confederation using language of individual rights. The limited guarantee to individuals that states would not discriminate on the basis of state residence was a reasonable provision for federalism, but a national guaranty of fundamental rights would be inconsistent with the jealousy for state sovereignty the Articles manifested.

The constitutional provision came directly from the Articles of Confederation. It is a part of an article that deals almost exclusively with problems of federalism rather than individual rights.[1] It provides a right for the individual, but the context demonstrates that the rights were granted to promote interstate harmony rather than from concern for the individual. No court ever struck down a state law under this clause because it violated a fundamental right. The context for any discussion of natural rights was as a limitation on the number of statutory and common law rights that had to be extended to citizens of other states.

The Supreme Court continues to follow the position established in *Paul* that Article IV protects against discrimination and does not establish natural law rights:

[I]t has come to be the settled view that Article IV, § 2, does not import that a citizen of one State carries with him into another fundamental privileges and immunities which come to him necessarily by the mere fact of his citizenship in the State first mentioned, but, on the contrary, that in any State every citizen of any other State is to have the same privileges and immunities which the citizens of that State enjoy. The section, in effect, prevents a State from discriminating against citizens of other States in favor of its own. (Baldwin v. Montana Fish and Game Commission, 1978, quoting Hague v. C.I.O., 1939)

Privileges Are Not Portable: Corporations Are Not Citizens

Prior to the Civil War, the court had said that corporations were not citizens under Article IV, but that was dictum not necessary to the decision. Chief Justice Taney had said that citizens could not get the advantages of the laws of a state they passed through without accepting the disadvantages (Bank of Augusta v. Earle, 1839). Justice Stephen J. Field cited *Bank of Augusta* in his opinion in *Paul*, but he stressed another aspect of Article IV. Justice Field wrote that the word *citizens* in Article IV "applies only to natural persons, members of the body politic, owing allegiance to the State, not to artificial persons created by the legislature, and possessing only the attributes which the legislature has prescribed." Since Article IV is limited to prohibiting discrimination against citizens of other states, a state need not give nonresidents the privileges from their home state. If privileges are not portable, a corporation need not be recognized in another state because its existence is dependent on the law of the state of its incorporation.

Unlike the human beings who invest in it and act on its behalf, a corporation has no physical existence. It is an abstract entity created by law. Incorporation grants special privileges to the incorporators and shareholders, enabling them to act as though they were a single individual for certain purposes while avoiding individual liability. State law regulates the entire structure of corporate ownership and obligation. Justice Field argued in *Paul* that to require a state to treat a foreign corporation as a citizen would impose one state's law upon another. The issue resembled the antebellum conflict over whether slaveowners could retain their slaves while travelling in northern states that had abolished slavery; the answer after the Civil War was clear. Field said in *Paul*, "It was not intended by the provision to give to the laws of one State any operation in other States. They can have no such operation, except by the permission, express or implied, of those states."

The Court has never reconsidered its decision that corporations are not citizens for the purposes of the privileges and immunities clause of Article IV. Even when the Court found a law violated the privileges and immunities of individuals, it dismissed a companion suit brought by a corporation (Blake v. McClung, 1898). The artificial nature of the entity disables it from claiming citizenship under Article IV. Thus, the Court found that associations or trusts are not citizens for Article IV purposes (Hemphill v. Orloff, 1928).

The Court has created an anomaly—corporations are treated as citizens of a state under Article III, which extends federal judicial power to controversies between citizens of different states, but are not citizens of a state for purposes of claiming privileges under Article IV. Nevertheless, the court's position is solidly based in the language and history of the clause.

The framers of the privileges and immunities clause did not consider corporations to be citizens for the purposes of the clause. Madison argued in *The Federalist Papers* Number 42 that the grant to Congress of power to make uniform rules for naturalization was an important element in improving the function of Article IV in the Constitution, because the power of a state to confer citizenship on an individual had been a source of friction for Article IV of the Articles of Confederation. Recognition of corporations as citizens under Article IV of the Constitution would directly contradict the thrust of this argument.

The various drafts of the article as it wound its way into the Articles of Confederation referred to the protected class as *inhabitants*, *citizens*, and *free inhabitants*. The standard of protection was variously the privileges of *natives*, *natural born free citizens*, and *free citizens*. These terms, especially the adjective *free*, are applied to human beings and not abstract entities. The term *citizen* in the Constitution bears no indicia of an alteration to give it a special meaning applicable to corporations.

When Article IV was adopted, the corporation was an exceptional mode of doing business. Legislatures were suspicious of the corporate form because individuals could avoid personal liability and a small number of individuals could control the aggregate power and wealth of many. States granted charters only for exceptional purposes such as educational institutions, canals, and water companies. If one state's grant of corporate status imposed that corporation on other states, every state in the union would have bitterly opposed the clause.

Although the history of Article IV demonstrates that corporations were not considered *citizens* for Article IV purposes when the Constitution was adopted, the corporation has substantially altered its place in American society since that date. Exclusion of corporations from the ambit of Article IV had little significance in 1787; there were few corporations, and they were local in scope. Almost all business was conducted by individuals or partnerships. Corporate status is no longer a jealously guarded special privilege; it is a readily available status used by almost every type of business. *Paul* suggested that a state could condition entry of a foreign corporation on whatever terms the state thought proper, but that is no longer true. The Court has written that "The combination of general incorporation laws and equal protection necessarily undermined the doctrine of Paul v. Virginia" (Western and Southern Life Ins. Co. v. State Bd. of Equalization of California, 1981).

Although the Court has not yet held that states are forbidden to exclude foreign corporations from intrastate business, it has held that the state may not condition the entry of foreign corporations on compliance with unreasonable conditions. The discriminatory bond requirement of *Paul* would probably be unconstitutional under this standard. Thus, many commentators have argued that the Court should overrule what remains of *Paul* and hold that corporations are citizens for Article IV purposes in order to assure the vindication of the overriding purpose of nondiscrimination.[2]

The primary reason commentators seek to overrule *Paul* has been their objection to dormant commerce clause theory: the idea that the grant of power to Congress to regulate interstate commerce deprives the states of power to impose discriminatory or otherwise impermissible burdens on interstate commerce unless Congress affirmatively permits it. The commerce clause does not expressly restrict state regulation. Congressional silence, critics say, neither supports nor detracts from state power. The critics of the dormant commerce clause would prefer to use the privileges and immunities clause as a curb to state power but fear that it would be ineffective unless extended to corporations.

The argument that the privileges and immunities clause of Article IV should be used to stop discrimination in trade violates its language as well as its history. The clause does not protect goods or trade, but citizens. Laws do not turn on citizenship when they prohibit the importation of goods from other states or subject them to higher fees or more stringent regulation. If a Maryland businessman must pay a high fee to import grain from Pennsylvania, the Pennsylvania businessman charged the same fee has not been subjected to discrimination. The law may have a discriminatory effect against Pennsylvania businessmen because they are more likely to deal in the goods of that state, but it is hard to parse the constitutional language to find that such discrimination denies them a privilege that a Maryland citizen has. If the privilege of citizenship is to sell goods of your own state, then Maryland could presumably impose a fee on Pennsylvania citizens selling Maryland goods—directly contrary to the sense and the language of the clause. And if the Court struck down the fee on Pennsylvania citizens in both situations, the citizen of Pennsylvania would have more rights than the Maryland citizen.

Madison's criticism of the violations of the Articles of Confederation privileges and immunities clause was leveled at state laws that taxed vessels at a differential rate based on both the owner's and the crew's state of citizenship. The practice of port states taxing the imports of other states trading through them, however, he said resulted from the lack of a general commerce power. Although the privileges and immunities clause prohibited discrimination based on the residence of the trader, it did not appear to affect discrimination based on the place of origin or destination of goods sold. Instead of protecting free trade, the clause protected only the recognition of common citizenship that had existed before independence.

Eliminating the dormant commerce clause and reversing Article IV interpretation to protect corporations against discrimination in interstate commerce is not only inconsistent with the history and language of the clauses, it is unnecessary. Companies incorporated in other states are adequately protected already. When they are engaged in interstate commerce, discrimination against them violates the commerce clause. The only situations where that clause fails to protect are (1) when Congress authorizes the discrimination or (2) when the discrimination does not interfere with interstate commerce because the out-of-state corporation is only precluded from commerce that takes place wholly within the state. Even then, the equal protection clause offers sufficient protection from parochial extremes. For example, in Metropolitan Life Ins. Co. v. Ward (1985), the Court held that "promotion of domestic business within a State, by discriminating against foreign corporations that wish to compete by doing business there, is not a legitimate state purpose." At the same time, the Court allowed a state to prohibit the acquisition of local banks except by regional banks from states with a reciprocal regional permission law, citing the need to promote competition while maintaining a close relationship between those who provide credit and those who need it (Northeast Bancorp, Inc. v. Board of Governors of Federal Reserve System, 1985).

Finally, a shift in interpretation could curtail existing flexibility. Under the commerce clause, businesses have no constitutional right to be free of discrimination. Congress may allow state laws that protect local industries if it finds them desirable. Article IV, however, confers a constitutional right. It says citizens of a state "shall be entitled." Congress might argue that federal approval satisfies the policy concerns that underlie the clause, so state laws that would be invalid under Article IV should escape scrutiny if incorporated as federal law. Nevertheless, the right is phrased as an individual right, and Congress cannot authorize the deprivation of a constitutional right. A congressional majority might be mustered for provincialism, but that would destroy the sense of national citizenship that Article IV was designed to foster.

The application of Article IV results in an individual right that Congress cannot remove. It is an appropriate protection of our federalism for citizens of the states. Corporations, however, are adequately protected by other constitutional provisions. The extension of Article IV to these artificial creatures of a state would be unwise, because that would restrict congressional discretion. The Court is unlikely to overturn its own precedents of more than a century and a half in order to do so.

Community Membership: Privileges and Immunities Do Not Include Politics or Public Funding

Membership in the political community of the state justifies exclusive rights in some situations. The Court often states that such rights are not privileges or immunities under Article IV, although the reason behind the definition is that the distinction between residents and nonresidents is justified. Thus *Campbell* excluded the franchise from privileges and immunities, whereas *Corfield* excluded rights to property held in common by the people of the state. The Court has consistently held that Article IV privileges and immunities do not apply to political rights. The difficulty lies in defining political participation. The Court rejected the proprietary interest in fisheries on which *Corfield* relied, because it denied citizens of other states the opportunity to pursue an occupation. Nevertheless, the Court does permit states to restrict some public goods to residents. To a large degree, the state can spend its money on public benefits for its own citizens, provided that the expenditure is not needed for the protection of the person or property of the citizen of another state passing through.

Political Power Can Be Restricted to Residents

Although Justice Bushrod Washington listed the elective franchise as a privilege or immunity of citizenship in *Corfield*, the Court subsequently dismissed any notion that the franchise was subject to Article IV. When Virginia Minor challenged Missouri's gender discrimination in voting as a violation of the Fourteenth Amendment, the Court rejected her challenge with a comment about Article IV:

If suffrage is necessarily a part of citizenship, then the citizens of each State must be entitled to vote in the several States precisely as their citizens are. This is more than asserting that they may change their residence and become citizens of the State and thus be voters. It goes to the extent of insisting that while retaining their original citizenship they may vote in any State. This, we think, has never been claimed. (Minor v. Happersett, 1874)

The Constitution envisioned the state as a separate political community with autonomous power to set government policy. The state can therefore limit the making of policy to members of the community—as voters and as officials entrusted with discretion. "No one would suggest that the Privileges and Immunities Clause requires a State to open its polls to a person who declines to assert that the State is the only one where he claims a right to vote. The same is true as to qualification for an elective office of the State" Baldwin v. Fish and Game Commission of Montana (1978).

Lawyers are not state officers, however, and states cannot restrict bar membership to their residents (Supreme Court of New Hampshire v. Piper, 1985). The Court invalidated New Hampshire's exclusion of nonresidents despite the state's argument that lawyers were officers of the court whose activities were an integral part of the making of state policy. Analogizing to equal protection cases involving aliens, the Court said that a lawyer is not an "officer of the State" in any political sense, and it found all other justifications for discriminating against nonresidents insufficient. The Court followed *Piper* when it struck down a Virginia law that allowed only permanent residents to be admitted to the bar on motion without taking the bar examination (Supreme Court of Virginia v. Friedman, 1988). Similarly, the Court invalidated a residency requirement for admission to the bar in the Virgin Islands on the grounds that Congress made the privileges and immunities clause applicable to the territory of the Virgin Islands (Barnard v. Thorstenn, 1989).

The Court is likely, as it did in *Piper*, to follow its equal protection decisions when it distinguishes positions that exercise policy-making power from other positions. The distinction is designed to allow a state to limit core policy-making decisions to the political community of citizens of the state while protecting access to job opportunities for those excluded from the polity. Neither aliens nor citizens of other states are members of the political community of a state unless the state decides to include them. The Court has permitted states to exclude aliens from public school teaching (Ambach v. Norwick, 1979) or from acting as police (Foley v. Connelie, 1978) or probation officers (Cabell v. Chavez-Salido, 1982), because it found these positions involved significant discretion in making or implementing the policy of the state. On the other hand, it invalidated citizenship restrictions for state civil service (Sugarman v. Dougall, 1973), membership in the bar (Supreme Court of New Hampshire v. Piper, 1985), or acting as a notary public (Bernal v. Fainter, 1984), saying either that the position was not that of a public official or the job did not call for significant policy-making decisions. A decision that a particular job involves making significant state policy decisions is likely to serve as precedent for both aliens and citizens of other states, because the function of the political community distinction is the same. They should be treated differently only when the decision does not turn on membership in the political community or the relevant community for the classification is a national one.

A citizen of another state is still a citizen of the United States, and that common citizenship may be sufficient to distinguish the citizen from an alien with respect to eligibility for public school teaching. A narrowly divided court found in Ambach that aliens could be excluded because public school teachers prepare young persons for participation in self-governance and foster and preserve societal values, including those related to self-governance. The rationale does not apply as well to citizens of other states because those values are equally concerns of the nation.

However, if residency is a reasonable qualification for a state position for reasons unrelated to membership in the political community, the alien could be entitled to an opportunity properly denied to the citizen of another state. The alien may be a resident of the state and may contribute to its tax base. If a job for the state did not have a significant policy component, aliens could not be barred from civil service positions (Sugarman v. Dougall, 1973). The state could not use the policy-making excuse to bar a citizen of another state from those positions, but it might be able to justify limiting some positions to residents by the need to conserve state money for state residents to address unemployment in the area (See United Bldg. and Constr. Trades Council of Camden County and Vicinity v. Mayor and Council of City of Camden, 1984). The next section addresses the degree to which states have power to limit expenditures to residents.

States May Spend Money on Their Own Citizens

Membership may have its privileges, but it also has its responsibilities. Citizens of a state are subject to its jurisdiction and may be taxed on their income and property, regardless of where it may be. Residents, in general, are more significant contributors to the state's resources than nonresidents, who may only be taxed on activities and property within the state. The greater support from and power over the state's own citizens creates a special relationship with the state. This relationship justifies some preferences for citizens of a state in the allocation of state-owned resources. At first, the court treated citizens of a state as joint proprietors of all state-owned resources, but the proprietary analysis proved too disruptive of federalism. Subsequent decisions strike a balance to protect citizens from other states in their opportunities to visit and do business while preventing them from leeching off the contributions of the citizens of the state. Questions remain over the extent to which a state's ownership of property permits it to favor its own citizens when it buys or sells goods or services.

Commercial versus recreational access to wildlife and other resources

Although the Court has always rejected Justice Washington's characterization of the elective franchise as a privilege or immunity, it was initially led astray by his statement in *Corfield* that a fishery is the common property of all citizens of a state and all others may be excluded from it. Relying on *Corfield*, a unanimous court held in an opinion by Chief Justice Morrison Waite that oyster beds were the common property of the citizens of the state and not a privilege or immunity of citizenship. Waite distinguished between the privileges of general citizenship and those of "special" citizenship that could be restricted to citizens of the state (McCready v. Virginia, 1876).

The state's claim to a property interest in wild animals and fish was rooted in the sovereign's power over the land and waters where they may be caught. This raised the issue of whether the state could exclude citizens of other states from access to state lands or waters or whether it could impose special conditions on that access. The Court held that taking shrimp from the state's coastal waters within three miles of shore was within the purview of the privileges and immunities clause (Toomer v. Witsell, 1948). If states could exclude nonresidents from fishing, it would exclude them from a major occupation. The Court saw this as a threat to the function of the privileges and immunities clause, saying that "one of the privileges which the clause guarantees to citizens of State A is that of doing business in State B on terms of substantial equality with the citizens of that State."

Fish and game not reduced to possession are not the normal form of property. The Court went even further and said, "The whole ownership theory, in fact, is now generally regarded as but a fiction expressive in legal shorthand of the importance to its people that a State have power to preserve and regulate the exploitation of an important resource." Although *McCready* was not specifically overruled, its thrust was blunted. The regulatory power of the state over wild animals and fish does not trump the privileges and immunities clause concern for nonresident access to business opportunities. The Court said that Article IV:

> does bar discrimination against citizens of other States where there is no substantial reason for the discrimination beyond the mere fact that they are citizens of other States. But it does not preclude disparity of treatment in the many situations where there are perfectly valid independent reasons for it. Thus the inquiry in each case must be concerned with whether such reasons do exist and whether the degree of discrimination bears a close relation to them. (Toomer v. Witsell, 1948)

The purpose of the clause, Chief Justice Fred Vinson wrote in *Toomer*, "is to outlaw classifications based on the fact of non-citizenship unless there is something to indicate that non-citizens constitute a peculiar source of the evil at which the statute is aimed." The Court indicated that a state could charge nonresidents a differential to compensate the state "for any added enforcement burden they may impose or for any conservation expenditures from taxes which only residents pay." However, the differential of a fee one hundred times greater than that charged residents was not justified. "We would be closing our eyes to reality, we believe, if we concluded that there was a reasonable relationship between the danger represented by non-citizens, as a class, and the severe discrimination practiced upon them." *Toomer* was subsequently applied to fishing in territorial waters on the basis that Congress did not authorize the territorial government of Alaska to treat citizens of states in a way that states could not treat citizens of sister states (Mullaney v. Anderson, 1952).

Toomer established the nonresident's right to equal access to state lands and waters to engage in commercial activities, subject to the state's power to charge nonresidents to equalize the burden of conserving the resources. The Court demanded a careful accounting of the burden in *Toomer* to prevent the state from favoring local commercial interests. However, the Court has not demanded such an accounting when commercial exploitation of the resources was not at issue. The Court found a lingering impact to the proprietary theory of *Corfield* and *McCready* in the state's control over wildlife in the absence of federal regulation (Baldwin v. Fish and Game Commission of Montana, 1978).

In *Baldwin*, nonresident hunters challenged a Montana law that required them to pay far more than residents for a license to hunt elk. The state made no showing that the cost differential reflected any specific dollar amount attributable to harm peculiar to nonresidents. The majority held that the differential did not violate the privileges and immunities clause, because recreational elk hunting was not a privilege or immunity of citizenship.

Justice Harry Blackmun's majority opinion gave a new sense to Justice Washington's reference to *fundamental* privileges. Washington spoke of those "which belong, of right, to citizens of all free governments," but Blackmun discounted this apparent reliance on natural rights and focused on the specific rights Washington listed. He said Washington "used the term 'fundamental' . . . in the modern as well as the 'natural right' sense." In other words, a privilege or immunity is fundamental when interference with it would frustrate the purposes of the formation of the Union. Blackmun wrote:

> Some distinctions between residents and nonresidents merely reflect the fact that this is a Nation composed of individual States, and are permitted; other distinctions are prohibited because they hinder the formation, the purpose, or the development of a single Union of those States. Only with respect to those *privileges* and *immunities* bearing upon the vitality of the Nation as a single entity must the State treat all citizens, resident and nonresident, equally. (Baldwin v. Fish and Game Commission of Montana, 1978)

Justice Blackmun said that the pursuit of a common calling, the ability to transfer property, and access to the courts were privileges and immunities: "With respect to such basic and essential activities, interference with which would frustrate the purposes of the formation of the Union, the States must treat residents and non-residents without unnecessary distinctions." Other activities, however, did not require justification for treating nonresidents differently. Justice Blackmun concluded that equality in access to Montana elk was "not basic to the maintenance or well being of the Union." Consequently, the Court held that elk hunting by nonresidents was not a fundamental right protected by the privileges and immunities clause.

The majority's use of Justice Washington's "fundamental" distinction is problematic in many ways. Too many different uses of that word already exist. It is easily confused with the natural law theory that gave it birth. It may also be confused with equal protection doctrine, which continues to distinguish between fundamental interests and other interests. For example, voting is fundamental for equal protection analysis but not for purposes of privileges and immunities. At the same time, many activities subject to Article IV, like carrying on a trade, are not fundamental for equal protection purposes.

Categorizing activities as fundamental is different from categorizing laws as interfering with the purposes of the formation of the Union. A focus on the activity will indicate that activities of minor significance are not fundamental, but a focus on whether discriminatory laws interfere with the purposes of the formation may result in finding a regulation of that same activity interferes with the purposes of the formation of the Union. Every dog knows the difference between being stumbled over and being kicked. Discriminating against nonresidents with respect to every minor trivial incident in a state would cumulatively undermine national citizenship.

The *Baldwin* dissenters argued that an inquiry into whether a given right is fundamental made no sense. Instead they urged the Court to focus on the State's justification for its discrimination. An unjustified discrimination against nonresidents frustrates the purposes of the Union, regardless of the discrimination's subject matter.

The Court could abandon its two-step analysis without overruling *Baldwin* by elaborating on that decision. The majority in *Baldwin* offered little analysis of how to determine whether an activity is fundamental. Suppose a state were to impose higher fees on nonresidents who enter state parks to shoot elk with a camera. Nonresidents pose no special danger to the residents' interest in photographing nor to the supply of elk, so the reason for higher fees would be to raise money from citizens of other states. That undercuts the vitality of the Union. Yet, in the abstract, photography may be no more fundamental than killing the elk. *Baldwin's* focus on the activity offers little help in predicting the outcome of such a case.

The reason the law in *Baldwin* did not threaten the purposes of the Union was that nonresidents were distinguishable from residents for the purposes of licenses to hunt elk. The Court's equal protection analysis shows it recognized this. Elk are not owned by the state, in anything but a fictional fashion. Nevertheless, the state spends money it collects from general tax revenues to maintain and conserve the elk herd, and it forgoes the revenues that might come from commercially more profitable uses of elk habitat. Thus the resident stands in a different relationship from the nonresident with respect to this resource. The need for conservation means that nonresident hunting reduces the amount of elk available to the resident. The nonresident is not excluded from elk hunting but must pay a substantial fee that is likely within range of the nonresident elk hunters who have traditionally engaged in this sport. Some commentators have suggested that the appropriate result would have been to allow discrimination only to the extent that the state could prove the additional cost.[3] That burden is too heavy. A perfect accounting of the costs to the state of maintaining this resource would be a nightmare because many of the costs (e.g., expenditures made and opportunities forgone) involve multiple purposes. These differences should suffice to justify discriminatory licensing when little impact on trade or commerce occurs and thus less reason exists to suspect real antipathy to the nonresident.

The Court's reference to fundamental privileges should be recast as having been a shorthand way of stating that a differential in specific limited circumstances will not threaten the purposes of the Union. Where the noncitizen is a "peculiar source of the evil at which the statute is aimed," the court may relax its concern for the substantiality of the relationship to that "evil" when the regulation poses no significant threat to the Union. Here, the nonresident was not precluded from access, the activity in question was recreational rather than commercial, it involved natural resources not owned privately, the nonresident would be profiting from resident assets if fees were the same, and an accurate allocation of fees that considered all possible economic implications would be difficult to manage.

State subsidies for citizens permitted

Baldwin suggests that citizens of a state have a legitimate interest in the disbursement of state revenues that they lack for the regulation of private activity. The state affords its own citizens a whole array of benefits that it either totally denies to nonresidents or for which it charges them higher fees such as welfare, public education, and even cash grants. Little case law with respect to these benefits is under Article IV because the state's right to spend its money on its own citizens is widely accepted. Cases have focused on durational residence requirements, not on whether residence itself was a legitimate requirement.

The Court has been very clear that education is a resource that can be limited to state residents. In Martinez v. Bynum (1983), the Court upheld a requirement of bona fide residence in a district for public school education. The Court has also summarily affirmed residence requirements for differential tuition at the college and graduate school level (Starns v. Malkerson, 1971; Sturgis v. Washington, 1973). The challenges have been based on the equal protection clause, in part because plaintiffs have recognized that a residence requirement is legitimate even while challenging its duration. Similarly, the Court has assumed that the state could properly restrict payments of surplus revenues to its own residents, even though it held that the state wrongly discriminated among its residents on the basis of the duration of residence (Zobel v. Williams, 1982).

The question remains why distinctions between residents and nonresidents are permissible in access to many public benefits. The Court said in *Baldwin* that privileges and immunities are only those where discrimination based on state residence would harm the union, and in *Toomer* that disparate laws are permitted where the nonresident can be said to represent "a peculiar source of the evil at which the statute is aimed." Where nonresidence poses a special problem for the political community, narrowly targeted laws do not undermine the Union. In this sense, *Baldwin's* fundamental rights collapse into the more appropriate rationale of whether legitimate justifications for differential treatment exist. Thus practical and theoretical justifications for restricting certain public benefits to residents satisfy the language of Article IV.

The difficulty is to determine which justifications are proper and which reasons violate the spirit and the purpose of the constitutional provision. The Court tends to decide on the facts of particular cases without setting forth much guidance on why particular residence restrictions on public good distribution do or do not threaten the union. Thus scholars may be more helpful than the Court in understanding the issue.

A practical reason for allowing state governments to exclude nonresidents from benefits conferred from state resources is that the state will not provide the benefits unless they can be restricted. The citizenry is unlikely to expend tax resources collected largely from residents for benefits that must be given to nonresidents passing through. Resentment of "free riders" is likely to undermine rather than support the union. From excellence in education to programs for the disabled and needy, New Hampshire citizens are unlikely to create programs if Massachusetts residents reap most of the benefits. This rationale does not apply to self-funding programs (whether from fees or special taxes) or resources where nonresident access benefits the citizens of the state (e.g., fire protection prevents nonresidents' property from endangering neighboring properties; roads give residents' access to nonresident friends and commerce). Similarly, this rationale does not apply to a benefit or service that is so important to the citizens of a state that the state would provide it at the same level whether available to noncitizens or not, although the free rider concern remains.

Natural resources do not come from the taxpayer's pocket, but the state may have an interest in preserving their existence. Preserving a natural resource by forbidding changes from its native state may impact residents of other states (e.g., diversion of water streams), but those laws do not turn on the residence of persons who wish to appropriate the natural resource, and are usually analyzed under the dormant commerce clause. Preservation, however, may involve the expenditure of public monies. Whether nonresident access to the resource poses a danger to state funding of preservation may depend on whether the resource is an item of commerce and whether the nonresident's access impacts the resident significantly.

Professor Mark Gergen has suggested a more elaborate and pragmatic approach to permitting preferences. He urged an analysis of the public benefit preference for residents based on maximization of economic utility for the whole society. Gergen proposed two principles to distinguish permissible from impermissible preferences: "First, a state may not interfere in the market to deny resources to outsiders. Second, a state may favor its own in the allocation of state-provided goods for which some redistributional or other interest justifies allocation by communal affiliation rather than through market transactions."[4] These principles reconcile most of the cases on state-provided goods and services, although, as Gergen admits, they do not resolve every decision because the public-private line is not always clear. His suggestions are less rooted in the language and history of the clause than in perceptions of good policy, but they may still be appropriate principles to approach the public benefit issue.

An alternative approach to the issues of preferences for residents in the allocation of public goods and services is more tightly connected to federalism principles. Theoretically, the vulnerability of residents to taxation and jurisdiction and the unavailability of nonresidents suggest that residence is a good proxy for determining who provided the resources to create the state's public goods. Jonathan Varat argued from this premise to a variety of specific principles to determine whether a particular public good should be available to nonresidents.[5] He contended that the contribution of residents to the state's resources gives them a strong claim to those resources, but the goal of national unification and interstate equality limits the claim. Although Professor Varat offered an impressive effort to delineate the lines of demarcation, the Court has not followed him in several areas.

Varat considered various factors in weighing the interests of the state residents against the interests of national unity: (1) the relative abundance of the resource and (2) the nonresident's need for the state-created resource, including its intrinsic importance, its importance in providing access to opportunities whose availability is guaranteed, and whether it is available elsewhere. Varat argued that the state may subsidize private business, and it may purchase goods and services from residents in a preferential manner, including resident-only hiring practices. Similarly, he would permit restriction to residents of state-created goods and services where the state does not have a monopoly, such as state educational institutions and goods manufactured by state enterprises. Varat distinguished between various state-owned natural resources on the basis of whether they can be reproduced. He argued that monopoly control requires state-owned resources that cannot be reproduced be open on a nondiscriminatory basis. He would allow the state to favor its residents in allocating natural resources that can be reproduced and have been reduced to property (e.g., state ranches and farms). He characterized the elk hunting in *Baldwin* as a state monopoly and therefore disagreed with the Court's holding, but his suggestions are consistent with case law when the resource is to be used for commercial purposes. Finally, he argued that the state should not be able to leverage its distribution of state resources to cause private persons to prefer state residents in their private dealings.

Both Varat's balancing scheme and Gergen's economic analysis support the current understanding of the Court. States may subsidize residents and provide facilities and institutions limited to state residents unless the limitation threatens the ability of citizens of other states to take full advantage of the nongovernmental opportunities and unique natural resources of the state. The Court, however, seems more uncertain when the state attempts to limit its contracts to state residents.

State contracting preference for citizens limited

The state cannot regulate the market to prefer its own citizens, but it can provide resources like welfare and education and cash grants to its citizens alone. The states have also argued that they can use their property for their own citizens. The Court has been concerned that a state may attempt to use its control over resources to accomplish impermissible regulation. For example, Alaska once enacted a statute that governed firms that got leases from the state to engage in oil and gas exploration, their contractors, subcontractors, and suppliers to the contractors, and subcontractors of the lessees. A unanimous court invalidated the law's requirement that all these firms give preference in employment to Alaska residents (Hicklin v. Orbeck, 1978). Alaska argued that the statute was designed to deal with widespread unemployment within the state, but the Court saw no showing that nonresidents were a "peculiar source of evil." The high unemployment was the result of lack of education and geographical remoteness. Further, the statute was not tailored to prefer only those citizens who were unemployed or lacked training. Ownership of resources was an insufficient basis for the statute's reach. *Hicklin* left open, however, whether state ownership might justify a more restricted preference in buying or selling.

The state may choose to buy goods or services from, or to sell to, residents exclusively without implicating the dormant commerce clause (Reeves v. Stake, 1980). A requirement that companies contracting with the state be located there might also escape the privileges and immunities clause. As long as the employees of the business can reside out of state, laws favoring businesses operating within the state will be difficult to challenge. However, Article IV applies to preferences based on the residence of the company's employees and management rather than on its state of incorporation or primary place of business. The corporation lacks Article IV rights, but its employees may claim that the state's market decisions deny those rights to them.

A union raised just such a claim on behalf of nonresident workers seeking construction jobs in Camden, New Jersey (United Bldg. and Constr. Trades Council of Camden County and Vicinity v. Mayor and Council of City of Camden, 1984).

A city ordinance required that at least 40 percent of the employees of contractors and subcontractors working on city construction projects be Camden residents. Camden argued that the privileges and immunities clause did not apply to this kind of restriction, both because it was a city and because it was acting in a proprietary capacity. The Court held that the clause applied, but remanded for further evidence on whether the discrimination was justified. The remand hinted that cities may have a lower burden of justification for preferring residents in public works project hiring, but the Court made no definitive ruling.

The Supreme Court held that municipal ordinances are subject to the privileges and immunities clause because the authority of the municipality is derived from the state (United Bldg. and Constr. Trades Council of Camden County and Vicinity v. Mayor and Council of City of Camden, 1984). The state court had found no violation of the clause because citizens of other states had all the privileges and immunities of citizens of New Jersey that did not live in Camden. The Court responded that the person from another state does not enjoy the same rights as a person from New Jersey who lives in Camden and pointed out that New Jersey residents outside of Camden had a political remedy not available to residents of other states. The key to the decision, however, was in a footnote where the majority noted that Camden's ordinance was followed elsewhere in the state. Regional preferences throughout a state effectively reserve employment to state citizens while excluding citizens of other states completely. That would frustrate the objective of the privileges and immunities clause. Thus the *United Building* majority concluded that a municipal preference should be considered a privilege of state citizenship that must be extended to nonresidents unless sufficiently justified.

Counsel for Camden argued that the privileges and immunities clause did not apply to state contracting decisions, citing the Court's decision that the imposition of a resident hiring preference on companies performing work within the state for the state was not a regulation of commerce and did not violate the commerce clause (White v. Massachusetts Council of Construction Employers, Inc., 1983). The Court, however, held that the opportunity to obtain employment with a company doing business for the state was a privilege or immunity of citizenship. Article IV does not have the free trade focus of the commerce clause, for which the state's regulatory or participatory character is relevant. Thus state contract decisions are subject to Article IV privileges and immunities when they require employees to be residents, even on public works (United Bldg. and Constr. Trades Council of Camden County and Vicinity v. Mayor and Council of City of Camden, 1984).

Payment for goods and services is not the kind of subsidy to residents that the Court considers not problematic. The citizen of another state is not a parasite draining monies from the state but someone who provides equivalent value for the money received. Further, nonresident access to contract opportunities does not affect whether the state will engage in the activity. The state could directly subsidize companies that employ local residents with tax breaks and grants that would make them more competitive. It might argue that a preference for its own citizens restricts supply (or demand) and thus affects the price like a subsidy, but this small subsidy functions by prohibiting contracting with the citizen of another state—it is a regulation, not a grant. Thus the Court demands the state justify any requirement that a party contracting with it employ residents.

Camden argued that a resident preference was needed to deal with urban flight in a decaying city. Because no trial had occurred, the Court said it would be inappropriate for it to make findings of fact or to take judicial notice of Camden's decay. Thus the *United Building* Court remanded the case to determine whether the nonresidents constituted a "peculiar source of the evil at which the statute is aimed." The remand suggests that residence requirements are more easily justified for public works than in other areas. Remedying urban decay would not justify a law requiring all companies in the state employ residents. That would destroy the ability of a citizen of another state to pursue an occupation. The Court would be very skeptical of such a justification, as it was in dealing with Alaska's claim of uniquely high unemployment in *Hicklin*. If remedying urban decay justifies a resident preference in public works projects, the Court must believe that state expenditures are at least a factor supporting state preferences that reduces the degree of justification required.

The Court has not ruled on whether state employment in a non-policy-making position is a privilege or immunity. It has upheld the residence requirement for municipal employment when challenged under the equal protection clause (McCarthy v. Philadelphia Civil Service Commission, 1976). In doing so, the Court stated that its cases did not support a claim of a constitutional right to be employed by a city while a resident in another state and that it had never questioned the validity of a rule that an applicant for municipal employment be a resident of a city. *United Building* cited *McCarthy* for the proposition that government employment was not a fundamental right under equal protection, but employment itself is not a fundamental right for purposes of the equal protection clause. Thus the Court still has not committed itself on whether municipal employment may be considered a privilege or immunity, but the Court is likely to find that it is not. The Court could easily say that state or municipal government jobs, as opposed to jobs with companies doing business with the government, are not matters that "bear upon the vitality of the Nation as a single entity."

Even if the Court were to find that government employment is a privilege or immunity of citizenship, the *United Building* justification would still apply, and the closer tie to the state might well reduce the burden of justification even further than for public works contracts. A state job hiring preference for residents is permissible to deal with problems of local unemployment; the state can create jobs for the unemployed rather than make welfare payments, and it should be able to use its job opportunities in this way. A targeted law would easily satisfy the privileges and immunities clause. A preference for residents that did not consider whether they had been unemployed, however, would not satisfy *Toomer's* requirement of a close relation between the degree of discrimination and the reasons for it. Nevertheless, the Court would probably lower the standard for justification in the limited setting of direct employment by the state and permit the residence requirement.

Justifications: Equalization, Procedural Distinctions, and Lack of Forum Connection

The determination that a law burdens a privilege or immunity does not end the inquiry. The Court has said, "The Clause does not preclude discrimination against nonresidents where (i) there is a substantial reason for the difference in treatment; and (ii) the discrimination practiced against nonresidents bears a substantial relationship to the State's objective" (Supreme Court of New Hampshire v. Piper, 1985). Differences between residents and nonresidents in the ability of the state to reach them with process and to tax them could give an advantage to the nonresident if the law took no notice. Laws may need to treat residents and nonresidents separately to create equality in their situations. Thus the Court has established a test of substantial equality in taxation and reasonable and adequate access to the courts.

The Court upheld a number of classifications in earlier cases on the basis of a false dichotomy between residence and state citizenship, which it subsequently repudiated. Nevertheless, the cases that used mistaken reasoning may still be viable, because the particular classification in question was justifiable on other grounds. For example, the situs of the marriage relationship may be relevant to property rights because it creates expectations between the parties and may affect security of title. The state's interest in the security of real property transactions has justified distinguishing nonresidents whose claims are based on marriage. Further, where the parties and activities giving rise to a cause of action are out of state, the nonresident may be in a better position to sue elsewhere. State laws designed to compensate for its citizens' problems in bringing actions within the state may be unnecessary for the nonresident.

Substantial Equality in Taxation

The Constitution "requires equality of burden, and forbids discrimination in State taxation when the power is applied to the citizens of the other States" (Ward v. Maryland, 1870). The state can only tax the nonresident on activities and property within the state, and the amount can be no greater than the state imposes on its own citizens with respect to such activity or property. Calculations may take into account the differences in the situation as long as they produce an equivalent rate. The line between permissible distinction and prohibited discrimination has not always been easy to determine.

Ward demonstrates both the problems of equality and the Court's protection of the citizen from another state. In that case, Maryland acknowledged that it imposed a higher license tax on nonresident traders, but the state contended that it did not discriminate. Maryland argued that its tax was designed to compensate for the difference between residents and nonresidents in taxes paid to the state. Resident traders paid rent and local taxes, but nonresident traders who operated by catalog or sample had no permanent place of business and could avoid local taxes. The Court noted that the state charged resident traders less than nonresident traders for a license to sell the goods of others, and it struck down the law. The liability of residents for other forms of taxation did not affect whether the differential in a tax based on the right to trade was discriminatory.

The argument that differences in taxation may be justified as equalizing was more successful when the incidence of the tax was on the same property—shares of stock in Connecticut corporations (Travellers Ins. Co. v. Connecticut, 1902). Connecticut had an unusual system for taxing stockholders of Connecticut corporations. It left the assessment of residents to the local communities where they resided, but the state taxed nonresident shareholders because local communities had no jurisdiction over them. The rates for residents varied with the local community although the average rate for all communities approximated the rate the state assessed nonresidents. Thus some residents paid less than the nonresident whereas others paid more. The Court found that the state had distributed the burdens in a reasonably fair manner and had not intentionally discriminated against nonresidents.

The principle that different treatment may be based on residence where it produces an equivalent result was elaborated in four cases decided in 1919 and 1920. The Court showed some confusion over the distinction between residence and citizenship. However, the Court's real inquiry examined the state's justification for using residence as a basis for classification. When citizens of other states received different treatment that did not advantage the state's own citizens, the Court upheld the law. If the distinction was designed to favor residents, the Court struck it down.

The Court first struck down a state statute that imposed higher taxes on construction companies whose chief office was outside the state (Chalker v. Birmingham & N.W. Ry. Co., 1919). The state argued that the statute did not distinguish on the basis of citizenship, but only on where the person conducted business. The Tennessee resident who had his chief office in another state would be taxed at the higher rate and the citizen of another state whose chief office was in Tennessee would pay the lower one. The Court responded that the chief office of an individual is usually in the state where he resides, so the practical effect of the statute discriminated against citizens of other states. Because no reason other than impact on nonresidents existed for the tax differential, the Court struck it down as violating privileges and immunities.

The next term, the Court upheld a transfer tax on the property within the state of nonresident decedents (Maxwell v. Bugbee, 1919). New Jersey used a graduated rate premised on the size of the estate. It calculated the rate for nonresident decedents based on their entire estate, although the rate was applied only to property within the state. Executors of estates of nonresident decedents claimed the law violated the privileges and immunities clause, arguing that the nonresident would be charged a higher rate than the resident for transfer of the same amount of property within the state. Although *Chalker* made it clear that discrimination based on residence must be justified, the Court in *Maxwell* dismissed the privileges challenge with the comment that the clause did not apply because the difference was based on residence and not citizenship. The Court's discussion of the equal protection clause, however, supplied the justification. It found that the New Jersey statute created substantial equality. Residents' estates paid transfer taxes on the entire intangible and usually most of the tangible property of the decedent wherever located, but nonresidents' estates paid it only for property within the state. Persons with the same total estate paid the same rate, but nonresidents paid it on less property. Any disparity in the rate paid on the same amount of property within the state was not a result of hostility to the nonresident, but incidental to the attempt to treat parties equally.

The Court faced two more challenges to state taxes in 1920. In Shaffer v. Carter (1920), Oklahoma taxed nonresidents on income earned in the state, allowing them to take business deductions only for expenses in the state. Nonresidents made two arguments that the tax violated the privileges and immunities clause. First, they argued that the incidence of the tax was different for nonresidents because citizens were taxed on their persons, whereas nonresidents were taxed on property and business within the state. The Court quickly dismissed this claim because the tax on citizens included all income derived from property and business within the state plus income from other sources. The second argument was not as easily dismissed. Nonresidents argued that residents could deduct losses they suffered out of state, whereas nonresidents were limited to losses in the state. A resident might have a deductible out-of-state loss without conducting any income-generating business out of state. A similarly situated nonresident would not have that deduction. Nevertheless, the court upheld the law (Shaffer v. Carter, 1920). The difference, it said, arose naturally from the extent of jurisdiction of the two classes of cases. The nonresident could only be taxed on business in the state and thus should be limited in offsetting its losses to those suffered in the state. The resident can be taxed on income wherever earned and thus properly should be able to deduct losses wherever suffered. The difference related to the differences in jurisdiction and not to any hostility or discrimination.

The same day that the Court upheld Oklahoma's limitation on nonresident deductions in *Shaffer*, it struck down the limitations in a similar scheme in New York. New York imposed an income tax on its residents and taxed nonresidents on their income from sources within the state. Nonresidents were allowed deductions only when the deduction related to the production of income within the state. Thus they could not claim personal exemptions for themselves or dependents. The statute permitted nonresidents to claim a credit for taxes paid to their home state on the income only if their home state permitted similar credits for New York citizens who earned money there. The Court upheld the imposition of an income tax on nonresidents as it did in *Shaffer*, and similarly upheld limiting deductions to those incurred in connection with income arising within the state, but it struck down the failure to allow personal exemptions (Travis v. Yale & Towne Mfg. Co., 1920).

New York also argued that the failure to allow personal exemptions did not create inequality because nonresidents had several advantages: they were not taxed on income from interest on bank deposits or bonds, they might have untaxed income out of state corresponding to the amount that residents use their exemptions to offset, and New York allowed a credit for taxes paid to the nonresident's home state to the extent it taxed their New York earnings. The Court noted that New Jersey and Connecticut did not have income taxes, so the credit did not benefit the vast majority of nonresidents who worked in New York. Further, New York failed to show that nonresidents had significant business income outside of New York, and the reason New York did not tax nonresidents on the interest on bank deposits or bonds was to maintain its position as a financial center rather than to equalize tax burdens. In short, the Court focused on the actual impact of the tax differences. The deductions meant that New York residents paid lower tax than nonresidents on income earned in the state, and therefore the Court held the tax invalid under Article IV.

Travis resolved most of the privileges and immunities issues of taxation. Nonresidents could be taxed only for activities for which residents were taxed. However, they could be taxed at a different rate if the actual impact of the tax on nonresidents was reasonably equivalent to its impact on residents. These principles continue to govern taxation by one state of income earned by citizens of other states.

The next major issue arose in 1975, when New Hampshire imposed a tax on nonresidents that had no impact on their total tax burden. The state argued that it did not deny a privilege or immunity because it did not cause any net harm to an individual. The Court, however, held that Article IV prevented a state from imposing a tax on citizens of other states from which its own citizens were immune (Austin v. New Hampshire, 1975).

In *Austin*, Maine imposed a tax on its residents on income wherever earned but gave residents a credit for taxes paid on income earned elsewhere. New Hampshire had no state income tax, but it instituted a commuter tax that applied only when the commuter's home state imposed a tax that gave a credit for amounts paid to New Hampshire. Maine could retain the benefit of the tax by changing its law. Without such a change, a Maine citizen would contribute to the resources of New Hampshire rather than Maine for an activity that was not taxable if done by New Hampshire residents.

Standing was an issue because paycheck withholding was the only impact of the tax on the nonresident plaintiffs. The amount paid to New Hampshire was identical to the amount they would have paid Maine. Justice Blackmun argued that no violation of the privileges and immunities clause occurred because no taxpayer was injured. The rest of the Court, however, saw that New Hampshire required nonresidents to pay a tax to the state that residents did not have to pay and held that it violated the privileges and immunities clause of Article IV (Austin v. New Hampshire, 1975). Justice Thurgood Marshall wrote that the cases established "a rule of substantial equality of treatment for the citizens of the taxing state and nonresident taxpayers." Because this tax fell only on nonresidents, it was invalid. Despite the plausibility of the argument that New Hampshire did not increase the tax liability of the nonresident, Marshall said "it cannot be squared with the underlying policy of comity to which the Privileges and Immunities Clause commits us."

The Court has continued to scrutinize closely any differences in taxation between residents and nonresidents. It held that New York's denial to nonresidents of a deduction on the state income tax violated the privileges and immunities clause (Lunding v. New York Tax Appeals Tribunal, 1998). The mechanism that produced a differential deduction was somewhat complicated. First, taxpayers computed their tax as if they were residents of New York using the federal adjusted gross income. Then this tax was multiplied by a fraction whose numerator was the income derived from New York sources and whose denominator was the federal adjusted gross income. Because alimony payments were deducted from federal gross income and not from the state derived income, the numerator could exceed the denominator, and a nonresident would have to pay more than a resident. The nonresident taxpayer challenged the failure to allow the alimony deduction from the state-derived income. The Court said, "the Privileges and Immunities Clause affords no assurance of precise equality in taxation between residents and nonresidents of a particular State." Nevertheless, it held the scheme invalid. "States may limit nonresidents' deductions of business expenses and nonbusiness deductions based on the relationship between those expenses and in-state property or income," but cannot limit personal deductions categorically without a substantial justification. The state claimed the alimony payments were linked to personal activities outside New York, and it could legitimately limit deductions to those linked to the state. However, the majority cited *Travis* for the proposition that personal deductions must be allowed in parity with residents. Justice Sandra Day O'Connor's opinion for the majority noted that amount of alimony is affected by total income wherever earned.

Chief Justice William Rehnquist and justices Ruth Bader Ginsburg and Anthony Kennedy dissented on grounds that the basic issue was allocation of income between parties for taxation. The state ultimately taxes the income regardless of who gets it. If parties both reside in New York, the resident ex-spouse receiving alimony will be taxed, and the deduction avoids taxing the same sum twice. If both are nonresidents, the state has no jurisdiction to tax the alimony recipient; therefore income earned in New York would not be taxed at all unless the nonresident is denied a deduction. The majority's problem with this analysis was that the deduction was not related to the residence of the wife receiving alimony. Thus a New Jersey resident earning money in New York and paying alimony to a New York spouse ended up with double taxation. New York taxed the New Jersey resident because no deduction was made, and the New York payee was taxed because the alimony was income in the state. However, the New York resident paying alimony to a New Jersey spouse was not taxed on the sum at all by New York.

Although the Court has articulated the same principle—allowing different schemes of taxation as long as they equalize inherent differences—it may require more demonstrable equality today. The rough justice that the Court upheld in *Traveller's Insurance* bespeaks a different attitude than the insistence in *Lunding* that the tax levied must be more evenhanded.

Reasonable and Adequate Access to the Courts

The Court has been careful to assure citizens of other states equality in the substantive rights of property and contract possessed by a state's citizens, but it has tended to view procedure as incidental. Recognizing the differences between residents and nonresidents in amenability to the jurisdiction of the state courts, the Court in its early decisions merely required that states provide citizens of other states reasonable and adequate access to the courts, not necessarily the same access.

The "reasonable and adequate" test comes from cases that are now quite old and has not been restated recently. The Court might well rephrase it today to require the state to show that nonresidents pose problems that justify procedural differences. In fact, nonresidence does pose problems for process in state courts. The state lacks jurisdiction over nonresidents unless they are present in the state or have committed an act in the state that is the subject of the litigation. Even if the nonresident is subject to personal jurisdiction in the state, enforcement of any judgment may require additional proceedings in the nonresident's home state. These jurisdictional problems may enable nonresidents to avoid paying debts incurred within a state. Finally, the opportunity to litigate in other states is more appropriate for them than for residents.

Requiring security for costs as a condition of access

The Court drew a distinction between substance and process in a number of cases. Perhaps the most prominent involved a preference given to Tennessee creditors of a bankrupt British corporation. The Court held that the discrimination violated the privileges and immunities clause (Blake v. McClung, 1898). However, Justice Harlan wrote:

> We must not be understood as saying that a citizen of one State is entitled to enjoy in another State every privilege that may be given in the latter to its own citizens. There are privileges

that may be accorded by a state to its own people, in which citizens of other states may not participate, except in conformity to such reasonable regulations as may be established by the state. (Blake v. McClung, 1898)

Harlan said that certain procedural differences did not violate the privileges and immunities clause, because they did not violate fundamental rights:

For instance, a state cannot forbid citizens of other states from suing in its courts, that right being enjoyed by its own people; but it may require a nonresident, although a citizen of another state, to give bond for costs, although such bond be not required of a resident. Such a regulation of the internal affairs of a state cannot reasonably be characterized as hostile to the fundamental rights of citizens of other states. . . . It has never been supposed that regulations of that character materially interfered with the enjoyment by citizens of each State of the privileges and immunities secured by the Constitution to citizens of the several States. (Blake v. McClung, 1898)

Why were such regulations not hostile to fundamental rights? Resident plaintiffs who fail to pay costs of litigation will have process issued against them and their income and property will be attached, but the nonresident may run home without paying. Although access to the courts may be a privilege of citizenship, at the end of the nineteenth century the court thought it appropriate for states to condition the use of their courts by nonresidents on payment of a bond for costs. Any court that distinguished between residents and nonresidents today might have a more difficult time in sustaining a bond requirement. Obstacles to suits by nonresidents should raise a presumption of protectionism. Judgments are given full faith and credit, and modern communications make their collection in other states far easier than a century ago. Thus the justification for imposing a bond requirement on nonresident plaintiffs that is not imposed on the resident may not be as substantial today.

Making nonresident defendants amenable to process

Injured parties seek recourse in a state against persons who have caused injury there or who own property there that could be used to satisfy a judgment. The resident can easily be reached with service of process and punished for failure to appear. The citizen of another state is likely to be out of reach of both process and threats of jail. Early state decisions asserted that this difference made it appropriate to allow attachment of the property of the nonresident to compel appearance (Campbell v. Morris, Md., 1797).

States attempted to get around the problem of serving papers on someone who was outside their jurisdiction by forms of service within their jurisdiction. Nonresidents challenged the service of process in a number of cases, claiming that the state violated due process when it asserted jurisdiction without personal service of court papers. They sometimes also argued Article IV because the resident was always subject to personal service. The Court appreciated the difference in the situation of the parties, and upheld these forms of serving process where jurisdiction was otherwise appropriate. "Personal service upon non-residents is not always within the State's power. Its process is limited by its boundaries. Constructive service is at times a necessary resource" (Ballard v. Hunter, 1907). Thus the court upheld constructive service by publication for a nonresident with respect to litigation over land within the state.

One method to serve a party within a state is to condition a right within a state on appointment of a person on whom service can be made. The Court upheld a New Jersey law that made it a condition of driving in the state that nonresidents appoint a state official for purposes of service of process connected to litigation over driving there (Kane v. New Jersey, 1916). Because the resident can be served at home, the appointment of an official for service of process simply made the resident equally subject to suit. The Court said: "It is not a discrimination against nonresidents, denying them equal protection of the law. On the contrary, it puts nonresident owners upon an equality with resident owners."

The primary argument in cases that involved constructive service has been whether it satisfied due process. For example, the Court found that a plaintiff could bring suit against a nonresident principal by serving process on his agent within the county when the suit was for acts arising out of that agency (Henry L. Doherty and Co. v. Goodman, 1935). The special statute for the service of process on the nonresident's agent enabled the injured plaintiff to reach the nonresident as well as the resident, and the Court spent little time discussing Article IV. The opinion focused on the reasonableness of the statute and the contacts within the state, finding that it satisfied due process.

Statutes of limitation

Citizens of a state have a natural interest in bringing suit where they reside, so it is an appropriate forum for them. The state then has a legitimate interest in making suit possible for its citizens. This may lead to statutes of limitation that take account of the difficulties of suit in the jurisdiction. The Court permits a state to create special rules for its citizens if citizens of other states have reasonable and adequate access to the forum. There is no need to give nonresidents the extended statute, because they have opportunities elsewhere.

Two cases upheld different periods for residents and nonresidents. In both cases, the nonresident was free to bring suit within the period of the statute of limitations, but the statute applicable to resident plaintiffs extended longer. Both statutes seemed designed to prevent forum shopping and in that sense expressed deference to the interests of other states. In the first case, a New York plaintiff was barred by Wisconsin's ten-year statute of limitation for actions brought on a judgment (Chemung Canal Bank v. Lowery, 1876). The Wisconsin defendant had only come to the state nine years earlier. While a defendant was out of state, Wisconsin tolled the statute of limitations for resident plaintiffs, so that period was not counted for purposes of determining the time within which a plaintiff must sue. The New York plaintiff complained that he should be entitled to the same privileges as a Wisconsin plaintiff.

The Court responded that the difference was justified. Where both plaintiff and defendant were out of state, Wisconsin lacked any real connection to the matter—no reason was evident for suit to be brought there nor for tolling a statute designed to keep claims fresh in that state. Where the plaintiff was from Wisconsin, the state had an interest in being a forum, but the absence of the defendant from the state made it difficult to bring him within the state's jurisdiction. It would not be fair, however, to let the nonresident plaintiff pounce on the defendant who happened to be going through the state long after the statute of limitations expired. Justice Bradley also argued that the judgment debtor had an obligation to pay the creditor at the creditor's residence, and therefore it was the law of the creditor's residence that should be concerned with the absence of the debtor from the jurisdiction. In short, it was not hostility to the nonresident plaintiff, but the propriety of being the forum for decision between nonresidents that influenced this decision.

Nearly half a century later, the Court upheld a Minnesota statute that applied, on behalf of its own residents, Minnesota's longer statute of limitations to suits arising out of state that were barred in that other state by its statute of limitations (Canadian Northern Ry v. Eggen, 1920). Minnesota argued that it had an interest in the vindication of the rights of its citizens to recover damages for their injuries, regardless of the policy of the state where events involving their citizen occurred. On the other hand, Minnesota had no interest in litigation involving a nonresident for an event that occurred out of state. Allowing the nonresident to sue under Minnesota's statute would simply permit forum shopping to avoid the policies of the state where the accident occurred. The Court said:

> The principle on which this holding rests is that the constitutional requirement is satisfied if the non-resident is given access to the courts of the State upon terms which in themselves are reasonable and adequate for the enforcing of any rights he may have, even though they may not be technically and precisely the same in extent as those accorded to resident citizens. (Canadian Northern Ry v. Eggen, 1920)

The Court required the nonresident to be given access to the courts on terms that are "reasonable and adequate." The twin tests do not require strict equality, but terms for access are not likely to be reasonable unless the difference from residents, including the degree of that difference, can be justified by some problem peculiar to nonresidents. The Court has continued to cite the *Canadian Northern Ry* decision for the proposition that a state need not always apply the same laws to anyone, resident or nonresident, who may request them (Baldwin v. Fish & Game Commission of Montana, 1978). It also cited *Canadian Northern Ry* for whether an interest is fundamental to the promotion of interstate harmony (United Bldg. and Const. and Trades Council of Camden County and Vicinity v. Mayor and Council of City of Camden, 1984). Thus it remains a viable precedent, although the test it articulated has not been repeated recently.

Classifications Not Based on State Citizenship: False Dichotomies and True Explanations

In a number of cases, beginning with Justice Curtis opinion in *Conner*, the court has stated that no privilege or immunity was involved because the classification was not based on state citizenship. In many of these cases, the classification turned on the residence of one of the parties, but the Court insisted that Article IV did not apply unless the classification was based on state citizenship. The Court subsequently repudiated this dichotomy, saying in *Hicklin*, "It is now established that the terms 'citizen' and 'resident' are 'essentially interchangeable,' Austin v. New Hampshire, . . . (1975), for purposes of analysis of most cases under the Privileges and Immunities Clause of Art. IV, § 2." Nevertheless, the Court has not repudiated the decisions based on this false dichotomy. The real reason for the court's decisions was that the rationale for the differential treatment was a peculiar problem posed by nonresidence and was not related to the desire to prefer citizens of a state. The underlying justifications therefore may survive the demise of the resident-citizen distinction.

Property incidents of the marriage relationship

Marriage is a legal status governed by the law of the state where the marriage occurred or the state to which the parties move. No violation of the privileges and immunities clause occurs in recognizing that the law governing the marital relationship of a nonresident is the law of that person's home state. Indeed, the Court upheld a state's requirement of one-year residence for marriage, because it supported the marital policies of other states with respect to their citizens (Sosna v. Iowa, 1975). It prevented persons from coming to the state just to get married and then return to their home state. On the other hand, property inheritance is a privilege of citizenship that must be afforded the nonresident. These principles collided in Conner v. Elliot (1856) where the Court held that a state could make spousal property rights within the state depend on situs of the marriage of the purchaser of land. The Court reasoned that a law that turned on the situs of the marriage did not discriminate on the basis of state citizenship, even though the situs of a relationship depends on where the parties reside and residence determines citizenship.

In *Conner*, a woman who married and then lived in Mississippi claimed land in Louisiana that her deceased spouse had purchased during their marriage. Louisiana community property law applied to couples that married in the state. It also applied to a couple that married elsewhere and moved to Louisiana with respect to property acquired after they moved. However, Louisiana did not apply its community property law to Louisiana property acquired by couples that did not marry there and were not living there at the time of acquisition. Instead it left the parties to look to the law of the state where they married or where they reside. The plaintiff argued that the law denied her the privileges of citizenship because a Louisiana citizen would have community property rights in the property. The Court found the differences in application of the law were not based on the citizenship of the parties, but on where the marriage occurred or was carried out. Justice Curtis said this was appropriate: "The law does not discriminate between citizens of the State and other persons; it discriminates between contracts only. Such discrimination has no connection with the clause in the constitution now in question" (Conner v. Elliot, 1856). Because the law was not based on the wife's state of citizenship, the rights asserted were not privileges of citizenship.

A similar issue arose when a wife challenged Oregon's statutes governing dower, the right of a spouse to a life estate in her deceased husband's property (Ferry v. Spokane, Portland &. Seattle Ry, 1922). Like community property, dower is a property right that depends on the marital relationship. Oregon permitted dower for residents in all lands that the husband held at any point in the marriage, but it allowed nonresidents dower only in the lands that the husband owned when he died. Any lands the husband conveyed during his life were free of dower unless his wife was an Oregon citizen. Citing *Conner*, the Court said that dower is not a privilege and immunity of state or federal citizenship (Ferry v. Spokane, Portland &. Seattle Ry, 1922).

The definitional approach, saying that rights dependent on the situs of the marital relationship are not privileges or immunities, is unsatisfactory. As the Court noted in *Chalker* and repeated in *Lunding*, a state law that has different applications to residents and nonresidents will treat citizens of other states differently than citizens of the state. A state could not impose higher taxes on income earned by couples who have a marriage situs out of state, and succeed in a claim that the tax did not discriminate against citizens of other states. The crucial question should be the legitimacy of the justification for the distinction. Professors Brainerd Currie and Herma Hill Kay suggested that *Conner* can be justified because the distinction protected the expectations of the parties to the marriage that their rights would be governed by common law rules.[6] *Ferry* was also a case for protecting expectations. Indeed the *Ferry* court noted that dower was an impediment to the transfer of land and that the statute was appropriate for security of title and the protection of innocent purchasers. When a husband disposes of land without his wife's consent, he probably portrays himself as single. If his wife is not a resident of the state, it is far more likely that the purchaser will not know of her existence. No record will be in the land or marriage office within the state to alert the purchaser, especially with respect to land that has passed through several hands. Thus residence is connected to security of title, and Oregon appropriately used it.

Concerns for avoidance of scrutiny

The state has a legitimate interest in assuring that its licensees operate properly, but the limitations on its jurisdiction may mean that citizens of other states pose different problems than its own citizens. The citizen of another state may escape the jurisdiction of the state more easily than its own citizen, and this makes it easier for them to avoid payment and to engage in improper activities relating to that state. Where the Court is convinced that the statute is targeted to the peculiar problem posed by the nonresident, it may uphold it. This excuse, however, could prove too much, destroying the equality of opportunity that Article IV was designed to provide. Thus the Court today will scrutinize such justifications carefully to demand that they be substantial.

At one time the Court was rather lenient to discrimination justified by the difficulty of supervision of persons outside the state. For example, in LaTourette v. McMaster (1919), South Carolina prohibited the sale of insurance by nonresidents. It argued that it could best supervise insurance agents when they were residents. La Tourette claimed this restriction violated Article IV, but the Court found that the act did not discriminate against citizens of other states. It held that residence and citizenship are different things, and the act depended on residence. The Court acknowledged that the use of the word "residents" was not dispositive, but said that its constitutionality depended on whether the act intended to use resident as synonymous with citizen of the state (LaTourette v. McMaster, 1919). The justification for the restriction was not to benefit the commercial interests of the local agents but to enhance the supervision of the industry. Thus the court determined that it was not the political tie of citizenship but the physical fact of residence that underlay the statute.

The Court would find the distinction insufficient today. It would require a substantial interest to repel the inference that a regulation denying a job opportunity to nonresidents was designed to benefit local interests. For example, the Court has dismissed as not substantial the concern that attorneys have a connection with the state of their practice based on residence (Supreme Court of New Hampshire v. Piper, 1984). The Court has consistently held that states may deal with the peculiar problems posed by citizens of other states, but it repudiates the significance of the residence-citizenship distinction, and it demands the justification be substantial when a state law interferes with the opportunities of citizens of other states to do business within the state.

Forum non conveniens

Citizens of other states may wish to sue in a state where they have no particular connection because the rules of that forum are particularly favorable to their case, although no reason otherwise exists for that action. Where no connection is made between a state and a cause of action, denial of a forum may be justified.

The Court has permitted a state to refuse to hear a cause of action where there was no strong connection between the parties or cause of action and the state. In Chambers v. Baltimore & O. R. Co. (1907), the Court found that the state could refuse to extend its law to the nonresident, and in Douglas v. New York, N. H. & H. R. Co., (1929), the state could deny its forum. Both decisions were badly reasoned, but the outcome can be justified.

In *Chambers*, an Ohio statute allowed parties to sue for the wrongful death of an Ohio resident whose death occurred outside the state if suit was permitted by the laws of the state where the death occurred. Mrs. Chambers sued the B&O Railroad, which had offices in Ohio, for the death of her husband. She and her husband lived in Pennsylvania, and his death occurred there. The Court upheld Ohio's decision to dismiss her case (Chambers v. Baltimore & O. R. Co. 1907). The majority said that the statute did not turn on the citizenship of the plaintiff, only that of plaintiff's decedent. The majority's distinction is not terribly convincing. The dissent pointed out that the law reserved privileges for the estate of the citizen over that of the noncitizen, and argued the distinction violated privileges and immunities. The state had jurisdiction over the person of the defendant and would be applying Pennsylvania law rather than its own to determine whether the death was wrongful. Thus the dissent saw the statute as foreclosing a privilege of citizenship in the right to sue. Nevertheless, the decision makes some sense as a forum non conveniens (the doctrine allowing a court with jurisdiction of a case to decline to hear it because the location is inconvenient for the witnesses and the parties and the interest of justice would be better served if the case were brought in a court having proper jurisdiction in another venue). No good reason existed for Ohio to be the forum in this case, so it should have been able to avoid it.

The same kind of mischaracterization of the nature of the issue to reach a sensible result soon occurred again (Douglas v. New York, N. H. & H. R. Co., 1929). The Court upheld a law that gave New York courts discretion on whether to hear or reject a suit brought by a nonresident against a foreign company, although the courts would be required to hear suits brought by residents. The Court cited *LaTourette*, asserting that the statute was not a violation of the privileges and immunities clause because it was based on residence rather than citizenship, and residence means where one lives regardless of domicile. However, the residence-citizenship distinction makes sense only as a way of saying that the use of residence as a classifying device must be justified by a characteristic sufficiently tied to a legitimate reason for distinction. Justice Holmes tried to do this in *Douglas*, saying: "There are manifest reasons for preferring residents in access to often overcrowded courts, both in convenience and in the fact that broadly speaking it is they who pay for maintaining the Courts concerned." However, preferring residents to nonresidents in most instances would violate the rights of the citizens of other states.

It is only where neither party is a resident of the state and the state's law is inapplicable that the nonresident plaintiff may be denied access. Under those circumstances, forum closure not only protects the state court operations from being burdened, but it prevents the state from appearing to meddle in the affairs of other states and supports the application of the law by the more appropriate state. In those limited circumstances, denying the nonresident access to the state court enhances the union rather than undermines it. Thus although states cannot reserve their courts to residents without violating a basic premise of the privileges and immunities clause, the court is willing on forum non conveniens grounds to allow states to close their courts to nonresidents where no connection to the state exists except for the happenstance that a nonresident party has a presence in the state when sued.

Right to Travel

The Court has stressed that Article IV is essentially a nondiscrimination clause, but the cases have moved away from the original understanding that the clause also protected movement. The Articles of Confederation specifically protected the right of "free ingress and egress to and from any other state." Article IV of the Constitution did not repeat the phrase, but the concept continued and early cases said so. Justice Washington mentioned in his listing of privileges and immunities in *Corfield*: "the right of a citizen of one state to pass through, or to reside in any other state, for purposes of trade, agriculture, professional pursuits, or otherwise." Justice Taney used it in *Dred Scott* to reason that African-Americans are not citizens: "It would give to persons of the negro race, who were recognized as citizens in any one State of the Union, the right to enter every other State whenever they pleased, singly or in companies, without pass or passport, and without obstruction, to sojourn there as long as they pleased." In *Paul*, the Court said Article IV gives citizens of a state "the right of free ingress into other states, and egress from them," and in *Ward*, the Court said: "[T]he clause plainly and unmistakably secures and protects the right of a citizen of one state to pass into any other state of the Union, for the purpose of engaging in lawful commerce, trade, or business, without molestation." As late as 1920 in *Wheeler*, the Court still considered Article IV the source for the right to travel applied against the state. The Court said Article IV fused into one the right to reside peacefully in, and to have free ingress into and egress from one's own state and other states (United States v. Wheeler, 1920).

Justice O'Connor cited this history when she concurred in invalidating durational requirements for an Alaska resident credit (Zobel v. Williams, 1982). Justice O'Connor argued that the privileges and immunities of Article IV applied to protect new residents of a state, unless the new residency was shown to be a peculiar source of the evil at which the statutory distinction was aimed. The rest of the Court, however, appeared to believe that the clause applies only to protect the citizen of a state while in other states. Thus the clause would not forbid discrimination by a state against its own residents, even in preventing a citizen from leaving.

Justice O'Connor's history and linguistic reading was sensible. Article IV does not limit the entitlement of a citizen of a state to the privileges and immunities of citizens in "other states" but "in the several states." Literally that would include the state of which the individual is a citizen. The privilege to which the citizen would be entitled in the citizen's home state would be the right of ingress and egress and to become a citizen of a state by residence. The Articles of Confederation guaranteed this expressly; denial prevents the individual from access to the privileges and immunities of citizenship in the several states; and the guarantee is consistent with the language of Article IV. The privileges and immunities of the citizens of a state in the several states would be to be able to travel among the several states, to reside in the state of choice and become a citizen there, and to be free of discrimination based on state citizenship while traveling among the states.

Despite the logic, historic support, and linguistic consistency, the Court has decided not to rest the right of travel in Article IV. It has divided the right into separate components, leaving the right to enter and leave a state with no certain linguistic home. After an interesting peregrination, the Court has rooted the right to become a citizen of another state in the privileges and immunities clause of the Fourteenth Amendment instead of Article IV. Thus only rights not to be discriminated against because of residency in another state are protected through Article IV.

AMENDMENT XIV: PRIVILEGES OR IMMUNITIES

The debates on the Fourteenth Amendment provide support for the argument that it protected unenumerated fundamental rights, made personal rights in the U.S. Constitution binding on the states, and required laws to be equal. The Supreme Court has interpreted the amendment to do just that. The debates suggest that the amendment's framers expected the privileges or immunities clause to be the source for these rights, but the Court used the due process and equal protection clauses instead.

From its very first decision on the privileges or immunities clause of the Fourteenth Amendment, the Court has rendered the enactment of the clause futile. According to the Court, the clause created no new rights; it merely recognized existing privileges and immunities of citizens of the United States—rights that the states never could abridge. When the Court did invalidate a law for violation of the privileges or immunities clause in Colgate v. Harvey (1935), it reversed the decision within five years (Madden v. Kentucky, 1940). The next invalidation was in 1999, when the Court struck down a California welfare law that treated new residents differently from old residents (Saenz v. Roe, 1999). Although the Court referred to the privileges or immunities clause of the Fourteenth Amendment, the theory of the case was that California violated a privilege that had existed from the formation of the union and would preclude the law even if the Fourteenth Amendment had never been adopted.

This section traces the cases that stripped the Fourteenth Amendment's privileges or immunities clause of any force and examines the content that remains.

The *Slaughter-House Cases*: The Rejection of Fundamental Rights

Everyone who spoke in Congress during the framing of the Fourteenth Amendment assumed that the privileges and immunities of United States citizens protected in the amendment referred to the same fundamental rights that were secured from discrimination against nonresidents by the privileges and immunities clause of Article IV. Nevertheless, when the Court considered the new amendment, a majority rejected this history and the arguments of counsel on both sides. They held that the privileges and immunities of the Fourteenth Amendment were totally different than those of Article IV (*Slaughter-House Cases*, 1873).

The first case argued under the privileges or immunities clause of the Fourteenth Amendment reached the Court on January 11, 1872. A group of butchers challenged a Louisiana statute that gave the Crescent City Live-Stock Landing and Slaughter-House Company a monopoly on the ownership of a slaughterhouse in New Orleans. The monopoly was as rank as the smell of the slaughter, procured allegedly by bribing the legislature, but was it a violation of the federal Constitution? Former Supreme Court Justice John A. Campbell argued on behalf of the butchers. He acknowledged the state legislature's power to regulate occupations by general rules, but he contended that monopolies were special privileges that deprived others of the privilege and immunity of pursuing an occupation on terms applicable to everyone.[7]

The slaughterhouse monopoly insisted that restrictions on property ownership and the practice of an occupation did not abridge the privileges and immunities of citizens when imposed for the public benefit; that the legislature rather than the Court should determine the nature of such public benefits; and that the only effect of the Fourteenth Amendment was to proscribe racial discrimination in fundamental rights.[8] The defendant monopoly argued that a broad reading of the amendment would block all exercises of the police power over the conduct of business. They agreed with the plaintiffs that the Fourteenth Amendment's privileges or immunities clause included the privileges and immunities protected by Article IV, but the defendant insisted the amendment should be construed in light of its history as "limited to the investiture of blacks with all the rights and immunities of whites, whatever these may be, and to protect them in their lives, liberties and properties just as whites are protected."[9]

Justice Samuel F. Miller, writing for the majority, noted that the Fourteenth Amendment specified two types of citizenship: state and national. Article IV protected the privileges and immunities of state citizenship, whereas the Fourteenth Amendment protected those of national citizenship. The privileges of state citizenship, said Miller, were the fundamental rights that all men have in a free society, whereas the privileges of national citizenship are limited to those rights arising out of a citizen's special relationship to the federal government—rights "which owe their existence to the Federal government, its National character, its Constitution, or its laws" (*Slaughter-House Cases,* 1873).

The distinction between the two citizenships did not necessarily imply that fundamental rights were not privileges and immunities of federal citizenship. Most fundamental rights in relation to government might be components of both state and federal citizenship while a few specific relationships applied only to one or the other. For example, the ability to institute and maintain suits should be a fundamental right in any governmental relationship, but protection in foreign relations is solely a federal matter, and rights to publicly owned resources relate to state citizenship.

The Court majority, however, rejected this interpretation. They said that neither Congress nor the ratifying states intended the amendment to have the profound consequences that would result if it forbade abridgment of fundamental rights by the states. If the fundamental right of property ownership was a privilege of state citizenship (as it was under Article IV), the state defined property rights. If it were one of national citizenship, Congress could arguably define it. As intimated in debates on the Enforcement Act in 1871 and on Sumner's Civil Rights bill in 1872, Congress might then claim power to enact federal contract, property, and criminal law enforced through the federal courts under Section 5 of the Fourteenth Amendment, which gave Congress power to enforce the other provisions of the amendment. The majority did not believe that the amendment conferred such power on Congress.

The Court did not go into great detail on the problems of a fundamental rights view, but it is possible to see why the framers might have thought the clause was limited yet Congress and the Court saw fundamental rights as a threat to federalism. The framers of the Fourteenth Amendment may have expected that each state would afford fundamental rights through its own laws, and Section 5 only enabled Congress to deal with state failures. A privilege such as the right to property or to sue exists only in general terms so that each state's property law may afford the fundamental right to property despite differing in specifics from other states. Although this interpretation seems to reconcile the protection of fundamental rights with the traditional role of the state, it could still result in congressional statutes on contract, property, or criminal law.

Unlike equal protection, which provides its own measure for relief, fundamental rights of contract and property lack fixed contours. If a state appeared to deny a basic right to all its citizens, a court would have difficulty in providing a remedy. The law could afford the right in a variety of ways, and a court would have difficulty choosing one. Ordering the state to enact a law would threaten state sovereignty and present overwhelming enforcement problems. A specific federal statute as a default rule would directly assure citizens' fundamental rights, but a default rule is still a federal law supplanting traditionally local law and raises the question whether states with different laws abridge the privilege. Thus even a requirement of state violation as a prerequisite for federal power would not avoid a shift from state to federal government of ultimate responsibility for enacting municipal law.

At least two ways were available for getting out of the dilemma posed by the logic of a fundamental rights interpretation. One was to apply the clause as its logic dictated, even though its framers may not have considered how far it would reach. Justice Miller chose the other option:

> The argument, we admit, is not always the most conclusive which is drawn from the consequences urged against the adoption of a particular construction of an instrument. But when, as in the case before us, these consequences are so serious, so far reaching and pervading, so great a departure from the structure and spirit of our institutions; where the effect is to fetter and degrade the State governments by subjecting them to the control of Congress, in the exercise of powers heretofore universally conceded to them of the most ordinary and fundamental character; when in fact it radically changes the whole theory of the relations of state and Federal governments to each other and of both these governments to the people; the argument has a force that is irresistible, in the absence of language which expresses such a purpose too clearly to admit of doubt. (Slaughter-House Cases, 1873)

Miller concluded that the privileges and immunities of citizens of the United States were not the fundamental rights of a citizen detailed in *Corfield.* State regulations of property rights and business activities did not involve privileges or immunities of citizens of the United States, and therefore the privileges or immunities clause did not apply to the New Orleans monopoly. Justice Miller said that he did not need to define the privileges or immunities of citizens of the United States, because they were not involved in this case. Nevertheless, he listed some "which owe their existence to the Federal government, its National character, its Constitution, or its laws." First, he set forth the right to travel within the United States "protected by implied guarantees of its Constitution" to have access to federal institutions and transact business governed by federal law. Justice Miller then pointed to rights derived from the federal role beyond the territories of the United States:

> Another privilege of a citizen of the United States is to demand the care and protection of the Federal government over his life, liberty, and property when on the high seas or within the jurisdiction of a foreign government. Of this there can be no doubt, nor that the right depends upon his character as a citizen of the United States. (Slaughter-House Cases, 1873)

Justice Miller next pointed to rights that could be found expressly in the Constitution:

The right to peaceably assemble and petition for redress of grievances, the privilege of the writ of habeas corpus, are rights of the citizen guaranteed by the Federal Constitution. (*Slaughter-House Cases,* 1873)

These rights limited the federal government, but they had not been applied to the states. This created a fundamental ambiguity.[10] Were the rights that citizens had with respect to limits on the federal government now applicable to the states, or were these privileges merely references to the status quo? The rest of Justice Miller's specific privileges or immunities of federal citizenship referred to existing rights and intimated no change. He concluded his list by saying:

The right to use the navigable waters of the United States, however they may penetrate the territory of the several States, all rights secured to our citizens by treaties with foreign nations, are dependent upon citizenship of the United States, and not citizenship of a State. One of these privileges is conferred by the very article under consideration. It is that a citizen of the United States can, of his own volition, become a citizen of any State of the Union by a bona fide residence therein, with the same rights as other citizens of that State. To these may be added the rights secured by the thirteenth and fifteenth articles of amendment, and by the other clause of the fourteenth, next to be considered. (*Slaughter-House Cases,* 1873)

Justice Miller's enumeration of the privileges and immunities of citizens of the United States included matters relevant to the federal government alone. For example, the prohibition against denying the privileges and immunities of citizens of the United States did not mean that states must afford care and protection to citizens on the high seas or within the jurisdiction of a foreign government. That right surely remained only one against the federal government. Similarly, Justice Miller may have mentioned the rights of assembly and habeas corpus as examples of privileges of citizenship without altering their character from restrictions of federal power to restrictions of state power. Justice Field's dissent supports this interpretation of Justice Miller's opinion. Field said:

If this inhibition has no reference to privileges and immunities of this character, but only refers, as held by the majority of the court in the opinion, to such privileges and immunities as were before its adoption specifically designated in the Constitution or necessarily implied as belonging to citizens of the United States, it was a vain and idle enactment, which accomplished nothing. . . . (*Slaughter-House Cases,* 1873, Field dissenting)

In other words, Justice Field understood Justice Miller to say that the privileges or immunities clause did not alter the existing law. The privileges or immunities of citizens of the United States were those that existed when the Constitution was adopted and were either expressly stated or implied from the federal institutions and structural relationships created by the document. The clause created no new ones. States were already prohibited from depriving citizens of the United States of their privileges or immunities, because those rights were derived from the Constitution, and the supremacy clause (U.S. Const. Art. VI, § 2) made the Constitution and laws of the United States "the supreme Law of the Land." Thus Justice Field charged that Miller's opinion stripped the privileges and immunities clause of any effect.

This construction of the privileges and immunities clause was not original. Senator Lyman Trumbull, debating with Senator Carpenter over the Enforcement Act in April of 1871, had set forth the same proposition.[11] The construction was linguistically possible, and it preserved the original relationship between the states and the federal government unless the state violated due process or equal protection. Justice Miller went on to find that the Louisiana statute did not violate either clause.

The majority opinion in the *Slaughter-House Cases* in effect destroyed the privileges and immunities clause as a significant source of protection to the rights of African-Americans. It left them only the more limited safeguards of due process and equal protection. There was some ambiguity about whether the privileges and immunities clause made any of the amendments restricting the federal government applicable to the states, but none over whether the clause applied to the fundamental rights of citizens to contract, sue, or hold property.

Several cases argued at the time of the *Slaughter-House Cases* were decided on the basis of that case. Those arguments had focused on fundamental rights premises that the *Slaughter-House Cases* decision rejected. For example, Matthew Carpenter argued the *Slaughter-House Cases* on behalf of the slaughterhouse monopoly, stressing that the privileges and immunities clause was designed to prevent racial discrimination. The next week, representing Myra Bradwell, who had been denied admission to the Illinois bar because of her gender, he argued that the privileges and immunities clause went beyond race to strike down gender barriers.[12] He made no mention of the equal protection clause, apparently because he regarded it as applicable only to laws protecting the individual from the infliction of injury to life, liberty, or property by other individuals.[13] He relied solely on privileges and immunities. Assuming that racial qualifications would be impermissible for licensing attorneys, he argued that the privileges and immunities clause secured the privilege of pursuing that avocation for everyone with the requisite intelligence and integrity.[14]

The court did not interpret privileges and immunities as Carpenter expected, and he had no opportunity to consider how to respond to the unexpected position of the court. Mrs. Bradwell lost her suit in an opinion delivered right after the *Slaughter-House Cases* (Bradwell v. Illinois, 1873). Admission to the bar was not a privilege or immunity of citizens of the United States but only a privilege of state citizenship.[15] It followed that freedom from racial discrimination in the privileges of state citizenship was also not a separate privilege or immunity of federal citizenship.

The same fate awaited a liquor seller who attempted to use the privileges and immunities clause to attack an Iowa prohibition law. The case was submitted on printed arguments, and decided the year after the *Slaughter-House Cases*. The Court said that states could always regulate alcohol, "in any event, the right to sell intoxicating liquors, so far as such a right exists, is not one of the rights growing out of citizenship of the United States" (Bartemeyer v. Iowa, 1874).

The Court suggested that the statute might have deprived the defendant of property without due process of law if he owned the liquor when the law was passed, but the record was unclear on when he obtained it. Although the Court found the issue was not properly presented, it hinted that the due process clause might be pressed into service for substantive principles for which the privileges and immunities clause initially seemed more suited. The *Slaughter-House Cases* dissenters, Justices Field, Swayne, and Bradley, concurred, explaining that state regulation of alcohol was wholly appropriate, but the *Slaughter-House Cases* monopoly was unjustified by health concerns.

After *Bartemeyer*, counsel attempted to use the privileges and immunities clause in numerous cases to claim that the state had regulated a business inappropriately, but the court rejected the claim in every case. A number of cases raised issues of sale or consumption of alcohol unsuccessfully (Crowley v. Christensen, 1890; Giozza v. Tiernan, 1893; Cox v. Texas, 1906; Crane v. Campbell, 1917).

Counsel often tried to claim that a regulation was unreasonable. If the Court found that an unreasonable regulation violated due process or equal protection, it would also violate the privilege or immunity of citizens of the United States to have government abide by the provisions of the Constitution. However, the privileges or immunities clause had no independent significance; that would have contradicted the *Slaughter-House Cases*. In some instances the Court rejected the privileges and immunities claim because the activity regulated was not a privilege of federal citizenship. In other cases, the response that the regulation was reasonable resolved all the Fourteenth Amendment claims without having to distinguish whether the activity regulated was a privilege or immunity or whether freedom from unreasonable regulation was itself a privilege or immunity (*See* In re Lockwood, 1894—practice of law; Iowa Central Ry. v. Iowa, 1896—fair process; Plessy v. Ferguson, 1896—segregation is reasonable; Holden v. Hardy, 1898—reasonable regulation of hours; Orient Ins. Co. v. Daggs, 1899—reasonableness of fire insurance regulation; Cumming v. Board of Education, 1899—school tax for segregated school; Orr v. Gilman, 1902—state transfer tax on inheritance; Halter v. Nebraska, 1907—use of American flag on beer bottle; Wilmington Star Mining Co. v. Fulton, 1907—mine safety regulation; Western Union v. Commercial Milling Co., 1910—prohibition on telegraph companies limiting liability; Missouri Pacific Ry. Co. v. Castle, 1912—comparative negligence in railway regulation; Rosenthal v. New York, 1912—stolen goods receiver law; Waugh v. Board of Trustees, 1915—Greek letter societies in universities; Porter v. Wilson, 1915—demurrer procedure;

Prudential Ins. Co. v. Cheek, 1922—right to choose employees not a federal privilege or immunity; Hamilton v. Regents of the University of California, 1934—attendance at University).

In short, the fundamental rights argument that the privileges of U.S. citizenship are the same privileges and immunities as those of state citizenship has shown from the first little success. The Bill of Rights as a privilege of U.S. citizens is perhaps the only fundamental rights argument that appeared to have a chance for success.

The Rejection of Incorporation and the Move to the Due Process Clause

The first eight amendments to the Constitution were intended to restrict the federal government and did not apply to the states. Chief Justice John Marshall affirmed this in Barron v. Baltimore (1833). The adoption of the Fourteenth Amendment raised the possibility that the situation would change. Both Congressmen Bingham, the author of the language, and Senator Howard, who presented it in the Senate, stated that the privileges and immunities clause made the first eight amendments applicable against the states. On the other hand, several congressmen specifically said that the amendments did no more than constitutionalize the Civil Rights Act of 1866, and no one other than Bingham and Howard specifically stated that the Fourteenth Amendment would make the first eight amendments applicable.

On its face, Justice Miller's opinion for the majority in the *Slaughter-House Cases* was somewhat ambiguous as to whether the Fourteenth Amendment made the individual rights of the first eight amendments applicable to the states. Nevertheless, the decision foreclosed a major route to that result when it rejected fundamental rights.

Justice Joseph Bradley dissenting, joined by Justice Noah Swayne, would have incorporated the Bill of Rights as examples of fundamental rights protected by the privileges and immunities clause. He contended that *privileges or immunities* referred to fundamental rights inherent in citizenship, and argued that the specific provisions on individual rights in the federal constitution were examples of such fundamental rights. Justice Bradley's fundamental rights incorporation theory was not restrictive; it left room to protect rights not specifically mentioned in the Constitution. This fundamental rights argument reflected Howard's speech, which said that privileges and immunities included all those matters Justice Washington spoke of in *Corfield*. Justice John Marshall Harlan championed this theory when he came to the Court, and a number of scholars—most notably Michael Curtis—have argued that it is the most appropriate way to interpret the language and history of the amendment. This view was consistently argued throughout the last quarter of the nineteenth century and into the beginning of the twentieth century. Just as consistently, the Court rejected it. This interpretation is flatly inconsistent with Justice Miller's opinion in the *Slaughter-House Cases*, which said that the fundamental rights that belong to all citizens were privileges of citizens of a state and not of citizens of the United States.

The fundamental rights view of the privileges and immunities of citizenship did not require the Court to find that every right against the federal government applied against a state. Arguably, the presence of a right in the Constitution did not demonstrate that it was fundamental. Some rights, like free speech, might be fundamental, whereas others, like the civil jury, would not be. Thus application to the states of some, but not all, of the Bill of Rights would be consistent with the fundamental rights articulation of proponents of the Fourteenth Amendment. It would also explain the failure to object to the privileges or immunities clause in the ratification conventions of states that did not provide all of the procedures specified in the Bill of Rights. However, the *Slaughter-House Cases* made this option for selective incorporation virtually impossible by denying that fundamental rights were privileges of citizenship of the United States. This led the Court to turn to the due process clause to accomplish the same function, with the result that the rights were not limited to citizens.

The *Slaughter-House Cases* decision that privileges or immunities under the Fourteenth Amendment were limited to those that had their genesis in the federal nature of the government left two alternatives: (1) the term referred only to matters in the Constitution itself (the individual rights applicable against the federal government) and made them applicable to the states or (2) the term did not change the effect of any provision of the Constitution. The first interpretation would limit judicial ability to find new rights, which endeared it to Justice Hugo Black when he began to make this argument in the middle of the twentieth century. It was consistent with Justice Miller's reference to the right to petition and assembly and to habeas corpus in his opinion in the *Slaughter-House Cases*. However, total incorporation limited to the specific constitutional provisions already applicable to the federal government was inconsistent with the debates, which used fundamental rights language throughout.

The Court ultimately chose the view that the words have no reference to fundamental rights and that they do not change the effect of any individual rights provision in the Constitution. Linguistically, this fit Miller's statement that fundamental rights are matters of state citizenship only, and privileges and immunities of national citizenship arise out of the federal relationship. It also fulfilled Justice Field's condemnation that the *Slaughter-House Cases* rendered the clause useless. The Court's current position is tolerable only because it has used other provisions to achieve the purposes originally intended for the privileges and immunities clause.

The fears that drove Justice Miller to reject a fundamental rights interpretation of privileges or immunities have less force with respect to incorporation of the Bill of Rights. Fundamental rights reasoning remains controversial, but at least selective incorporation of the first eight amendments is now generally accepted. However, the Court and litigants have found it easier to use due process than privileges or immunities as a basis to pick and choose among rights.

The first time the incorporation argument was relevant to a Supreme Court case, counsel did not even mention it. Members of the Court referred to the argument in somewhat ambiguous dicta in the *Slaughter-House Cases*, but they unequivocally rejected total incorporation shortly thereafter—first in dicta in a unanimous opinion the following year, then in two more cases in 1876. By 1878 the parties shifted their arguments on incorporation to the due process clause as the more promising avenue for the criminal procedure and property claims before the Court. The linguistic argument for privileges and immunities tended to support a literal application of each of the specified individual rights, whereas a due process claim seemed more easily framed to permit application of only those rights the Court found essential. When counsel returned to the privileges or immunities clause at the turn of the century to argue for incorporation of the first eight amendments against the state, the Court rejected the arguments. Justice Black's mid-century efforts to use the clause were deflected into selective incorporation by the due process clause. The Court has left the privileges and immunities clause today to the battalion of scholars who futilely insist it was intended to serve as the vehicle for incorporation.

Rejection by Silence and Dicta

During the first decade after the adoption of the Fourteenth Amendment, the Court either ignored the possibility of incorporation or denied it, with the exception of the dissenters in the *Slaughter-House Cases*. Professor Stanley Morrison argued that this indifference demonstrated that the amendment was not intended to incorporate the Bill of Rights.[16] Critics have responded that the cases in the first decade were consistent with incorporation or at least reveal that a substantial body of people believed in it. They contend that Justice Miller's opinion in the *Slaughter-House Cases* supported incorporation.[17] Indeed, during the first decade after the Fourteenth Amendment, the court never rejected incorporation in any case where the proposition was argued and was necessary to decision. Nevertheless, it is a strain to believe that the justices supported incorporation. They did not.

The first time counsel could have argued the Fourteenth Amendment incorporated rights against the state, the attorney failed to do so. Six months after the adoption of the Fourteenth Amendment, George S. Twitchell, Jr., and his wife were indicted for murdering his mother-in-law, Mary Hill. As permitted by a Pennsylvania statute, the indictment did not specify how the victim was murdered. Although his wife was acquitted, George Twitchell was convicted, the Supreme Court of Pennsylvania affirmed, and he was sentenced to hang on April 8, 1869. Eight days before the execution date, Twitchell's lawyer filed a motion for a writ of error (a document issuing from the Supreme Court to the state courts that would stop the state proceedings and enable the Court to set the case for full argument on the merits of a claim that the state statute conflicted with the Constitution). Normally, a single justice would hear the motion, but the full court agreed to hear argument "because of the urgency of the case, and the momentous importance of the result to the petitioner" (Twitchell v. The Commonwealth, 1869). Twitchell's counsel argued the motion for the writ on April 2. He claimed that Pennsylvania's statute was repugnant to the Fifth and Sixth Amendments, especially the Sixth Amendment's requirement that the accused be informed of the nature and cause of the accusation. Therefore, he argued, the warrant for the execution was not "due process" of law. Chief Justice Salmon P. Chase responded for a unanimous court that the Fifth and Sixth Amendments did not apply to state governments, citing *Barron*. Consequently, Chase found that the court did not have appellate jurisdiction to hear a challenge to the state statute on that basis (Twitchell v. The Commonwealth, 1869).

Counsel apparently failed to raise the new Fourteenth Amendment, either the due process or the privileges or immunities clause, as a basis for applying the Fifth and Sixth amendments. The justices' concern for the capital case led them to the irregular procedure of a full bench hearing of the motion. If they thought the principles of the Fifth and Sixth Amendments applied through the privileges or immunities and/or the due process clauses, they could have said so to save Twitchell's life. Lawyers today, however technically incorrect, often refer to a First Amendment right in contesting a state law abridging speech. The Court could have found that Twitchell's counsel employed the same shorthand, if they were anxious to reach the incorporation argument. On the other hand, they may have ignored the argument because it would have done no good to raise it; the allegation of murder was probably sufficient notice to satisfy the Sixth Amendment.

The *Slaughter-House Cases* was the first decision to discuss the Fourteenth Amendment. Incorporation was, of course, not strictly relevant to the case. Nevertheless, at least two justices said the Bill of Rights applied to the states, and no judge specifically rejected the argument. Justice Miller's opinion was ambiguous. Justice Field's opinion, in which Justices Chase, Swayne, and Bradley concurred, was also unclear. Field spoke of the natural and inalienable rights that belong to all citizens, but he did not specifically mention those in the first eight amendments. Justice Bradley, however, with Justice Swayne concurring, specifically pointed to habeas corpus and the early amendments including free speech and trial by jury as among the privileges and immunities protected by the Fourteenth Amendment in the *Slaughter-House Cases* (1873):

> But we are not bound to resort to implication, or to the constitutional history of England, to find an authoritative declaration of some of the most important privileges and immunities of citizens of the United States. It is in the Constitution itself. The Constitution, it is true, as it stood prior to the recent amendments, specifies, in terms, only a few of the personal privileges and immunities of citizens, but they are very comprehensive in their character. The States were merely prohibited from passing bills of attainder, ex post facto laws, laws impairing the obligation of contracts, and perhaps one or two more. But others of the

greatest consequence were enumerated, although they were only secured, in express terms, from invasion by the Federal government; such as the right of habeas corpus, the right of trial by jury, of free exercise of religious worship, the right of free speech and a free press, the right peaceably to assemble for the discussion of public measures, the right to be secure against unreasonable searches and seizures, and above all, and including almost all the rest, the right of not being deprived of life, liberty, or property, without due process of law. (*Slaughter-House Cases,* 1873, J. Bradley dissenting)

Although Justice Bradley noted rights protected "in express terms" only against the federal government, he indicated that all the privileges and immunities applied against the states because they were fundamental. He said "even if the Constitution were silent, the fundamental privileges and immunities of citizens, as such, would be no less real and no less inviolable than they now are." Further, Justice Bradley suggested that due process included "almost all the rest" of the Bill of Rights. Thus, Justices Bradley and Swayne appeared to support incorporation in 1873, although Bradley's opinion only specifically listed some of the individual rights in the Constitution as fundamental.

Nevertheless, the following year the Court's unanimous opinion rejected the argument that the Fourteenth Amendment made the Seventh Amendment's right to a jury trial in civil cases applicable to the states (Edwards v. Elliott, 1874). The defendant argued that a lien on a ship being built was a maritime lien and that states had no jurisdiction. The defendant also contended the state lien law conflicted with the right of trial by jury, saying:

The State law in effect takes away or obstructs the right of trial by jury, and so abridges one of "the privileges or immunities of citizens of the United States. It, in this case, also "deprives him of his property without due process of law," and it denies to a person residing in New Jersey "the equal protection" of the laws of his State. These matters all fall within the fourteenth amendment.[18]

Unfortunately, the record did not indicate that this challenge had been specifically made in the courts below. Opposing counsel said the argument was an afterthought and needed no reply. Then, citing the *Slaughter-House Cases*, he said "the constitutional provisions referred to did not profess to control the power of the State governments over the rights of its own citizens, but only to declare that as the States grant them to their own citizens . . . the same, neither more nor less, shall be the measure of the rights of citizens of other States within their jurisdiction."[19] In other words, the right to trial by jury and other protections of the Bill of Rights were fundamental rights and privileges applicable to citizens as citizens of a state through Article IV and not privileges of U.S. citizenship except against violation by the federal government. The "due process" claim applied only if trial by jury was a constitutional right against the state.

Justice Nathan Clifford found that the Fourteenth Amendment issue was not raised below in state court, and he rejected the argument for that reason; but Clifford also said that the Seventh Amendment does not apply to trials in state court citing *Twitchell*, *Barron,* and cases following *Barron* that had been decided prior to the Fourteenth Amendment. He said both arguments disposed of the civil jury trial claim: "(1) That it does not apply to trials in the State courts. (2) That no such error was assigned in the Court of Errors, and that the question was not presented to, nor was it decided by, the Court of Errors."

Justices Bradley and Swayne may have disagreed with Clifford's jury trial comments, but they did not respond, perhaps because the issue was not properly before the Court. Nevertheless, Clifford's statements created an obstacle for incorporation arguments in subsequent cases.

The Court soon intimated that the privileges and immunities clause did not incorporate other rights from the Bill of Rights, including freedom of assembly and the right to bear arms (United States v. Cruikshank, 1876). African-Americans in Colfax, Louisiana, had organized to defend against an expected attempt by white Democrats to seize control of government after a disputed gubernatorial election. Armed white citizens overwhelmed them, killing a large number, including a group who laid down their arms under a flag of surrender. A jury found William Cruikshank and others guilty of depriving colored citizens of the rights secured to them by the Constitution and laws of the United States, but the Court discharged the defendants. The Court dismissed counts charging conspiracy to interfere with the citizens' rights to peaceably assemble, to bear arms for lawful purposes, and not to be deprived of life and liberty without due process. Chief Justice Morrison Waite stated that the freedom of assembly guaranteed by the First Amendment and the right to bear arms in the Second Amendment did not apply to the states, although he did not expressly say that the Fourteenth Amendment did not incorporate them.

Chief Justice Waite focused on whether the federal government had power to legislate against private acts of violence interfering with assembly or carrying weapons. He characterized the right of the people to assemble as "one of the attributes of citizenship under a free government." Under the reasoning of the *Slaughter-House Cases*, a fundamental right of that nature would be a privilege of state citizenship and not federal citizenship. Waite discussed the constitutional provisions of the Bill of Rights before the Civil War as restraints on Congress. The right of assembly was not guaranteed by the First Amendment "except as against congressional interference," and the power to protect the fundamental right of assembly was placed in the states and "has never been surrendered to the United States." (United States v. Cruikshank, 1876). Congress would have power to protect freedom of assembly only if the assembly and petition related to Congress itself or was otherwise connected to performance of national duties. Thus petitioning Congress might be a privilege of U.S. citizenship but not because it was mentioned in the Constitution. With respect to assembly generally or bearing arms, the federal government had no power to legislate against private action and only the states could act.

This suggested that the rights were not made applicable to the states by the Constitution. If the Bill of Rights did not secure the rights but only guaranteed them against federal violation, only the right against federal violation would be a privilege of citizenship of the United States. The reasoning leads to the conclusion that the Fourteenth Amendment did not apply the first eight amendments of the Constitution to the states. Nevertheless, since the state was not alleged to have denied assembly or the right to bear arms in the case, the Court did not need to decide that issue, and the reference may have been limited to the First amendment's reach.

That same year, in another case from Louisiana, Chief Justice Waite and the Court seemed to slam the door shut on incorporation through the privileges or immunities clause. The Court held that the Seventh Amendment was not made binding on the states by the Fourteenth (Walker v. Sauvinet, 1876). The force of the precedent was weakened, however, because Walker's counsel did not even argue in his brief before the court that the Fourteenth Amendment made the right of trial by jury applicable.

A number of ironies were in *Walker*. Charles Sauvinet, sheriff of Orleans Parish, had been the foreman of the grand jury that indicted Cruikshank under laws that sought to extend the reach of the Fourteenth Amendment.[20] In *Walker*, he sought to persuade the court that the amendment did not apply, transposing the usual racial impact of the Fourteenth Amendment. Sauvinet sued Joseph Walker under a Louisiana statute that provided a civil action for denying a person equal rights in a place of public resort. Walker had refused to serve Sauvinet at the bar of his coffeehouse. Although Walker did not give a reason, Sauvinet was reputed to be a person of color. Sauvinet testified at trial that he did not know himself whether he was. The jury deadlocked. Pursuant to a provision in the statute that allowed the judge to decide if the jury failed to agree, the judge found for Sauvinet and awarded $1,000 damages. Walker moved for a new trial, assigning numerous errors, including that the Fourteenth Amendment guaranteed him a right to trial by jury. Although the point was preserved for appeal, Walker's counsel did not argue it in the brief before the Court. They argued that the statute abridged the privileges and immunities clause of the Fourteenth Amendment, but they based their claim on the contention that Walker had a constitutional right to choose with whom he would do business, a privilege without foundation after the *Slaughter-House Cases*.

Chief Justice Morrison Waite said that the only federal question decided below was the rejection of the trial by jury claim. He then proceeded to rule that it did not apply here.

> By Article 7 of the amendments it is provided that "in suits at common law, where the value in controversy shall exceed twenty dollars, the right of trial by jury shall be preserved." This, as has been many times decided, relates only to trials in the courts of the United States.

Edwards v. Elliott, 21 Wall. 532, 557. The States, so far as this amendment is concerned, are left to regulate trials in their own courts in their own way. A trial by jury in suits at common law pending in the state courts is not, therefore, a privilege or immunity of national citizenship, which the States are forbidden by the Fourteenth Amendment to abridge. A State cannot deprive a person of his property without due process of law; but this does not necessarily imply that all trials in the state courts affecting the property of persons must be by jury. This requirement of the Constitution is met if the trial is had according to the settled course of judicial proceedings. (Walker v. Sauvinet, 1876)

Waite's opinion was clear that the privileges and immunities clause did not change the application of the first eight amendments, but it suggested some potential for due process. Justices Clifford and Field dissented without opinion, but Clifford's opinion in *Edwards* suggests that the dissent was not over the incorporation issue. Justices Miller and Bradley were in the majority in both *Cruikshank* and *Walker*. Miller's stance corroborates the view that his *Slaughter-House Cases* opinion repudiated incorporation. Bradley seems to have conceded to the majority view on privileges and immunities, leaving incorporation arguments to the due process clause.

The Move to Due Process

By 1878 the Court held that state actions were constitutional on several occasions despite assuming that the same behavior by the federal government would violate provisions of the Bill of Rights. Parties could still argue that the privileges or immunities clause of the Fourteenth Amendment incorporated the Bill of Rights and applied it to the states, because that issue had not been necessary to the decision of any case in which the parties briefed and argued it. On the other hand, the Court had specifically stated that trial by jury in civil suits was not a privilege or immunity of U.S. citizenship. Justice Miller's opinion for the Court in Davidson v. New Orleans (1878) raised the possibility that a different provision might prove more successful as a basis for applying any of the first eight amendments to the states.

In *Davidson*, landowners challenged assessment of a real estate tax whose proceeds were to be used to drain swamp land in the city of New Orleans. Their counsel attempted to get around the effect of the *Slaughter-House Cases* by arguing that the decision in that case had not focused on due process considerations. Justice Miller acknowledged that due process had not been fully defined, and he agreed that "due process" imposed constraints on the legislature. He wrote:

It seems to us that a statute which declares in terms, and without more, that the full and exclusive title of a described piece of land, which is now in A., shall be and is hereby vested in B., would, if effectual, deprive A. of his property without due process of law, within the meaning of the constitutional provision. (Davidson v. New Orleans, 1878)

Justice Miller's hypothetical involved a statute that transferred property without a judicial proceeding to determine whether any fact existed that would warrant transferring title under the statute. The existence of procedures might be sufficient, however, even if the underlying law was draconian. The Court held that a tax imposed for a public purpose did not violate due process if the state law provided the taxpayer with a chance to contest it in a fair trial. Miller's opinion even seemed to suggest that the due process clause of the Fourteenth Amendment could not be used to incorporate other provisions of the Bill of Rights against the states. He said:

> If private property be taken for public uses without just compensation, it must be remembered that, when the fourteenth amendment was adopted, the provision on that subject, in immediate juxtaposition in the fifth amendment with the one we are construing, was left out, and this was taken. (Davidson v. New Orleans, 1878)

Justice Miller's comments might seem to turn parties toward the privileges or immunities clause as the basis for incorporation. Privileges and immunities incorporation avoids the linguistic problem that Justice Miller pointed out with using due process as a basis for applying other provisions. The due process clause applies to all persons including aliens and corporations; the privileges or immunities clause is limited to citizens of the United States. Even if citizens of the United States were entitled to due process through incorporation of the Fifth Amendment by the privileges and immunities clause, a separate provision in the Fourteenth Amendment would be necessary to give aliens due process rights against the states.

Nevertheless, Justice Miller's opinion in *Davidson* left the door ajar for the use of due process, because it had given some substance to due process. He also added that the term would be elaborated gradually:

> But, apart from the imminent risk of a failure to give any definition which would be at once perspicuous, comprehensive, and satisfactory, there is wisdom, we think, in the ascertaining of the intent and application of such an important phrase in the Federal Constitution, by the gradual process of judicial inclusion and exclusion, as the cases presented for decision shall require, with the reasoning on which such decisions may be founded. (Davidson v. New Orleans, 1878)

Due process seemed quite an appropriate ground to argue that a particular procedure forbidden by the Bill of Rights violated a constitutional restriction on the state. Thus counsel in the next major decision on incorporation focused on due process (Hurtado v. California, 1884). The defendant claimed that California had violated due process because it proceeded by information (a formal accusation of crime issued by the prosecuting attorney) instead of grand jury indictment. The Court held that it did not. Justice Stanley Matthews said that it was a principle of interpretation that terms of a document should not be construed to be superfluous. On that basis, the specific provisions of the Fifth Amendment were not subsets of due process, their violation would not violate due process and that was the only clause applicable against the states. Justice John Marshall Harlan, who had joined the Court in 1877, took up the cudgels for incorporation—a position he continued to press throughout his time on the Court. He maintained that the provisions of the Fifth Amendment were all basic components of due process.

The failure of the due process argument in *Hurtado* sent parties back to the privileges or immunities clause. For example, when Illinois indicted Herman Presser and others for associating together and drilling or parading with arms in a municipality without legal authorization, the defendants urged that they had a privilege or immunity to parade with guns (Presser v. Illinois, 1886). However, Presser, represented by Lyman Trumbull, did not argue privileges and immunities incorporation. Instead, he argued that the right to bear arms was a privilege of U.S. citizenship because the possession of guns was necessary if the federal government called out the militia. The Court found that the portion of the law of Illinois in question did not interfere with the federal ability to raise the militia. It held the law, which had been adopted to control the Ku Klux Klan, did not infringe the right of the people to keep and bear arms (Presser v. Illinois, 1886). The Court cited *Cruikshank* for the proposition that the right to bear arms in the Second Amendment did not apply to the states. It noted that the only clause that might have a relationship to the claim to associate with others was the First Amendment's right of assembly. "But it was held in the same case [*Cruikshank*] that the right peaceably to assemble was not protected by the clause referred to, unless the purpose of the assembly was to petition the government for a redress of grievances."

Cruikshank did not involve state regulations, but *Presser* did. Thus the assertion of *Cruikshank* as support for the decision that neither the Second nor the First Amendment applied to the states extended *Cruikshank's* reasoning and put the court squarely in opposition to the use of the privileges and immunities clause to incorporate the Bill of Rights, even though counsel had not argued for incorporation.

A Failed Campaign for Fundamental Rights Incorporation: The First Justice Harlan

Counsel did argue the next year, in an appeal from a conviction in the Haymarket Square trial, that the privileges and immunities clause applied the first eight amendments to the states. The Court said that even if he was correct, the trial would not violate the Sixth Amendment, but the Court also indicated that the Sixth Amendment did not apply to the state (Spies v. Illinois, 1887).

Justices Harlan and Field revived the *Spies* argument in dissent two years later (O'Neil v. Vermont, 1892). The majority claimed O'Neil failed to properly raise the federal question, so they did not pass on incorporation. Vermont applied its prohibition law to an out-of-state seller by treating each individual sale of alcohol to a Vermont resident as a separate offence. The cumulation of violations produced a very long jail sentence. Justices Field, Harlan, and Brewer would have found this a cruel and unusual punishment in violation of the privileges and immunities of citizens of the United States.

Although Harlan, Field, and Brewer offered hope for a revived privileges and immunities argument, Justice Harlan had even more success with the due process clause of the Fourteenth Amendment. He used it to convince a majority of the Court that states were bound by the Fifth Amendment's principle that no private property shall "be taken for public use, without just compensation" (Chicago, B. & Q. R. Co. v. Chicago, 1897). Citing *Davidson*, Justice Harlan for the court said the concept of due process required compensation when property was taken for a public purpose. If giving one person's property to another violates due process, "it must be that the requirement of due process of law in that amendment is applicable to the direct appropriation by the State to public use and without compensation of the private property of the citizen." Thus citing the very case in which Justice Miller suggested due process did not include the right to compensation for a taking, the Court found that it did (although the Court affirmed the decision below on the grounds that the railroad received just compensation). This revived the due process clause as a vehicle for arguing that other individual rights provisions applicable to the federal government were part of due process.

By the turn of the century, it was clear that the Court would not incorporate the Bill of Rights against the states as a whole, but it might find some individual right was part of due process. Justice Harlan was the sole dissenter in the major cases confronting the issue (Maxwell v. Dow, 1900; Twining v. New Jersey, 1908).

The most extensive examination of the claims of incorporation through the privileges and immunities clause occurred at the turn of the century. In a case brought by information, Maxwell was convicted of robbery by an eight person jury. He argued that this violated his right to a jury trial, citing both the privileges and immunities clause and the due process clause as incorporating the jury trial guarantee (Maxwell v. Dow, 1900). The court rejected his contention.

Justice Harlan dissented, arguing that the amendments applied against the states through the privileges and immunities clause of the Fourteenth Amendment:

> [I]f prior to the adoption of the Fourteenth Amendment it was one of the privileges or immunities of citizens of the United States that they should not be tried for crime in any court organized or existing under National authority except by a jury composed of twelve persons, how can it be that a citizen of the United States may be now tried in a state court for crime, particularly for an infamous crime, by eight jurors, when that amendment expressly declares that "no State shall make or enforce any law which shall abridge the privileges or immunities of citizens of the United States"? (Maxwell v. Dow, 1900, Harlan J. dissenting)

Harlan also argued as he had in *Hurtado* that the due process clause applied, and that a jury of twelve was required by due process as well as the privileges and immunities clause. He cited the *Chicago, B. & Q. R. Co.* decision to show that mention of a specific right in the initial amendments did not preclude its application against the states under the Fourteenth.

Justice Rufus Peckham's opinion for the Court tried to deal with Harlan's arguments, but it was not a strong effort. Peckham quoted from the *Slaughter-House Cases* opinion and noted that Justice Miller failed to mention trial by jury as one of the rights of national citizenship. However, in the *Slaughter-House Cases*, Miller said he only mentioned some of the rights, and his general reference to rights guaranteed by the federal government would cover all the Bill of Rights. Trial by jury was clearly a right of national citizenship—the only question was whether it was a right limited to federal trials.

Peckham argued that the rights in the first eight amendments were not privileges of United States citizenship because they applied to all persons, regardless of whether they were citizens or aliens. Yet Justice Miller mentioned due process, habeas corpus and the right to peaceably assemble as privileges of citizens of the United States, although each right was applicable to aliens.

Justice Peckham deflated the intent of the framers argument reasonably well. He noted that counsel cited Senator Howard's references to incorporation when Howard presented the proposed amendment to the Senate. Peckham responded that Howard's speech did not show that other members of Congress agreed:

> A constitutional amendment must be agreed to, not only by Senators and Representatives, but it must be ratified by the legislatures, or by conventions, in three fourths of the States before such amendment can take effect. The safe way is to read its language in connection with the known condition of affairs out of which the occasion for its adoption may have arisen, and then to construe it, if there be therein any doubtful expressions, in a way so far as is reasonably possible, to forward the known purpose or object for which the amendment was adopted. This rule could not, of course, be so used as to limit the force and effect of an amendment in a manner which the plain and unambiguous language used therein would not justify or permit. (Maxwell v. Dow, 1900)

Even if other factors were more important than Howard's speech, however, Justice Peckham did not offer much to show that Howard's interpretation of the clause was wrong. He sought to show that contemporary opinion was against incorporation. After reciting the numerous cases in which the court, after the adoption of the Fourteenth Amendment, had held that specific amendments did not apply to the states, he said, "if the particular clause of that amendment, now under consideration, had the effect claimed for it in this case, it is not too much to say that it would have been asserted and the principles applied in some of them." (Maxwell v. Dow, 1900) Of course, the privileges and immunities clause incorporation argument had been asserted in earlier cases and had drawn support from several justices. It just never succeeded in the Court as a whole. The argument seems to be little more than a reliance on precedent.

Thus although appearing to fully address the substance of the privileges and immunities incorporation argument, the court ended by relying on precedent. The capstone in the line of cases discussing the application of the privileges and immunities clause to incorporation then asserted that precedent ended the argument (Twining v. New Jersey, 1908). This case ended hopes for privileges and immunities but left the door ajar for due process. Defendants claimed that the trial judge violated their privilege against self-incrimination when he commented negatively on their failure to take the stand. The claim had three aspects: (1) that the privilege against self-incrimination was a privilege of U.S. citizenship because it was a fundamental right, (2) that it was a privilege of U.S. citizenship applicable against the states because it was stated in the Fifth Amendment, and (3) that the judge's comment denied the defendants due process under the Fourteenth Amendment because the privilege against self-incrimination was a basic principle of justice.

The Court said that the incorporation question had already been decided. Justice William H. Moody analyzed the previous cases to support this proposition. First, he argued that before the Fourteenth Amendment, the right against self-incrimination was found in state constitutions. Thus "so far as the state courts are concerned, the privilege had its origin in the constitutions and laws of the States, and that persons appealing to it must look to the State for their protection." He went back to the *Slaughter-House Cases* dichotomy between privileges and immunities of citizens of a state and those of citizens of the United States, and Justice Miller's statement that fundamental rights were those that belonged to citizens of a state as such and were not the privileges and immunities of citizens of the United States. Moody said that the dissenting opinion of Justice Field made the distinction clear. The privileges and immunities of U.S. citizens were only those that existed before the amendment was adopted and therefore the amendment had no effect.

Justice Moody next cited *Cruikshank* for the proposition that the right of peaceable assembly for a lawful purpose (not relating to the National Government) was not a right secured by the Constitution, but a fundamental right that preexisted it. He argued that *Cruikshank*'s citation to the *Slaughter-House Cases* supported the argument that the right of assembly was a right of state citizenship rather than federal. If an exemption from self-incrimination is a fundamental right, "it is, so far as the States are concerned, a fundamental right inherent in state citizenship, and is a privilege or immunity of that citizenship only." (Twining v. New Jersey, 1908)

With respect to the claim that personal rights mentioned in the Constitution are among the privileges and immunities of citizens of the United States, Moody acknowledged the dissenting opinion of Justices Field, Brewer, and Harlan in *O'Neil* and Justice Harlan in *Maxwell,* and he admitted that at least some of the framers undoubtedly entertained the idea. However, he said that the question was no longer open, citing the cases that had rejected incorporation:

The right of trial by jury in civil cases, guaranteed by the Seventh Amendment (Walker v. Sauvinet, 92 U.S. 90), and the right to bear arms guaranteed by the Second Amendment (Presser v. Illinois, 116 *U.S. 252),* have been distinctly held not to be privileges and immunities of citizens of the United States guaranteed by the Fourteenth Amendment against abridgment by the States, and in effect the same decision was made in respect of the guarantee against prosecution, except by indictment of a grand jury, contained in the Fifth Amendment (Hurtado v. California, 110 U.S. 516), and in respect of the right to be confronted with witnesses, contained in the Sixth Amendment. West v. Louisiana, *194 U.S. 258.* In Maxwell v. Dow, supra, where the plaintiff in error had been convicted in a state court of a felony upon an information, and by a jury of eight persons, it was held that the indictment, made indispensable by the Fifth Amendment, and the trial by jury guaranteed by the Sixth Amendment, were not privileges and immunities of citizens of the United States, as those words were used in the Fourteenth Amendment. (Twining v. New Jersey, 1908)

Justice Moody stressed the *Maxwell* opinion as the definitive discussion of the incorporation argument under the privileges or immunities clause of the Fourteenth Amendment:

The discussion in that case ought not to be repeated. All the arguments for the other view were considered and answered, the authorities were examined and analyzed, and the decision rested upon the ground that this clause of the Fourteenth Amendment did not forbid the States to abridge the personal rights enumerated in the first eight Amendments, because those rights were not within the meaning of the clause "privileges and immunities of citizens of the United States." If it be possible to render the principle which governed the decision more clear, it is done so by the dissent of Mr. Justice Harlan. We conclude, therefore, that the exemption from compulsory self-incrimination is not a privilege or immunity of National citizenship guaranteed by this clause of the Fourteenth Amendment against abridgment by the States. (Twining v. New Jersey, 1908)

Justice Moody then went on to analyze the due process claim. "[I]t is possible that some of the personal rights safeguarded by the first eight Amendments against National action may also be safeguarded against state action, because a denial of them would be a denial of due process of law." He concluded that the privilege against self-incrimination was not a fundamental principle of liberty and justice.

Harlan once more was the lonely dissenter. He continued to insist that the Fourteenth Amendment secured fundamental rights against the states and that the protections of the amendments against federal invasion were fundamental: "The privileges and immunities mentioned in the original Amendments, and universally regarded as our heritage of liberty from the common law, were thus secured to every citizen of the United States and placed beyond assault by any government, Federal or state." (Twining v. New Jersey, 1908, Harlan J. dissenting)

When Justice Harlan died in 1911, the privileges or immunities incorporation argument was not heard again for decades. The court was content to rely on the due process formula of ordered liberty that Moody discussed in *Twining*. Thus the Court used the due process clause to find freedom of speech applied to the states (Gitlow v. New York, 1925). Indeed, in Hague v. C.I.O., (1939), Justice Stone's concurring opinion took the majority to task for using privileges and immunities in a case that he perceived to be freedom of speech. The CIO and some of its members sued the mayor and officials of Jersey City for preventing them from holding meetings in open air and public places to discuss the National Labor Relations Act. The federal trial judge found that the defendants had interfered with the plaintiffs' rights and violated the Fourteenth Amendment. Defendants appealed to the Court. Justice Owen Roberts, joined by Justice Hugo Black, wrote an opinion for the Court that found the federal court could hear an action for deprivation of any privilege secured by the Constitution and that the right to discuss matters growing out of national legislation was a privilege inherent in citizenship of the United States.

This was enough to uphold the order below (with minor modifications), but Justice Harlan Fiske Stone joined by Chief Justice Charles Evans Hughes objected strenuously to the use of privileges and immunities rather than due process. They saw the privilege of U.S. citizenship as too narrow and unsuited to the facts, which did not allege that plaintiffs were citizens. Instead, these concurring justices insisted that the defendants had breached free speech rights under the due process clause, which applied to all persons regardless of citizenship:

> It has been explicitly and repeatedly affirmed by this Court, without a dissenting voice, that freedom of speech and of assembly for any lawful purpose are rights of personal liberty secured to all persons, without regard to citizenship, by the due process clause of the Fourteenth Amendment. . . . . [cases omitted]. It has never been held that either is a privilege or immunity peculiar to citizenship of the United States, to which alone the privileges and immunities clause refers, *Slaughter-House Cases,* . . . [other cases omitted], and neither can be brought within the protection of that clause without enlarging the category of privileges and immunities of United States citizenship as it has hitherto been defined. (Hague v. C.I.O., 1929, Stone J. concurring)

The *Hague* concurrence illustrated how completely due process had replaced privileges or immunities as a basis for arguments on the application of the Bill of Rights to the states.

Justice Black: The Successful Failure of Incorporation by Reference

In the middle of the twentieth century, Justice Black became the standard bearer for the idea of incorporation of each of the amendments of the Bill of Rights. It did not matter much to him whether the due process clause or the privileges or immunities clause was the vehicle for incorporation, but he argued that history demonstrated the framers of the Fourteenth Amendment intended to incorporate the Bill of Rights.

In Adamson v. California (1947), the *Twining* issue was raised again. Both the judge and the prosecutor commented on the defendant's failure to take the stand in a state criminal case. The Court affirmed the conviction by a narrow margin. Four justices (Frank Murphy, Wiley Rutledge, Hugo Black, and William O. Douglas) dissented, contending that the Bill of Rights applied to the states. Justice Black wrote a lengthy dissent contending that the Bill of Rights was applicable to the states, but only those rights specifically set forth in the Constitution limited the states, rejecting vigorously what he designated as the "natural law" theory of fundamental principles supported by the majority. Black included a lengthy appendix to support his position, but he did not limit the text for incorporation to any single provision: "one of the chief objects that the provisions of the Amendment's first section, separately and as a whole, were intended to accomplish was to make the Bill of Rights applicable to the states." (Adamson v. California, 1947, Black J. dissenting)

Justice Black continued his fight for incorporation throughout his years on the Court, but *Adamson* marked the high point for the theory. On the other hand, he was successful in getting majorities to incorporate one by one most of the Bill of Rights using a due process fundamental right approach. For example, in Duncan v. Louisiana (1968), the court held that the Sixth Amendment right to trial by jury in criminal trials was fundamental to the American scheme of justice. The second Justice John Marshall Harlan, a judge with very different views from his grandfather, dissented. Harlan stated in a footnote that the language of Section 1 of the Fourteenth Amendment "would have been an exceedingly peculiar way to say that 'The rights heretofore guaranteed against federal intrusion by the first eight amendments are henceforth guaranteed against state intrusion as well.'" Mr. Justice Black replied:

> . . . the words "No State shall make or enforce any law which shall abridge the privileges or immunities of citizens of the United States" seem to me an eminently reasonable way of expressing the idea that henceforth the Bill of Rights shall apply to the States. What more precious "privilege" of American citizenship could there be than that privilege to claim the protections of our great Bill of Rights? (Duncan v. Louisiana, 1968)

However, the Court did not follow Justice Black's theory and has not accepted total incorporation. In that respect, he failed. On the other hand, Justice Black's steady vote for the application of each of the amendments to the states was largely successful in practice because other justices found them to be part of due process. The court continues to approach the issue through the idea of fundamental principles of ordered liberty embodied in the due process clause, leaving some issues undecided and the civil jury and grand jury indictment clauses inapplicable.

Federal Privileges and Immunities

The decisions rejecting either a fundamental rights interpretation or incorporation of any of the amendments of the Bill of Rights destroyed any function for the privileges or immunities clause. Privileges or immunities that "owe their existence to the Federal government, its National character, its Constitution, or its laws" exist apart from the clause. The Fourteenth Amendment privileges or immunities clause does not create them, and the supremacy clause of Article VI precludes states from denying them. Similarly, Congress has power to secure the privileges or immunities of citizens of the United States by legislation without relying on Section 5 of the Fourteenth Amendment. Thus the privileges and immunities clause is an empty provision, but that does not mean that the concept of privileges and immunities is vacuous. Privileges and immunities of citizens of the United States exist, and they can be enforced. They are both express and implied. There are express rights from the Constitution, laws, and treaties of the United States. There are also rights implied from the national character of the federal government. The Court's latest discussion of privileges or immunities focused on the right to travel, including the right to migrate and become a citizen of another state.

Rights Expressly Based on Laws, Treaties, and the Constitution

Few constitutional rights are expressly limited to citizens of the United States. In *Dred Scott*, Chief Justice Taney argued that only citizens of the United States could claim the rights of citizens of a state under the privileges and immunities clause of Article IV. The Fourteenth Amendment reinforced that result when it defined citizens of the United States and said they are citizens of the state where they reside. The Fifteenth Amendment prohibition of racial discrimination with respect to the right to vote applies only to citizens, but the privileges or immunities of citizens of the United States are not defined solely by rights that only citizens may have. Justice Miller's list of privileges of citizens of the United States included a number of constitutional rights that were not limited to citizens, including "the right to peaceably assemble and petition for redress of grievances, the privilege of habeas corpus . . . rights secured by the thirteenth . . . amendment, and by the other clause of the fourteenth next to be considered" (*Slaughter-House Cases*, 1873). Citizens of the United States have privileges or immunities because the Constitution or federal government provides them rights, even though the rights may be available to noncitizens as well. They are privileges or immunities of citizens of the United States because they are rights common to citizens of the United States. On the other hand, the privileges or immunities clause does not affect their scope.

In addition to constitutional rights, any right that the federal government secures for its citizens by statute or treaty may be a privilege or immunity of citizenship. For example, a Vermont missionary could claim a right pursuant to treaties between the United States and the Cherokee Indians to enter Cherokee land at the tribe's invitation without a license from the state of Georgia. This was a privilege of a citizen of the United States (Worcester v. Georgia, 1832). A complete list of the privileges and immunities of citizens of the United States would be enormous, but it would be outdated the moment it was finished. Privileges or immunities secured by statute or treaty are contingent; government is free to alter them at will. To enforce express rights, the citizen must look to the statute, treaty, or constitutional provision that is their source; the concept of privileges and immunities of citizens adds little.

Structural Inferences: Federal Functions

The "Federal government and its National character" provide a basis both for invalidation of some state laws and legitimation of some federal government action. Even in the absence of a specific statute, the supremacy clause of Article VI precludes state interference with federal operations (McCulloch v. Maryland, 1819). Consequently, when the federal government provides any right to an individual, states cannot interfere. The federal government can secure its operations against interference by private individuals as well, but it must enact legislation to make that interference a criminal offense. In some instances, the federal legislation uses very general language, such as conspiracy to injure a citizen in the exercise of any right or privilege secured by the Constitution and laws of the United States. A court must then determine whether the alleged act interferes with a right or privilege. Under such general statutes, the Court has ruled specifically that privileges of U.S. citizens include the right of eligible voters to vote in federal elections (Ex parte Yarbrough, 1884; Wiley v. Sinkler, 1900), the right to occupy land obtained under federal law (United States v. Waddell, 1884), the right to personal security while in federal custody (Logan v. United States, 1892), the right to inform federal officials of the violation of federal law (In re Quarles, 1895), and the right to discuss federal laws and their administration (United States v. Cruikshank, 1876; Hague v. C.I.O., 1939).

The first attempt to seriously grapple with the *Slaughter-House Cases* definition of the privileges and immunities of citizens of the United States upheld the denial of voting rights to women. Virginia Minor sued the Missouri registrar of voters for refusing to register her to vote in a federal election. She argued that Missouri violated her privileges and immunities as a U.S. citizen to vote for President and other federal officers when it limited the franchise to men. Justice Washington's opinion in *Corfield* had mentioned the franchise as one of the privileges and immunities of citizenship. Although the Fifteenth Amendment only prohibited denial or abridgement on account of race, it referred to the right of a citizen to vote. Justice Miller's *Slaughter-House Cases* opinion said that the rights secured by that amendment were privileges and immunities of U.S. citizenship. Finally, if the *Slaughter-House Cases* demanded that a party point to a federal relationship, she had done so. Thus Minor argued that voting was a privilege of citizenship and voting in federal elections was a privilege that owed its existence to the federal government and its national character.

Chief Justice Waite's opinion for the Court agreed that women were citizens but insisted that "the Constitution of the United States does not confer the right of suffrage upon any one" (Minor v. Hapersett, 1874). States determined eligibility to vote, subject to the Fifteenth Amendment right not to have the vote denied on account of race. Thus voting was not a privilege or immunity of federal citizenship.

The next voting case challenged Sections 3 and 4 of the Enforcement Act of 1870, which made conspiracy to obstruct an election a federal crime. The law's purpose was to end the intimidation of African-American voters, but the challenged provisions were not limited to obstruction because of race. The Court struck down the statute, saying that the only federal privilege with respect to voting in state elections was to be free of state denial on the basis of race (United States v. Reese, 1876). The failure to allege that the intimidation was for racial reasons also proved fatal with respect to some counts in *Cruikshank.*

Reese and *Cruikshank* left open the question whether the federal government could protect the right to vote for federal offices from private interference as a federal privilege or immunity. This issue came before the court in *Ex parte Yarbrough.* The defendants had been convicted for beating a man because he voted in a federal election and was of African descent. They brought habeas corpus to challenge their conviction, arguing that Congress had no power to punish private interferences with voting because the Fifteenth Amendment applied only to state action. The offense was the act of private persons who injured another private person. The defendants argued that suffrage was not a federal right, pointing to the language in *Minor*. The Court, however, affirmed their conviction. Justice Miller distinguished between eligibility to vote and the exercise of the right to vote in federal elections by eligible voters. He said that the right to vote was not conferred by the Constitution alone, so it was not a right of citizenship:

> But the court did not intend to say that when the class or the person is thus ascertained, his right to vote for a member of Congress was not fundamentally based upon the Constitution, which created the office of member of Congress, and declared it should be elective, and pointed to the means of ascertaining who should be electors. (*Ex parte* Yarbrough, 1884)

Congress has power to protect any individual exercising any function or right which is dependent on the laws of the United States, and:

> . . . it is the duty of that government to see that he may exercise this right freely, and to protect him from violence while so doing, or on account of so doing. This duty does not arise solely from the interest of the party concerned, but from the necessity of the government itself, that its service shall be free from the adverse influence of force and fraud practised on its agents, and that the votes by which its members of Congress and its President

are elected shall be the free votes of the electors, and the officers thus chosen the free and uncorrupted choice of those who have the right to take part in that choice. (*Ex parte* Yarbrough, 1884)

The "duty" of government did not necessarily create a corresponding individual right to compel the federal government to act. The eligible voter's right to exercise the franchise in federal elections in this respect is a privilege of U.S. citizenship like the privilege to demand the care and protection of the Federal government when on the high seas or within the jurisdiction of a foreign government. It is protected against individuals only where the federal government acts, but it is still a privilege that will be encompassed by general references in legislation to interference with federal rights or privileges.

The citizen can claim privileges or immunities only insofar as they have a direct constitutional right or Congress has provided such a right. As the Court indicated in *Minor*, a federal relationship alone is not enough to create a privilege or immunity. A right must exist. Thus a reasonable regulation by a state of the use of the federal public domain does not violate a privilege or immunity of federal citizenship, because there is no right to use public lands (Omaechevarria v. Idaho, 1918). However, when federal law creates an individual right in the public domain, it creates a privilege or immunity of federal citizenship that the federal government can protect from private interference. For example, the federal Homestead Act provided rights to enter and occupy certain land. In United States v. Waddell (1884), the government alleged that defendant Waddell conspired to prevent another person from exercising his right to make an effectual entry. The Court upheld the application of federal law prohibiting interference with a federal right.

The crucial issue is whether the federal government and its functioning can be identified as the source of the right. Some horrendous behavior may violate all norms of civilized society, yet be beyond the reach of privileges and immunities of U.S. citizenship. Although Congress could enact laws against racially based lynching under its Thirteenth Amendment powers, in the absence of a specific statute, the Court held that a lynching did not violate a privilege or immunity of U.S. citizenship (United States v. Harris, 1883). Life, liberty, and property are matters of state concern and not privileges or immunities of federal citizenship; thus the federal government cannot punish private deprivations of these rights unless the deprivation involves a particular federal interest. The constitutional right is that the state not deny life, liberty, or property without due process or equal protection. A lynch mob may injure the state's interest in the enforcement of its laws, but it is the mob and not the state that acts. Thus the Court struck down a federal law against conspiracies to deprive persons of the equal protection of the laws as applied to private parties taking a state prisoner from the custody of state officers (United States v. Harris, 1883).

The Court reacted very differently to a lynch mob seeking to harm a person held by federal officials. The federal government has an interest in protecting prisoners in its custody. Prisoners not only have due process rights against the federal government, they have a privilege against being harmed by others while in federal custody. This reasoning supported the prosecution of members of a lynch mob for conspiring to injure prisoners in the custody of a U.S. Marshal:

[E]very right, created by, arising under or dependent upon, the Constitution of the United States, may be protected and enforced by Congress by such means and in such manner as Congress, in the exercise of the correlative duty of protection, or of the legislative powers conferred upon it by the Constitution, may in its discretion deem most eligible and best adapted to attain the object. . . .

In the case at bar, the right in question does not depend upon any of the Amendments to the Constitution, but arises out of the creation and establishment by the Constitution itself of a national government, paramount and supreme within its sphere of action. Any government which has power to indict, try and punish for crime, and to arrest the accused and hold them in safekeeping until trial, must have the power and the duty to protect against unlawful interference its prisoners so held, as well as its executive and judicial officers charged with keeping and trying them. (Logan v. U.S., 1892)

Protection of a federal prisoner from a lynch mob fit the description of a right arising under or dependent on the Constitution. The government has the ability to protect its own processes, and participation in those processes may be a privilege of citizenship. For example, in *In re Quarles*, Henry Worley told a U.S. Marshal that George Terry violated the revenue laws by carrying on the business of distiller without a bond. Terry's friends reacted to protect the Georgia moonshine business by beating up Worley. They were convicted of conspiracy to injure Worley in the exercise of a right secured by the Constitution and laws. Based on *Logan*, the court found federal citizenship includes the right to inform federal officials of violation of federal law, and it upheld the conviction.

Another federal privilege relating to the operation of government is the right of the citizen to discuss government activity. In *Cruikshank*, the Court distinguished between assembly for federal purposes and for other purposes:

The right of the people peaceably to assemble for the purpose of petitioning Congress for a redress of grievances, or for any thing else connected with the powers or the duties of the national government, is an attribute of national citizenship, and, as such, under the protection of, and guaranteed by, the United States. The very idea of a government, republican in form, implies a right on the part of its citizens to meet peaceably for consultation in respect to public affairs and to petition for a redress of grievances. If it had been alleged in these counts that the object of the defendants was to prevent a meeting for such a purpose, the case would have been within the statute, and within the scope of the sovereignty of the United States. Such, however, is not the case. The offence, as stated in the indictment, will be made out, if it be shown that the object of the conspiracy was to prevent a meeting for any lawful purpose whatever. (United States v. Cruikshank, 1876)

In other words, the federal privilege is to communicate on federal issues. States cannot interfere with that, and the federal government has the power to protect their citizens from private interference as well. On the other hand, the right to assemble and petition state government or discuss other matters is not a privilege of federal citizenship. It is a fundamental right committed to the states.

The Court picked up on this distinction in *Hague*. The majority opinion written by Justice Roberts held that discussion of labor matters under the National Labor Relations Act was a privilege and immunity of federal citizenship. In this connection, Roberts wrote his famous lines that:

Wherever the title of streets and parks may rest, they have immemorially been held in trust for the use of the public and, time out of mind, have been used for purposes of assembly, communicating thoughts between citizens, and discussing public questions. Such use of the streets and public places has, from ancient times, been a part of the privileges, immunities, rights, and liberties of citizens. The privilege of a citizen of the United States to use the streets and parks for communication of views on national questions may be regulated in the interest of all; it is not absolute, but relative, and must be exercised in subordination to the general comfort and convenience, and in consonance with peace and good order; but it must not, in the guise of regulation, be abridged or denied. (Hague v. CIO, 1939)

But this narrow right of petition and assembly had little practical importance because, as the concurring opinions indicated, freedom of speech and assembly were applicable against the states through the due process clause of the Fourteenth Amendment anyway.

Right to Travel: Saenz v. Roe

Most privileges and immunities of citizens of the United States result from express statutes. The right to travel, however, is not entirely expressed in either statute or Constitution. Justice John Paul Stevens has distinguished three different components of the right to travel—"the right of a citizen of one State to enter and to leave another State, the right to be treated as a welcome visitor rather than an unfriendly alien when temporarily present in the second State, and, for those travelers who elect to become permanent residents, the right to be treated like other citizens of that State" (Saenz v. Roe, 1999).

The right "to be treated as a welcome visitor rather than an unfriendly alien" was a reference to the privileges and immunities clause of Article IV. Some cases involving claims of alleged discrimination on the basis of residence raised Fourteenth Amendment privileges and immunities claims as well; however, those attempts to establish a right against discrimination beyond Article IV have been unsuccessful. For example, one group of cases sought to use the Fourteenth Amendment privileges or immunities clause in interstate claims of improper taxation. The decisions also analyzed the claims under Article IV, due process and equal protection and sometimes the commerce clause. When a state law arguably discriminated against nonresidents, the primary test was whether Article IV was satisfied. The Fourteenth Amendment privileges or immunities clause added nothing. It offered no escape for corporations from their inability to claim Article IV privileges, because the Court found they were not citizens of the United States for purposes of the Fourteenth Amendment either (Western Turf Ass'n v. Greenberg, 1907; Selover, Bates & Co. v. Walsh, 1912). Thus if the state discrimination against nonresidents did not offend Article IV, the privileges and immunities clause of the Fourteenth Amendment raised no difficulty (Ballard v. Hunter, 1907; Maxwell v. Bugbee, 1919. See also Armour & Co. v. Virginia, 1918: license tax on persons carrying on merchandise business with exemption for manufacturers to the extent they sell goods at the place of manufacture; Ownbey v. Morgan, 1921: foreign attachment special bond requirement not a due process or equal protection violation and parties privileges and immunities here have no federal origin).

The Fourteenth Amendment has played a much stronger role with respect to the other aspects of the right to travel mentioned by Justice Stevens—that is, the right to enter and leave a state and the right to migrate. The Court has limited the impact of the privileges and immunities clause of Article IV to the rights of nonresidents and forced individuals to turn elsewhere when their state of residence has arguably interfered with their right to travel. The Court has found a personal constitutional right to enter and leave a state that applies against private and state interference, but it has rejected any Fourteenth Amendment right to have a state treat activities by its residents in another state as it treats those activities at home. The citizen may, however, migrate and become a citizen of another state with all the rights that its citizens may have.

The right to enter and leave another state

The first major case on the right to travel arose before the adoption of the Fourteenth Amendment. It involved the claimed right of a citizen to enter and leave a state. Crandall, the agent for the Pioneer Stage Line, challenged Nevada's $1 tax on every passenger leaving the state by public conveyance. The Court expressed doubt whether the tax violated the commerce clause, but it struck down the tax anyway as a violation of the rights of citizens of the United States (Crandall v. Nevada, 1867).

Justice Miller, in his opinion for the majority of the Court, said that the government of the United States had the right to call its citizens to assist it in performing functions throughout the land, and the Supremacy clause precluded states from interfering with this right. He then insisted that the citizen had correlative rights to travel as part of his relationship to the federal government that the State could not abridge.

In the *Slaughter-House Cases*, Justice Miller referred to *Crandall* as demonstrating that the right to travel from state to state is a privilege or immunity of U.S. citizenship. Indeed, the right to travel was Justice Miller's first example of a privilege or immunity of U.S. citizenship:

> One of these [privileges or immunities of U.S. citizenship] is well described in the case of Crandall v. Nevada, 6 Wall. 36, 18 L. Ed. 745. It is said to be the right of the citizen of this great country, protected by implied guaranties of its Constitution, "to come to the seat of government to assert any claim he may have upon that government, to transact any business he may have with it, to seek its protection, to share its offices, to engage in administering its functions. He has the right of free access to its seaports, through which all operations of foreign commerce are conducted, to the subtreasuries, land-offices, and courts of justice in the several states." And quoting from the language of Chief Justice Taney in another case, it is said "that, for all the great purposes for which the Federal government was established, we are one people with one common country; we are all citizens of the United States;" and it is as such citizens that their rights are supported in this court in Crandall v. Nevada. (Slaughter-House Cases, 1873)

Litigants tried to use *Crandall* to prevent their home state from taxing their activities in other states. The cases began with the claim that a state may not tax its citizens on money earned in another state. The first case did not involve any discrimination, and the core issue was the due process concern with jurisdiction. The Court found that a tax imposed on assets of a resident could include money owed from an out of state business because the situs of the debt was with the creditor. Therefore the state was taxing a matter within its jurisdiction (Kirtland v. Hotchkiss, 1880).

Two decades later, the Court reviewed a tax imposed on emigrant agents who hired persons to work outside the state. The agent's citizenship did not affect the tax, but the tax operated only on agents who hired people to work in other states and not on employment agents who hired for jobs in the state. The agents claimed that the tax impaired the right to travel. The Court acknowledged the right to travel was constitutionally protected by the Fourteenth Amendment, but noted that the tax was not imposed on persons who traveled (Williams v. Fears, 1900). The Court held that the tax did not violate equal protection because there could be a legitimate reason for distinguishing between hiring for in-state and out-of-state work, such as the difficulty of supervising the work out of state to be sure the agent was acting ethically. Further, the court held that the activity of hiring people to work out of state was not interstate commerce because the agent was acting within the state.

The Court's analysis in *Williams* might not stand up today; the tax certainly affected the decision of workers to travel, and its commerce clause reasoning was questionable. Its basic proposition on the right to travel would survive, however, because the Court has held that a state can exempt from taxation local activities that it wishes to encourage or subsidize. The state cannot tax the activity of a nonresident outside the state, and Article IV requires that any tax exemption be available to citizens and nonresidents alike. Nevertheless, the state does not violate the privileges or immunities clause if it distinguishes in the tax on its own citizens between local activities and those done elsewhere. For example, Illinois imposed an inheritance tax on property within the state that exempted property bestowed on charities within the state. A charity outside the state challenged the tax, but the Court upheld the law as reasonable (Board of Education v. Illinois, 1906).

This deference to state subsidization of local activities changed temporarily in Colgate v. Harvey (1935). Vermont's state income tax allowed exemptions for interest from loans within the state. The taxpayer challenged the law as it applied to his income from loans and dividends outside the state. The Court said that a citizen's right to do business in a state other than his own was a privilege of national citizenship. Therefore, it reasoned, a state could not forbid its citizens from doing business in another state, and a discriminatory tax on doing business in other states would be equally bad unless a reasonable basis existed for it. Distinctions between income earned in state and out of state that were designed to equalize burdens and prevent double taxation were appropriate. For example, the Court upheld the distinction between dividends from corporations in the state and out of the state because the state had already taxed the in-state company. On the other hand, the state must offer a sufficient reason for differential taxation. The exemption for loans made within the state was not restricted to loans invested within the state, and the Court found no legitimate public purpose for it existed. (The Court noted that it might have a public purpose if the exemption required the proceeds from the loan to be invested in the state). States cannot exact taxes discriminating against goods brought from sister states. Thus a tax on business out of state should be equally bad.

Justices Harlan Fiske Stone, Louis Brandeis, and Benjamin Cardozo dissented. These justices objected to the tendency of the Court to second guess the reasonableness of legislative decisions in cases decided under the due process clause, and they brought the same view to privileges and immunities. They considered the exemptions reasonable. Encouraging residents to invest their funds at home is legitimate activity, they argued. Although states may not lay taxes on imports or burden interstate commerce, they can favor domestic interests by granting exemptions in the exercise of the taxing power. Investment capital was leaving the state, and the state should be able to preserve it with the inducement of a tax exemption. However the dissenters would have gone further than merely finding the state acted reasonably. They argued that *Crandall* should have been decided on dormant commerce clause grounds. At most, it should be limited to its rationale, and applied only to travel "in pursuance of the relationship between the citizen and the national government."

> The protection and control of intercourse between the states, not carried on in pursuance of the relationship between the citizen and the national government, has been left to the interstate commerce clause, to the due process and equal protection clauses of the Fourteenth

> Amendment, and to Art. IV, § 2, guaranteeing to the citizens of each state the privileges and immunities of citizens in the several states. *See Williams v. Fears,* 179 U.S. 270. In no case since the adoption of the Fourteenth Amendment has the privileges and immunities clause been held to afford any protection to movements of persons across state lines or other form of interstate transaction. (Colgate v. Harvey, 1935, Stone J. dissenting)

Within five years, the *Colgate* principle of a Fourteenth Amendment privilege to do business in other states was reversed. Kentucky imposed a personal property tax on its citizens' bank deposits that was five times higher for deposits in banks outside of the state. Justice Stanley Reed's opinion for the court found that the difference did not violate equal protection or due process because the difficulties and expenses of tax collection justified the distinction (Madden v. Kentucky, 1940). He then said, "the right to carry out an incident to a trade, business or calling such as the deposit of money in banks is not a privilege of national citizenship," and expressly overruled *Colgate*. His opinion did not discuss the right to travel or attempt to call *Crandall* in question as the dissenters in *Colgate* had done.

Madden appeared to deny any federal privilege to do business in other states under the same terms as in one's home state. *Crandall* had assured individuals can go from state to state, Article IV prevented the state where they went from discriminating against them, but national citizenship did not give a citizen of one state the ability to engage in activities in another state free from taxation or regulation by their home state.

With the right to travel limited to freedom to cross borders, the Court began to consider it more favorably. In the wake of the depression, California sought to prohibit the army of unemployed from coming there by penalizing anyone who brought a person into the state knowing that person was indigent. In Edwards v. California (1941), the Court struck down the statute as a violation of the negative implications of the commerce clause. It noted that relief of the poor was no longer solely the responsibility of local government, saying, "The theory of the Elizabethan poor laws no longer fits the facts." With cooperative federal-state arrangements, "the relief of the needy has become the common responsibility and concern of the whole nation." The Court rejected as outmoded earlier decisions that had suggested a police power rationale for excluding paupers: "Whatever may have been the notion then prevailing, we do not think that it will now be seriously contended that because a person is without employment and without funds he constitutes a 'moral pestilence.'"

Four concurring justices would have relied on a right of interstate travel. Justice William O. Douglas, joined by Justices Frank Murphy and Hugo Black, said, "The right to move freely from State to State is an incident of *national* citizenship protected by the privileges and immunities clause of the Fourteenth Amendment against state interference." Justice Douglas said that it was not limited to travel for federal purposes, nor was it derived from Article IV because it applied to states' regulation of their own citizens. Justice Robert Jackson agreed:

> This Court should, however, hold squarely that it is a privilege of citizenship of the United States, protected from state abridgment, to enter any state of the Union, either for temporary sojourn or for the establishment of permanent residence therein and for gaining resultant citizenship thereof. If national citizenship means less than this, it means nothing. (Edwards v. California, 1941, Jackson J. concurring)

The Court majority did not deny a right to travel; they simply ignored it and relied on the dormant commerce clause. Later decisions continued to mention the right to travel while resting any decision on commerce clause grounds, but the dormant commerce clause did not protect travel from private interference. That led to the Court's most far-reaching decision on the right to travel, in which it sustained an indictment for conspiracy to interfere with "the right to travel freely to and from the state of Georgia and to use highway facilities and other instrumentalities of interstate commerce within the State of Georgia" (United States v. Guest, 1966). Congress could have used its commerce power to protect travel by a statute that specifically made private interference criminal; however, it did not. The only applicable statute used the general language of rights secured by the Constitution and laws. Because no specific law could be cited the Court had to find that travel was a right secured by the Constitution to apply the general statute. Citing *Crandall* and *Edwards*, the Court noted "recurring differences in emphasis within the Court as to the source of the constitutional right of interstate travel," but it did not stop to resolve the differences because "All have agreed that the right exists." The unusual step for the Court was that it applied the right to travel against "interference from any source whatever, whether governmental or private."

Most constitutional rights are against government. Previous cases finding private interference with federal rights involved statutory grants or the functioning of federal institutions. Indeed, the Court had previously indicated that travel related rights were only applicable against the states. The question had arisen in United States v. Wheeler (1920), when the federal government attempted to prosecute defendants who had kidnapped labor organizers, put them in a boxcar that took them across state lines, and let them out with the warning that they should never return to Arizona. The federal government charged that this behavior violated the rights secured to the citizens by the Constitution to peacefully reside in a state and not be unlawfully deported. The Court noted the many cases that spoke of the privileges and immunities as including the right of a citizen of one state to pass through or to reside in any other state. Nevertheless, it held that the wrongful act of an individual that deprived a citizen of the ability to pass through or reside in a state was not a deprivation of a Constitutional right. The Court said that the states had power to deal with the wrongful behavior, and the constitutional right was only against state discrimination (United States v. Wheeler, 1920).

Justice Potter Stewart made a weak attempt to distinguish *Wheeler* in a footnote in *Guest*, saying *Wheeler* involved expulsion from a state rather than interference with interstate movement. But telling someone they cannot come into a state effectively interferes with their interstate movement. In reality, the Court simply took a different view of the right to travel in *Guest*. It argued that travel, like discussion of national matters, is a privilege that the federal government can protect against private interference.

The Court continues to avoid specifying the source of the right. In its most recent privileges and immunities decision, Justice Stevens said it was not necessary to identify the source of the right to enter and leave a state in the text of the Constitution, because the challenged law did not impose any obstacle to the right (Saenz v. Roe, 1999). He noted it was mentioned in the Articles of Confederation, but quoted *Guest*, which was vague on its source. If there is such a right, of course it is a privilege of citizenship, but the question is whether the source of the right is in the privileges of citizenship. It is arguably a liberty interest protected by due process, it could be a federally specific right inferred from the federal government as in *Crandall*, or it might be seen as implicit in Article IV as necessary for any citizen to be able to obtain the constitutional protection of Article IV in other states. Only the latter sustains the decision in *Guest*.

It is difficult to use the due process clause as a basis for a privilege to travel that can be protected against private interference—the right created by that provision is only to have state or federal governments afford due process. Indeed, the Fourteenth Amendment only creates rights against the state government, and the Court has been reluctant to find that it can be the source for federal legislation regulating private individuals.

Interference with the functioning of the federal government does interfere with rights or privileges created by federal law; hence, the access to government rationale for a right to travel creates a privilege that can be protected against private interference. However, individuals travel interstate for reasons unrelated to accessing federal government offices, and *Crandall's* reasoning does not apply on its face to travel for personal or commercial purposes.

This leaves Article IV as a potential source for finding that the right to travel is a privilege of federal citizenship. Many of the early decisions of the Court specifically mentioned interstate travel as a privilege or immunity of Article IV, even though the provision does not contain the Articles of Confederation's express statement that citizens have a right of ingress or egress. Thus, there is a strong historical warrant for finding it there. Even more persuasive than text and history is the argument that the relationship between the individual and the states created by Article IV requires a right to travel. If the Court inferred a right to travel from the need to cross state lines to gain access to the privileges of citizens in another state, travel would be a privilege of federal citizenship. The access protected is not to government offices, but to be within the jurisdiction of another state. If the right to interstate travel is rooted in any particular provision of the Constitution, therefore, it should find its home in Article IV.

Justice Douglas rejected Article IV as a source for the right to travel in his *Edwards* concurrence, because he thought the privileges and immunities clause of that article did not apply to the way a state treated its own citizens. Even if that were true, it does not prevent Article IV from being the basis for inferring a right from its structure. But it is also arguable that the language expressly applies to a state's treatment of its own citizens, insofar as any state seeks to prevent its citizens from receiving what the Constitution says they are entitled to—the privileges and immunities of citizens "in the several states."

The right of migration

Nondiscriminatory regulations of the police power which burden interstate travel (e.g., speed limits, anti-hitchhiking laws, environmental regulations) have never been considered a threat to the implied constitutional right to travel, and until the past two decades there was little litigation of interstate travel restrictions except for cases decided on commerce clause grounds. Then in 1969, the right to travel merged with evolving equal protection analysis to produce new doctrine. Plaintiffs challenged the rules of several states and the District of Columbia that required persons to have resided within the jurisdiction for at least one year before becoming eligible for welfare benefits. The Court found the residency requirements denied equal protection, because the classification impinged on the right to travel (Shapiro v. Thompson, 1969). Assuming that a state may limit benefits to its residents, the durational residency requirement was not shown to be necessary as a means of determining residence. It was apparent from the insubstantiality of the other reasons proffered that the real rationale for the statute was to discourage interstate immigration. Right to travel analysis alone was insufficient because states are not constitutionally required to provide welfare benefits and their lack is not a bar to travel. Equal protection analysis alone was insufficient because the regulations were rational. But the reason was contrary to the right to travel principle. Combining equal protection with fundamental rights, the Court struck down the statute.

Shapiro sired a host of cases challenging durational residency requirements under the equal protection clause, forcing the court to articulate the legitimate interest of states in making such distinctions. A state may require residency without violating the equal protection clause as a condition of providing specific benefits, such as public service jobs (McCarthy v. Philadelphia Civil Service Commission, 1976); voting (Rosario v. Rockefeller, 1973); public education (Starns v. Malkerson, 1971). The visitor may look to his or her home state for such benefits. The issue in these cases was whether the state could delay, for a period, providing benefits to a person who entered the state to reside there. The need to prevent fraudulent residence claims justifies durational requirements in each of these areas, but the period must be brief. However, the Court upheld a Texas law that permitted school districts to deny tuition for education to a child who lived apart from his parents or legal guardian if the child's presence in the district was for the primary purpose of attending school there (Martinez v. Bynum, 1983). The Court found the law imposed a bona fide residence requirement.

In general, the Court invalidated any durational residency requirements not designed to prevent fraud. For example, the Court struck down an Alaskan rebate program that paid each resident $50 per year of residence after 1959, finding no rational basis for the distinctions among residents (Zobel v. Williams, 1982). The Court also struck down a New York civil service law that gave an employment preference to veterans who served during time of war and were residents of New York when they entered military service (Attorney Gen. of New York v. Soto-Lopez, 1986). Four justices argued that the law was a permanent deprivation of a significant benefit based only on the fact of nonresidence at a past point in time, and that it "clearly operates to penalize appellees for exercising their rights to migrate." They concluded that all state interests could have been served by granting bonus points regardless of place of prior residence and thus struck the statute down. Two justices concurred on the basis that the statutory distinction was irrational, and they did not determine whether some form of heightened scrutiny was appropriate.

These rulings created a policy difficulty. States might be reluctant to provide benefits, particularly good welfare benefits, fearing the provision of the benefits would encourage immigration to take advantage of them. Congress supported this concern in the Personal Responsibility and Work Opportunity Reconciliation Act of 1996 (PRWORA). For a family who had been in a state less than a year, PRWORA authorized states to apply the welfare law including benefit levels of the state from which they came. California took advantage of the federal authorization, but newcomers from Oklahoma and Washington, D.C., challenged the California law. The case might easily have been decided on the basis of *Shapiro*, but the Court chose to focus on the source of the right to travel.

Justice Stevens said the newly arrived citizen's right to the same privileges and immunities enjoyed by other citizens of the state is a privilege or immunity of citizens of the United States. He noted that all the justices in the *Slaughter-House Cases* agreed that this component is a privilege or immunity:

> it has always been common ground that this Clause protects the third component of the right to travel. Writing for the majority in the *Slaughter-House Cases*, Justice Miller explained that one of the privileges conferred by this Clause "is that a citizen of the United States can, of his own volition, become a citizen of any State of the Union by a bona fide residence therein, with the same rights as other citizens of that State." Id., at 80. Justice Bradley, in dissent, used even stronger language to make the same point:
>
> "The states have not now, if they ever had, any power to restrict their citizenship to any classes or persons. A citizen of the United States has a perfect constitutional right to go to and reside in any State he chooses, and to claim citizenship therein, and an equality of rights with every other citizen; and the whole power of the nation is pledged to sustain him in that right. He is not bound to cringe to any superior, or to pray for any act of grace, as a means of enjoying all the rights and privileges enjoyed by other citizens." (Saenz v. Roe, 1999, quoting from Slaughter-House Cases, 1873)

Stevens said the impact on the right to travel as a deterrent to migration was irrelevant. The right itself is to equal treatment. The case raised no issue on the bona fides of the residence and there was "no danger that recognition of the claim will encourage citizens of other States to establish residency for just long enough to acquire a readily portable benefit like divorce or a college education that will be enjoyed after they return to their original domicile." (Saenz v. Roe, 1999)

The Court found that deterring welfare applicants from migrating to California was not a sufficient justification for the law for three reasons: (1) that the number of persons who migrate with that motive was small according to the empirical evidence, (2) the state represented to the court that it was not the purpose, and (3) "such a purpose would be unequivocally impermissible." The classification saves money, but any curtailment of welfare saves money. The Court said that interest did not justify the classification: "Neither the duration of respondent's California residence, nor the identity of their prior States of residence, has any relevance to their need for benefits." They are not relevant to allocation either because that would allow apportionment according to past contributions and similar rationing for police, schools, and so on. Finally, Congressional approval was irrelevant because Congress cannot authorize a violation of the Fourteenth Amendment. "Moreover, the protection afforded the citizen by the Citizenship Clause of that Amendment is a limitation on the powers of the National Government as well as the States." Stevens said, "Citizens of the United States, whether rich or poor, have the right to choose to be citizens 'of the State wherein they reside.' U.S. Const., Amdt. 14, § 1. The States, however, do not have any right to select their citizens."

Chief Justice Rehnquist dissented, joined by Justice Clarence Thomas. He agreed that the right to travel prohibits states from impeding the free interstate passage of citizens. Similarly, Article IV was correctly described, but inapplicable because it does not apply to persons changing residence. Finally, he said that citizens have a right to become citizens of another state, but it is a separate right. "At most, restrictions on an individual's right to become a citizen indirectly affect his calculus in deciding whether to exercise his right to travel in the first place, but such an attenuated and uncertain relationship is no ground for folding one right into the other." He resisted the line of cases striking down durational residency requirements. Instead, Chief Justice Rehnquist argued that the appropriate analysis should be based on "the right of individuals not to be subject to unjustifiable classifications as opposed to infringements on the right to travel." He argued that one-year durational requirements are appropriate as objective criteria to determine bona fide residence. Rehnquist contended that welfare payment benefits are just as portable as college education, and congressional approval supported the reasonableness of the durational requirement. Although welfare benefits may give a family breathing space that helps them later, Rehnquist did not convince a majority that they are as portable as education.

The decision in *Saenz* indicates that the Court will carefully scrutinize any distinctions between citizens of a state based on the length of their residence. It is likely to continue to examine the bona fides of claims of state citizenship and to support distinctions between education and welfare in terms of the criteria for determining whether a claim of change of residence is bona fide.

The Future of Privileges and Immunities

The discussion of the cases has set forth the road traveled and the current location of Fourteenth Amendment doctrine on privileges or immunities. This last section looks at the future for that clause. One fork in the road would revisit the questions from the *Slaughter-House Cases* and return the privileges and immunities clause to the place of prominence its framers intended. Alternatively, the court could follow its precedents and continue to develop the concept of privileges and immunities unique to citizens of the United States because they flow from the particular structure of our government.

Return to Original Intent: The Effect on Fundamental Rights and Incorporation

Justice Thomas' separate dissent in *Saenz* reopened the possibility of bringing back the original meaning of the privileges and immunities clause. He argued that privileges and immunities did not apply to public benefits, pointing to the fundamental rights distinction found in *Corfield.* He brought the meaning of fundamental rights in Article IV into the search for meaning of the Fourteenth Amendment:

> That Members of the 39th Congress appear to have endorsed the wisdom of Justice Washington's opinion does not, standing alone, provide dispositive insight into their understanding of the Fourteenth Amendment's Privileges or Immunities Clause. Nevertheless, their repeated references to the *Corfield* decision, combined with what appears to be the historical understanding of the Clause's operative terms, supports the inference that, at the time the Fourteenth Amendment was adopted, people understood that "privileges or immunities of citizens" were fundamental rights, rather than every public benefit established by positive law. Accordingly, the majority's conclusion—that a State violates the Privileges or Immunities Clause when it "discriminates" against citizens who have been domiciled in the State for less than a year in the distribution of welfare benefit appears contrary to the original understanding and is dubious at best. (Saenz v. Roe, 1999, Thomas J. dissenting)

He went even further in suggesting revised attention to the clause:

> Because I believe that the demise of the Privileges or Immunities Clause has contributed in no small part to the current disarray of our Fourteenth Amendment jurisprudence, I would be open to reevaluating its meaning in an appropriate case. Before invoking the Clause, however, we should endeavor to understand what the framers of the Fourteenth Amendment thought that it meant. We should also consider whether the Clause should displace, rather than augment, portions of our equal protection and substantive due process jurisprudence.

Thomas' call for a return to the framers' intent leads to the problems already chronicled. The framers intended to protect fundamental rights of citizens, but what are they?

One of the first modern commentators suggesting a revival of the privileges and immunities clause was Professor Philip Kurland.[21] He sought to root the right of privacy in the doctrine. In general he offered the clause as a limit on legislative and executive discretion in public education, welfare, and housing; police; fire; sanitation; and ecology. The limit would stress quality rather than equality, perhaps creating minimum standards.

Justice Thomas is unlikely to share a welfare state vision of fundamental rights. His concern with natural rights law is more likely to find a right to life in the unborn fetus and a stronger commitment to property rights.[22] One article he might find congenial argued that natural law could provide a more coherent privileges or immunities doctrine than currently exists. The authors insisted that privileges and immunities do not apply to government benefits because the clause only secures natural rights that antedate government.[23]

Another approach argues that fundamental rights under privileges and immunities poses an historical rather than a philosophical issue. Changing mores can change the application of the clause, but only claims that have attained widespread support and been confirmed with experience should be accepted.[24]

Supporters for revisiting the privileges and immunities clause are often economic libertarians who would like to shift to the state the burden of showing that regulations of business entry are needed for public health or consumer protection.[25] However, a wide variety of views on fundamental rights make the doctrine's revival attractive to both the left and the right.

Professor Lawrence Tribe argued for a core idea of the right to individual self-government.[26] Daniel Levin similarly argued that the clause secures rights in the structure of government rather than rights to be free of government. Levin said that the clause focuses on "the participatory privileges that make up a citizen's architectural role in the political and judicial process of civil government."[27] However, Levin did not take the line of argument to the extent that Tribe would take it.

The variety of theories cast doubt on Justice Thomas' belief that a fundamental rights analysis will produce a fairly limited doctrine. His insistence that welfare benefits are not among the fundamental rights protected runs up against Blackstone's Commentaries' reference to just such benefits as part of the right to security of the person. Further, if natural law includes the protection of property, it is not protecting a natural liberty but a right that is largely determined by government.

The switch to privileges and immunities rather than due process as the grounds for finding unenumerated substantive rights might be justified if it resulted in either clarity or better doctrine. However, it would do neither. Substantive due process has its own historical warrant, as Justice David Souter demonstrated in his concurring opinion in Washington v. Glucksberg (1997). Despite the oxymoronic sense of the language, the court has had little difficulty over the past century in using the due process clause for this purpose. A switch would limit protections to citizens of the United States and would exclude aliens from rights such as the use of contraceptive devices except as derivative rights from the equal protection clause.

Another difference between the clauses is that the due process clause uses the term "deprivation," whereas privileges and immunities may not be "abridged." This latter term may suggest that the unenumerated fundamental rights are absolutes.[28] The advantages for stronger protection for civil liberties, however, could be substantially offset by the disadvantages of precluding government from sensible regulations of behavior. If the court were to switch from due process to privileges and immunities, it would probably not distinguish between deprivation and abridgment and thus the switch would probably not affect the scope of the rights.

Professor Michael Curtis and others have urged the use of privileges and immunities as the basis for incorporating fundamental rights from the first eight amendments of the Constitution. They argue that the language of privileges and immunities requires total incorporation of every clause, as Justice Black insisted. The switch from due process to privileges and immunities as the basis for incorporation could have this effect, but that is not necessarily a point in its favor.

Curiously, many of the individual rights of the first eight amendments seem more appropriate for the due process clause than privileges or immunities because they are procedural in nature—jury trial, speedy trial, self-incrimination, and so on. If incorporation succeeds under the privileges and immunities banner, it might require states to adhere to provisions that the Court has previously considered out moded and nonessential, such as grand jury indictment and the civil jury. The current membership of the Court shows no signs of shifting the process of selective incorporation.

Most advocates for revival of the clause hope that the due process and equal protection clauses will make any substantive right found in privileges and immunities applicable to aliens and possibly corporations; however, if rights incorporated throughout the privileges and immunities clause apply to aliens, why was the clause limited to citizens in the first place? The issue of superfluity, which has dogged the clause, could produce here a restriction of the rights of aliens. That is particularly true in reaction to fears of terrorism.

In short, any attempt to return to the original meaning of the privileges and immunities clauses faces three problems: bad history, bad law, and bad policy. First, no single coherent understanding of fundamental rights and the meaning of the clause exists, so no original meaning can be returned to. Second, current law satisfies the underlying concerns of the framers reasonably well, and shifting to a new provision threatens to destabilize precedent with the potential to bring back the infamous *Lochner* decision, which invalidated maximum hour legislation as an unwarranted interference with freedom of contract (Lochner v. New York, 1905).

Finally, restricting rights to citizens would be politically unpalatable and unwise.[29]

Federal Relational Substantive Rights as International Human Rights

Saenz identified a familiar notion—the right of a citizen of the United States to migrate and become a citizen of another state—and gave it further definition. The decision was based on structural reasoning about the federal nature of this society. We can expect further testing of durational residency requirements to develop the legitimacy of the use of length of residence as a proxy for bona fide intent to reside.

The Court's failure to root the right to travel in the privileges or immunities clause may be temporary. *Crandall* established that interstate travel was a privilege or immunity of citizenship of the United States. It can logically be deduced from the privileges of Article IV, and the Court could move to that clause as a basis for finding that interstate travel is a privilege or immunity under the Fourteenth Amendment. The citizen's right to travel abroad has no express constitutional source; however, Justice Miller in the *Slaughter-House Cases* referred to the privilege of the citizen of the United States to the protection of the U.S. government when traveling abroad. The right to travel abroad may be a correlative of the U.S.'s role as the source of protection abroad. Thus state department limits on travel, which have been analyzed under due process, may need reexamination under a privileges or immunities analysis that could impose additional limits on the federal power.

The international relationship analysis of privileges and immunities may mean that the Court will deal with individual rights involving foreign relations as a Fourteenth Amendment privileges or immunities issue. Although the Fourteenth Amendment only restricts states, it indicates that unenumerated rights exist that arise out of the federal relationship. Because the relationship among nations is at the national level, citizens of the United States might be able to claim international human rights. This could apply against the states through the Fourteenth Amendment.

Of course, citizens of the United States have rights through treaties and other federal action. The incorporation of international law into domestic law is a complex subject. For example, treaties may be self-executing or they may require domestic legislation to be effective. Beyond specific treaties, however, there are also obligations of customary international law—that is, the customary law created through behavior that is habitually engaged in by most members of the international community because they believe they are legally obligated to do so. These obligations may be used within the state and federal court systems to support judicial decisions where no applicable statute or regulation is available. Professor Louis Henkin has argued that customary international law of human rights is also the law of the United States, and he attempted to make that part of the Restatement (3d) of the Foreign Relations Law.[30] But no decision of the Court has yet found that customary international law overrides a state's regulation of its own citizens. Customary international law has not displaced the power of either the federal government or the state government to enact conflicting legislation. It may be possible, however, to argue that customary international law has an impact on the nation to the extent that the federal government does not contradict it. Historically, customary law has focused on international relations, but acceptance is growing for international human rights applicable to the treatment by a country of its own citizens. The rights are obligations of all governments, but it is the national government that has obligations under international law. Thus the relationship of the individual to the federal government provides the basis for any claim of international human rights. This creates the possibility that international human rights should be considered privileges and immunities of citizenship of the United States, at least to the extent that the federal government does not specifically enact contrary laws. Under this theory, international human rights law would provide a standard that states cannot abridge under the Fourteenth Amendment.

International human rights law is still in an infant stage. A wide variety of treaties and United Nations declarations have varying amounts of support. The United States often agrees to such documents only with reservations. It is difficult to find a very large category of individual human rights that are generally accepted as customary international law, but voices are heard arguing for their recognition, and the future may see these rights grow. For example, the international condemnation of the death penalty as a violation of human dignity could at some point support an argument that abolition is a privilege or immunity of U.S. citizenship.[31] Although this tends toward the natural law (fundamental rights) doctrine that first caused the restrictive reading of the clause and that makes it unlikely for the Court to follow Justice Thomas' suggestion, an approach that proceeds from international standards reaches only as far as international consensus allows.

As these words are written, the future of the privileges and immunities clause is difficult to predict. It seems unlikely in the short term that the Court will displace conventional due process and equal protection doctrine. The development of the privileges and immunities clause in the short term therefore is likely to be primarily along the lines of the right to travel and to migrate. Whether the international legal system will insinuate its way into our constitutional law is, as yet, a distant prospect, but a doctrine that returned the clause to broadly recognized fundamental rights through a structural analysis of federal responsibilities under international human rights law would use a path of analysis set forth over a century ago to bring the clause back close to its origins.

NOTES

1. John M. Gonzales, "Comment: The Interstate Privileges and Immunities: Fundamental Rights or Federalism?" 15 *Capital University Law Review* (1986) 493, 499–50.

2. George F. Carpinello, "State Protective Legislation and Nonresident Corporations: The Privileges and Immunities Clause as a Treaty of Nondiscrimination," 73 *Iowa Law Review* (1988) 351–411; Martin Redish and Shane Nugent, "The Dormant Commerce Clause and the Constitutional Balance of Federalism," 1987 *Duke Law Journal* (1987) 569, 610–11; Julian Eule, "Laying the Dormant Commerce Clause to Rest," 91 *Yale Law Journal* (1982) 425, 451; Jonathan D. Varat, "State 'Citizenship' and Interstate Equality," 48 *University of Chicago Law Review* (1981) 487. Justice Antonin Scalia has been the leading voice on the Court for the proposition that the dormant commerce clause is not appropriate. See Tyler Pipe Indus. v. Washington Dept. of Revenue, 483 U.S. 232 (1987) (Scalia dissenting).

3. See Varat, "State 'Citizenship' and Interstate Equality," p. 560.

4. Mark P. Gergen, "The Selfish State and the Market," 66 *Texas Law Review* (1988) 1097, 1100.

5. Varat, "State 'Citizenship' and Interstate Equality."

6. Brainerd Currie and Herma Hill Schreter, "Unconstitutional Discrimination in the Conflict of Laws: Privileges and Immunities," 69 *Yale Law Journal* (1960): 1323.

7. *Landmark Briefs and Arguments of the Supreme Court of the United States: Constitutional Law* (Philip Kurland & Gerhard Casper eds.) vol. 6: 734–63.

8. *Landmark Briefs,* vol. 6: p. 587–614, 717–32 (Brief for Defendant by Charles Allen and Thomas Durant, and Brief for Defendant on Reargument by Thomas Durant).

9. *Landmark Briefs* vol. 6: 732 (Brief for Defendant on Reargument by Thomas Durant).

10. See Robert Palmer, "The Parameters of Constitutional Reconstruction: *Slaughter-house*, *Cruikshank*, and the Fourteenth Amendment," 1984 *University of Illinois Law Review* (1984) 739. Palmer argues that Miller's opinion in the *Slaughter-House Cases* favored interpreting the privileges and immunities clause as incorporating the Bill of Rights, and points to *Cruikshank* as a repudiation of Miller's reasoning. See also Kevin Newsom, "Setting Incorporationism Straight: A Reinterpretation of the Slaughter-House Cases," 109 *Yale Law Journal* (2000): 643. Newsom agrees that Miller intended to incorporate the Bill of Rights, but contends that *Cruikshank* was about state action issues and did not involve incorporation so did not repudiate incorporation.

11. *Globe, 42d Cong., 1st Sess.* 577 (1871).

12. Charles Fairman, *Reconstruction and Reunion 1864–88*, pt. 1 in *The Oliver Wendell Holmes Devise: History of the Supreme Court of the United States* (P. Freund, ed., 1971) vol. VI, p. 1341, 1365. Carpenter argued Slaughterhouse on January 11, 1872, and Bradwell on January 18. Slaughterhouse was reargued the following term, but Bradwell was not.

13. The equal protection clause received very little attention in debates. The reference to "equality" certainly forbade racial discrimination, but the prohibition applied only to the "protection of the laws." This did not mean that no law could discriminate, for proponents had been clear that section one of the fourteenth amendment did not apply to suffrage. Although Senator Howard said of the clause, "[T]his abolishes all class legislation in the states and does away with the injustice of subjecting one caste of persons to a code not applicable to another," he qualified the statement immediately by asserting it did not apply to voting. "The right of suffrage is not, in law, one of the privileges and immunities thus secured by the Constitution. It is merely the creature of law." *Globe, 39th Cong., 2nd Sess.* (1866) p. 2766. This suggests that Howard understood the "protection of the laws" to refer only to the "fundamental rights" secured by the privileges and immunities clause. Under this reading, it would first be necessary to establish that admission to the bar was a privilege

or immunity of citizenship before a court could find that gender restrictions violated the Fourteenth Amendment. See Raoul Berger, *Government by Judiciary* (1977); Jacobus Tenbroek, *Equal Under Law* (1965).

14. Bradwell v. Illinois, 21 *Lawyer's Edition* (1873) p. 444. (argument of Carpenter).

15. The *Slaughter-House Cases* dissenters, with the exception of Chief Justice Chase, concurred in *Bradwell*, joining in Justice Bradley's well-known opinion on the proper place of women.

16. Stanley Morrison, "Does the Fourteenth Amendment Incorporate the Bill of Rights? The Judicial Interpretation," 2 *Stanford Law Review* (1949) 140.

17. Palmer, Robert C., "The Parameters of Constitutional Reconstruction: *Slaughter-House*, *Cruikshank*, and the Fourteenth Amendment," 1984 *University of Illinois Law Review* (1984) 739–770; Newsom, Kevin Christopher, "Setting Incorporationism Straight: A Reinterpretation of the *Slaughter-House Cases*," 109 *Yale Law Journal* (2000) 643–744; Wildenthal, Bryan H., "The Lost Compromise: Reassessing the Early Understanding in Court and Congress on Incorporation of the Bill of Rights in the Fourteenth Amendment," 61 *Ohio State Law Journal* (2000) 1051–1173; Wildenthal, Bryan H., "The Road to Twining: Reassessing the Disincorporation of the Bill of Rights," 61 *Ohio State Law Journal* (2000) 1457–1528.

18. Edwards v. Elliott, 88 U.S. (21 Wall.) 532 (1874) (argument of D. McMahon for plaintiff in error 1874 Lexis 1393, p.22)

19. Edwards v. Elliott, (argument of A.Q. Keasbey, 1874 Lexis 1393, p. 31).

20. Charles Fairman, *Reconstruction and Reunion 1864–88,* pt. 2 in the *Oliver Wendell Holmes Devise: History of the Supreme Court of the United States* (P. Freund, ed., 1987) vol. VII, p. 263 n. 130.

21. Philip B. Kurland, "The Privileges or Immunities Clause: 'Its Hour Come Round At Last'?" 1972 *Washington University Law Quarterly* (1972) 405–420.

22. Kirk Kennedy, "Reaffirming the Natural Law Jurisprudence of Justice Clarence Thomas," 9 *Regent University Law Review* (1997) 33–87.

23. Kimberly Shankman and Roger Pilon, "Reviving the Privileges or Immunities Clause to Redress the Balance Among States, Individuals, and the Federal Government," 3 *Texas Review of Law & Policy* (1998) 1–48.

24. Michael McConnell, "The Right to Die and the Jurisprudence of Tradition," 1997 *Utah Law Review* (1997) 665–708. See also Derek Shaffer, "Note: Answering Justice Thomas in Saenz: Granting the Privileges or Immunities Clause Full Citizenship Within the Fourteenth Amendment," 52 *Stanford Law Review* (2000) 709–50.

25. See Steve France, Dusty Doctrines, *ABA Journal* (May 2001) p. 46–48.

26. Lawrence Tribe, "*Saenz* Sans Prophecy: Does the Privileges or Immunities Revival Portend the Future—Or Reveal the Structure of the Present?" 113 *Harvard Law Review* (1999) 110–98.

27. Daniel J. Levin, "Note: Reading the Privileges or Immunities Clause: Textual Irony, Analytical Revisionism, and an Interpretive Truce," 35 *Harvard Civil Rights—Civil Liberties Law Review* (2000) 569.

28. Lawrence Brenner, Marshall J.Hartman, Hon. Shelvin Singer, ret., "Criminal Justice in the Supreme Court: A Review of United States Supreme Court Decisions at the Close of the Millennium 1998–1999," 36 *California Western Law Review* (2000) 437.

29. See Jeffrey Rosen, "Translating the Privileges or Immunities Clause," 66 *George Washington Law Review* (1998) 1241–68.

30. Louis Henkin, "International Law as U.S. Law," 82 *Michigan Law Review* (1984): 1555; but see Philip R. Trimble, "A Revisionist View of Customary International Law," 33 *UCLA Law Review* (1985) 665 arguing that it is inappropriate to use it.

31. See James S. Gifford, "Jus Cogens and Fourteenth Amendment Privileges or Immunities: A Framework of Substantive, Fundamental Human Rights in a Constitutional Safe Harbor," 16 *Arizona Journal of International and Comparative Law* (1999) 481, 539. Note the references to international law in the decision in South Africa holding that the then interim constitution prohibited capital punishment. S v. Makwanyane, 1995 (3) SA 391 (CC).

Part III

Conclusion

The Court has consistently held that the privileges and immunities clause of Article IV only protects against discrimination by a state in favor of its own citizens. The two-part test of the court (whether a law involves a privilege or immunity of citizenship and whether different treatment is justified) is not a good approach. The inquiry into whether something is fundamental for purposes of the union breaks down into whether distinctions in the application of that law are justifiable, because unjustifiable distinctions would undermine the federal union.

The maintenance of the political community of the state justifies the restriction of political privileges to citizens of the state, and the contribution of residents to the resources of the state supports the restriction of certain state-provided goods and services to residents. Those include education, welfare, and other grants and subsidies. Where the services are critical to the ability of other citizens to come to the state and engage in commerce (e.g. police, roads, fire, etc.), they must be afforded to all. The state may have different rules for access to its courts to the extent that the procedural rules do not unreasonably impair the ability to vindicate substantive rights and are justified by the differences in amenability to process or by the lack of connection with the state as forum.

The Court has effectively repudiated any distinction between classification based on residence or state citizenship, recognizing that both pose the same danger to Article IV concerns and require justification. Article IV assures no discrimination by a state in the taxation of citizens of other states and in their access to business and job opportunities. The Court may someday use Article IV as the basis for the right to travel, but its current role is limited to protecting federalism through prohibiting discrimination against citizens of other states.

The privileges and immunities clause of the Fourteenth Amendment has no current role, because the tasks for which it was designed are being performed by the due process clause. Unless fear of aliens or a desire to revive a property-centered jurisprudence propels the Court to reverse more than a century of precedent, the near future will see only refinements on residency requirements with respect to the right to migrate. Nevertheless, before the twenty-first century ends, the clause may acquire global relevance and undergird the domestic application of international human rights. Until then it remains a spectator on the sidelines of the law, watching others battle in other ways for the fundamental human rights it was designed to secure.

Bibliographic Essay

PRIMARY SOURCE MATERIALS

No definitive work is available on the original meaning of privileges and immunities in English law at the beginning of colonization. The early colonial charters can be found in a fine collection edited by Francis N. Thorpe (*The Federal and State Constitutions, Colonial Charters, and Other Organic Laws of the States, Territories, and Colonies Now or Heretofore Forming the United States of America*, Francis N. Thorpe, editor. Washington, DC: GPO, 1909). The *Journals of the Continental Congress* contain the shifting drafts of Article IV of the Articles of Confederation (*Journals of the Continental Congress 1774–1789*, Worthington C. Ford, editor. Washington, D.C.: GPO, 1904–36). A small amount of discussion of those drafts by the delegates is contained in Edmund Burnett's classic collection of their letters (*Letters of the Members of the Continental Congress,* Edmund C. Burnett, editor. Washington, D.C.: Carnegie Institution, 1921–36). Paul Smith subsequently brought out an expanded collection of those letters (*Letters of Delegates to Congress*, Paul A. Smith, editor. Washington D.C.: Library of Congress 1976–85).

Max Farrand remains the best source for the records of the Constitutional Convention (*The Records of the Federal Convention of 1787*, Max Farrand, editor. 4 vols. New Haven, Conn.: Yale University Press, 1966). However, a nice edition of Madison's notes was brought out by Adrienne Koch (*Notes of the Debates in the Federal Convention of 1787 Reported by James Madison*, Adrienne Koch, editor. Athens, Ohio: Ohio University Press, 1966). *The Federalist Papers* are the most prominent source for contemporary discussion of the Constitution (*The Federalist Papers*, Clinton Rossiter, editor. New York: New American Library, 1961).

Alfred Avins' collection of the relevant sections of the debates from the Congressional Globe remains the most convenient collected source for reviewing the debates over the Fourteenth Amendment (*The Reconstruction Amendments' Debates: The Legislative History and Contemporary Debates in Congress on the 13th, 14th, and 15th Amendments*, Alfred Avins, editor. Richmond, Va.: Virginia Commission on Constitutional Government, 1967).

SECONDARY SOURCE MATERIAL

Article IV History

Only one book has been entirely devoted to the privileges and immunities clause of Article IV: Roger Howell, *The Privileges and Immunities of State Citizenship* (Baltimore: Johns Hopkins University, 1918). Dean Roger Howell argued that the clause could be traced to the treatment afforded alien merchants in England. In this connection, the King controlled the status of the foreigner and empowered aliens to engage in trade, but this can only be a small part of the origin, because the charter provisions go far beyond the privileges of aliens. Those privileges include the restrictions on the prerogative found in the Magna Carta. J.C. Holt, *Magna Carta* (Second Edition. Cambridge, England, Cambridge University Press, 1965, second edition 1992) is an excellent source for appreciating the Magna Carta's provisions in context. J.G.A. Pocock's groundbreaking work on the English appeal to the ancient constitution, *The Ancient Constitution and the Feudal Law* (Cambridge, England: Cambridge University Press, 1987), contains a nice discussion of the shift from appeals to history to Locke's appeal to reason. Locke's importance comes from the way in which he was understood, regardless of his intentions. Thus William Blackstone, *Commentaries on the Laws of England* (1765) (Special Edition 1983; The Legal Classics Library) is important evidence of privileges and immunities understanding.

One of the first works to address the history of the clause was David Bogen, "The Privileges and Immunities Clause of Article IV," 37 *Case Western Law Review* (1986–87) 794. Douglas Smith wrote a trio of articles on citizenship and the relationship of fundamental rights under Article IV to the Fourteenth Amendment privileges or immunities clause, "An Analysis of Two Federal Structures: The Articles of Confederation and the Constitution," "Citizenship and the Fourteenth Amendment," and "The Privileges and Immunities Clause of Article IV, Section 2, Precursor of Section 1 of the Fourteenth Amendment," 34 *San Diego Law Review* (1997) 249, 681, 809. Smith's articles canvas international jurisprudential works and he has an interesting discussion of the Roman law background for the phrase. Mortimer Sellers, *American Republicanism: Roman Ideology in the United States Constitution* (New York, N.Y.: New York University Press, 1994) demonstrates that the Roman model was important to American thought, but the book does not focus on the phrase in Article IV. James Kettner, *The Development of American Citizenship 1608–1870* (Chapel Hill, University of North Carolina Press, 1978) is the best work on the development of the concept of citizenship in America.

Privileges and immunities law has been tied to racial issues. Paul Finkelman, *An Imperfect Union: Slavery, Federalism and Comity* (Chapel Hill, N.C.: University of North Carolina Press, 1981) examined the impact of Article IV on interstate travel with slaves. The culmination of the relationship between citizenship and race was the Dred Scott decision. Donald Fehrenbacher, *The Dred Scott Case: Its Significance in American Law and Politics* (New York: Oxford University Press, 1978) is the leading historical treatment. Walter Ehrlich, *They Have No Rights: Dred Scott's Struggle for Freedom* (Westport, Conn.: Greenwood Press, 1979) is another good treatment that tracks the stages of the case. John Vishneski III, "What the Court Decided in Dred Scott v. Sandford," 32 *American Journal of Legal History* (1988) 372, analyzes the various justices' opinions to demonstrate that Chief Justice Taney had a majority for each point that he discussed in his opinion for the court.

Fourteenth Amendment History

There is virtual unanimity among scholars that the Court's interpretation of the privileges and immunities clause of the Fourteenth Amendment got it wrong. Thus scholarship tends to be devoted to an analysis of the history of the clause and proposals for change in the future. The unanimity among scholars that the Court misread history does not suggest any agreement about the correct interpretation of the clause or what role history should play in that interpretation.

The debates need to be put in a historical framework that understands the context of the times, the roles and politics of the various members of Congress, and the debates on ratification in the states including published discussion. A number of books and articles attempt to recount this history, although they come to quite different views of it.

The classic study of congressional intention in adopting the privileges and immunities clause by the courts was an article in the *Stanford Law Review* by Charles Fairman on the framer's intent, "Does the Fourteenth Amendment Incorporate the Bill of Rights? The Original Understanding," 2 *Stanford Law Review* (1949) 5. The article was intended to rebut Justice Black's contention that the amendment incorporated the Bill of Rights.

Raoul Berger has been the leader among scholars urging a narrow reading of the privileges or immunities clause. He contended that the Thirty-ninth Congress intended only to constitutionalize the Civil Rights Act of 1866. His main exposition is in Raoul Berger, *Government By Judiciary: The Transformation of the Fourteenth Amendment* (Second Edition. Indianapolis, Ind.: Liberty Fund, 1997). Berger cited Horace Flack, *The Adoption of the Fourteenth Amendment* (Baltimore, Md.: Johns Hopkins University Press, 1908) for the proposition that there was no statement at all on incorporation of the Bill of Rights in speeches and popular discussion concerning the Fourteenth Amendment during its ratification. Berger's position is supported by James Bond's study of ratification debates in several specific states,

"The Original Understanding of the Fourteenth Amendment in Illinois, Ohio, and Pennsylvania," 18 *Akron Law Review* (1985) 435. Bond's article indicated that discussion focused on the constitutionalization of the Civil Rights Act of 1866. Kenyon D. Bunch wrote "The Original Understanding of the Privileges and Immunities Clause: Michael Perry's "Justification for Judicial Activism or Robert Bork's Constitutional Inkblot?" 10 *Seton Hall Constitutional Law Journal* (2000) 321. This article supports Berger by contending that the clause should not be interpreted to mean more than the common minimal content that the supermajority necessary to pass a constitutional amendment would have agreed on. Bunch's theory has several problems, however, including the difficulty of assuming that radicals would have voted for a severely limited clause that could not expand.

In general, scholars supporting narrower views of the Fourteenth Amendment stress the racial prejudice among the moderate republicans that would have made them unwilling to support broad notions of equality beyond fundamental rights. Earl Maltz has written extensively on the antebellum understanding of Fourteenth Amendment concepts. He agreed with Berger on the narrowness of fundamental rights reflected from the Civil Rights Act of 1866, but he is more supportive of incorporation and more tolerant of ambiguity and uncertainty. His book is *Civil Rights, The Constitution, and Congress, 1863–1869* (Lawrence, Kan.: University Press of Kansas, 1990).

In *The Fourteenth Amendment: From Political Principle to Judicial Doctrine* (Cambridge, Mass.: Harvard University Press, 1988), Professor William Nelson took an equality-based approach to the interpretation controversy, relying on the references to privileges and immunities in Article IV. He argued that equality was the central notion of Fourteenth Amendment, and that the references to the Bill of Rights assumed that states had such rights in their own state constitutions so that an equality guaranty would make them applicable to everyone. Nelson contended that speakers rhetorically conflated equality guarantees with absolute rights, but he ultimately left open his position on interpretation. John Harrison, "Reconstructing the Privileges and Immunities Clause," 101 *Yale Law Journal* (1992) 1385, pressed the equality view of the Fourteenth Amendment more definitively.

Professor Michael Kent Curtis has been the leading scholar contending for incorporation of the Bill of Rights. He relies heavily on the statements of the leaders in both the House and the Senate (Bingham and Howard) who explicitly stated that they intended the Bill of Rights to be included in the meaning of privileges and immunities. Curtis has argued that Blackstone's characterization of basic liberties included historic rights from the Magna Carta, so that incorporation of basic individual rights from the Bill of Rights is reasonable. He convincingly demonstrated that the framers intended to apply the free speech clause of the Constitution to the states through Section 1 of the Fourteenth Amendment. Like Justice Black, Curtis found the specifics of natural rights much more problematic than incorporation. Curtis presents his argument in his book *No State Shall Abridge:*

The Fourteenth Amendment and the Bill of Rights (Durham, N.C.: Duke University Press, 1986).

Perhaps the greatest difficulty with Curtis' arguments has been the provisions inconsistent with the Bill of Rights in the statutes or constitution of several states that supported the Fourteenth Amendment ratification. The failure in those states to raise the inconsistency as an argument against the amendment suggests that they did not recognize any inconsistency. Only some form of selective incorporation would be consistent with that behavior. That is the result of Professor Akil Amar's most recent and much discussed approach to the privileges and immunities clause and the issue of incorporation, or "refined incorporation." Amar argues that the original Bill of Rights was strongly structural, designed to protect the central role of the states and the majority from the corruption of a government losing touch with the "people." In turn, Reconstruction changed the understanding of the problems to focus on individual liberties and worked a change on the provisions even as it incorporated them. Amar contends that "privileges and immunities" incorporate the provisions of the first ten amendments that were personal rights, while not affecting those concerned with federalism, recognizing that social changes before the Civil War affected whether a right was a personal right or a federalism concern. Amar's book is *The Bill of Rights: Creation and Reconstruction* (New Haven, Conn.: Yale University Press, 1998).

Not everyone agrees. Richard Aynes, supporting total incorporation, noted that the framers referred to the Bill of Rights and the bill included all eight amendments. See Richard Aynes, "Refined Incorporation and the Fourteenth Amendment," 33 *University of Richmond Law Review* (1999) 289. In his article "Akhil Amar on Criminal Procedure and Constitutional Law: 'Here I Go Down That Wrong Road Again,'" 74 *North Carolina Law Review* (1996) 1559, Donald Drips argued that Amar's use of privileges and immunities caused him to undervalue due process as the basis for incorporating criminal procedure safeguards. Drips does not adhere to incorporation, but would focus on needed safeguards. Others agree with Amar's basic proposition, but disagree over whether particular rights are those of federalism or individual rights. One example is Kurt Lash, "Two Movements of a Constitutional Symphony: Akhil Reed Amar's The Bill of Rights," 33 *University of Richmond Law Review* (1999) 485.

The distinction between framer's intent and the meaning of a clause has provoked a number of interesting discussions. An outstanding student note that provides perspective on the debate is Timothy M. Bishop's "Comment: The Privileges or Immunities Clause of the Fourteenth Amendment: The Original Intent," 79 *Northwestern University Law Review* (1984) 142. Members of Congress believed the clause protected only civil and not political rights, but Bishop argued there is no principled intentionalist method for choosing between competing versions of intent. Roderick Hills presents a similar argument in his article "Back to the Future? How the Bill of Rights Might Be About Structure After All. The Bill of Rights: Creation and Reconstruction. By Akhil Reed Amar," 93 *Northwestern University Law Review* (1999): 977. Hills argued that the ideas of the framers on what was necessary to protect federal liberties were incoherent and practically unworkable. For example, in Strauder v. West Virginia (1879), which involved the exclusion of African-Americans from the jury, one cannot protect the personal privileges and immunities (of a defendant) as the framers sought without disregarding the framers' command not to enforce the citizen's political rights (of the jurors). Brent Boyce questioned the utility of an originalist interpretation in "Originalism and the Fourteenth Amendment," 33 *Wake Forest Law Review* (1998) 909. In the article, he summarized and critiqued the originalist approaches of a host of current legal scholars—Akil Amar, Raoul Berger, Michael Curtis, John Harrison, Earl Maltz, and Michael McConnell. Boyce argued that originalism leads to bad results, noting that the radical constitutionalism which led to the Fourteenth Amendment was itself premised on a rejection of originalism.

Controversy Over the *Slaughter-House Cases* and Incorporation

For many years, it was assumed that the *Slaughter-House Cases* decision of Justice Miller denied any significance to the privileges and immunities clause. Stanley Morrison wrote the leading article in 1949 as a companion to Fairman's work on the intent of the framers. In his article, "Does the Fourteenth Amendment Incorporate the Bill of Rights? The Judicial Interpretation," 2 *Stanford Law Review* (1949) 140, he contended that the Court continuously denied that the Fourteenth Amendment incorporated the Bill of Rights. A half-century later, a number of articles have insisted that Miller supported incorporation in his *Slaughter-House Cases* opinion. Robert C. Palmer wrote an article, in which he argued that Miller reversed himself in *Cruikshank.* Palmer's article is entitled "The Parameters of Constitutional Reconstruction: *Slaughter-House*, *Cruikshank*, and the Fourteenth Amendment," 1984 *University of Illinois Law Review* (1984): 739. Kevin Christopher Newsom wrote "Setting Incorporationism Straight: A Reinterpretation of the *Slaughter-House Cases*," 109 *Yale Law Journal* (2000): 643. In the article, Newsom contends that Miller's decisions were consistent with incorporation, except possibly with respect to the civil jury. Bryan Wildenthal agreed with Newsom and Palmer that Miller initially supported incorporation, but Wildenthal concluded that Miller and the rest of the court abandoned that position within a few years. Wildenthal advanced this argument in "The Lost Compromise: Reassessing the Early Understanding in Court and Congress on Incorporation of the Bill of Rights in the Fourteenth Amendment," 61 *Ohio State Law Journal* 61 (2000) 1051. In another article Wildenthal traces the decisions that ultimately resulted in abandoning the privileges and immunities clause as a basis for incorporation to suggest that the issue remained a live one for decades. That article is entitled "The Road to Twining:

Reassessing the Disincorporation of the Bill of Rights," 61 *Ohio State Law Journal* (2000) 1457. The articles are all fine pieces of work supporting an alternative vision, but the consistent rejection of fundamental rights in Miller's opinion and the concerns voiced in the Reconstruction Congress are persuasive that later decisions correctly perceived Miller as rejecting any form of incorporation.

Article IV Analysis

Professor Chester Antieu has argued that the privileges and immunities clause of Article IV should guarantee to the citizens of each state the natural and fundamental rights inherent in the citizenship of all persons in a free society, following the views of some of the Republican congressmen in the debates on the Fourteenth Amendment. Antieu discussed this in "Paul's Perverted Privileges or the True Meaning of the Privileges and Immunities Clause of Article IV," 9 *William & Mary Law Review* (1967) 1. However, his idiosyncratic views have been rejected by the Court and other scholars. At most the fundamental rights concept limited the scope of the antidiscrimination reach of Article IV.

The idea of *fundamental rights* has had little appeal to scholars critiquing the decisions of the Court. The Court has repudiated the natural rights sense of the term, and the remaining sense of significance to the union is not a viable criteria. Professor Gary Simson was one of the first to effectively attack this new sense of the term as incoherent, and he urged the court to apply the clause to all residence distinctions and find that they are valid only if necessary to serve a significant state objective. Simson advances this argument in his article "Discrimination Against Nonresidents and the Privileges and Immunities Clause of Article IV," 128 *University of Pennsylvania Law Review* (1979) 379, Several years later, Jonathan Varat also attacked the fundamental interest distinction, pointing out the confusion with equal protection doctrine. His thoughtful discussion is the best article on the interests that could justify differences between residents and nonresidents with respect to public benefits. The article is "State 'Citizenship' and Interstate Equality," 48 *University of Chicago Law Review* (1981) 487. Another fine attempt to set forth the interests justifying differences is Mark Gergen, "The Selfish State and the Market," 66 *Texas Law Review* (1988) 1097. Gergen focused on a market efficiency rationale. Varat and Gergen are among a group of scholars who call for an end to the exclusion of corporations from the definition of citizen in Article IV. They were not impassioned on the point, however, because the clause was not central to their vision of maintaining free trade. Other scholars, like Julian Eule and George Carpinello, made reversal of the corporate exclusion central to their articles because they would give greater prominence to the economic impact of the privileges and immunities clause and diminish reliance on the dormant commerce clause. Their articles are George F. Carpinello, "State Protective Legislation and Nonresident Corporations: The Privileges and Immunities Clause as a Treaty of Nondiscrimination," 73 *Iowa*

Law Review (1988) 351; and Julian Eule, "Laying the Dormant Commerce Clause to Rest," 91 *Yale Law Journal* (1982) 425.

Finally, the leading work on the potential impact of the privileges and immunities clause of Article IV on conflict of laws is Brainerd Currie and Herma Hill Shreter, "Unconstitutional Discrimination in the Conflict of Laws: Privileges and Immunities," 69 *Yale Law Journal* (1960) 1323. After brilliantly attacking the resident-citizen distinction, Currie and Herma Hill Kay (then Shreter) reconciled most of the conflict of law cases, arguing that forum non conveniens is legitimate where neither party is in state and the state has no interest in case, and that statute of limitations cases are explicable as respecting policies of other states to the extent that forum state has no interest in the case.

Fourteenth Amendment Analysis

There are two types of articles on the current analysis of the privileges and immunities clause. One accepts the *Slaughter-House Cases* as controlling, and analyzes rights based on the structure of the Union, possibly limited to travel. Very few books or articles discuss in any detail what other inferences can be drawn from the structure of the Union as matters of individual rights. The cases rarely mention the clause, even when they make inferences from the structure of the Constitution, because the clause itself is not the source of the right. Thus articles on the individual rights recognized by the Court as privileges and immunities of U.S. citizenship discuss the right to travel.

William Cohen foretold the turn that the Court would take, while emphasizing the citizenship sentence of the Fourteenth Amendment in his article, "Discrimination Against New State Citizens: An Update," 11 *Constitutional Commentary* (1994) 73. Jide Nzelibe argued that the right to travel is designed to promote political and economic union against provincial state interests rather than protecting individuals. Thus he contended that states should be able to limit it where there is a substantial state interest, and that Congress should be able to authorize state limitations. Nzelibe's article is entitled "Free Movement: A Federalist Reinterpretation," 49 *American University Law Review* (1999) 433. The Court, however, took a different view in *Saenz*. Subsequently, Roderick Hills wrote an interesting analysis of right to travel issues, "Poverty, Residency, and Federalism: States' Duty of Impartiality Toward Newcomers," 1999 *Supreme Court Review* (1999) 277. In it, he argued that residency can be differently defined for redistributive and allocative functions. Hills pointed out that *Saenz* ignores difficult issues on defining residents. He contended that subsidy-motivated migrants undermine a state's incentives to maintain redistributive programs, so it should be legitimate to limit eligibility, much as the court has done under Article IV. On the other hand, it is not legitimate to treat newcomers as unwelcome strangers because of cultural or social hostility. Hills concluded that welfare durational rules are too likely to be based on the latter, so the outcome in *Saenz* was correct. Nan Ellis and Cheryl Miller argued that empirical evidence suggests that the race to the bottom has not occurred. Their article is entitled "Welfare Waiting Periods: A Public Policy Analysis of Saenz v. Roe," 11 *Stanford Law & Policy Review* (2000) 343.

Scholars not reconciled to *Slaughter-House* have urged a *fundamental rights* reading of the Fourteenth Amendment. The debate over incorporation has been largely historical. The debate over fundamental rights in the literature has been more forward looking. Prior to his elevation to the Supreme Court, Justice Thomas suggested invoking natural law in his essay, "The Higher Law Background of the Privileges or Immunities Clause of the Fourteenth Amendment," 12 *Harvard Journal of Law & Public Policy* (1989) 63. His subsequent opinions like *Saenz* suggest that Justice Thomas maintains this view, as anticipated in Kirk A. Kennedy, "Reaffirming the Natural Law Jurisprudence of Justice Clarence Thomas," 9 *Regent University Law Review* (1997) 33. Some conservatives believe that a natural law interpretation would be restricted by history and tradition while potentially reviving some protections against arbitrary government (likely to be particularly important with restrictions on contract and property). Kimberly Shankman and Roger Pilon urge the revival of the clause in "Reviving the Privileges or Immunities Clause to Redress the Balance Among States, Individuals, and the Federal Government," 3 *Texas Review of Law & Politics* (1998). Michael McConnell suggested the restraints of history while he was a professor in his article "The Right to Die and the Jurisprudence of Tradition," 1997 *Utah Law Review* (1997) 665. Derek Shaffer argued in a student note that the clause should be effective as a limit on government only where there is consensus: "Note: Answering Justice Thomas in Saenz: Granting the Privileges or Immunities Clause Full Citizenship Within the Fourteenth Amendment," 52 *Stanford Law Review* (2000) 709.

Scholars with a very different view of basic rights have also supported a fundamental rights interpretation of privileges and immunities. Philip Kurland began the modern academic consideration of the clause's potential with an article in the Wisconsin Law Review, "The Privileges or Immunities Clause: 'Its Hour Come Round At Last'?" 1972 *Wisconsin Law Review* (1972) 405. Kurland suggested that the clause might be used as a basis for the right of privacy and to secure minimum standards of quality in government-provided goods and services. Perhaps the most elaborate articulation comes in John Denvir, *Democracy's Constitution: Claiming the Privileges of American Citizenship* (Urbana: University of Illinois Press, 2001). Denvir argues that the Fourteenth Amendment privileges and immunities clause supports rights to assistance and voting rights because they are basic to citizenship. Lawrence Tribe also supports a broad range of rights based on citizenship in a liberal framework, which he finds based on a core notion of individual self-government. Tribe considered the potential for the court to shift in "Comment: Saenz Sans Prophecy: Does the Privileges or Immunities Revival Portend the Future—or Reveal the Structure of the Present?" 113 *Harvard Law Review* (1999) 110.

Academics who seek to go back to the original meaning of the privileges and immunities clause and make it do the work of due process and equal protection would disrupt precedent with only marginal gains possible. Thus Jeffrey Rosen has pointed out the questionable benefits of this interpretation in his article "Translating the Privileges or Immunities Clause," 66 *George Washington Law Review* (1998) 1241.

Table of Cases

Adamson v. California, 332 U.S. 46 (1947)
Ambach v. Norwick, 441 U.S. 68 (1979)
Amy v. Smith, 11 Ky. (1 Litt.) 326 (1822)
Armour & Co. v. Virginia, 246 U.S. 1 (1918)
Attorney Gen. of New York v. Soto-Lopez, 476 U.S. 898 (1986)
Austin v. New Hampshire, 420 U.S. 656 (1975)
Baldwin v. Fish and Game Commission of Montana, 436 U.S. 371 (1978)
Ballard v. Hunter, 204 U.S. 241 (1907)
Bank of Augusta v. Earle, 38 U.S. (13 Peters) 519 (1839)
Barnard v. Thorstenn, 489 U.S. 546 (1989)
Barron v. Baltimore, 32 U.S. (7 Pet.) 243 (1833)
Bartemeyer v. Iowa, 85 U.S. 129 (1874)
Bernal v. Fainter, 467 U.S. 216 (1984)
Blake v. McClung, 172 U.S. 239 (1898)
Bradwell v. Illinois, 83 U.S. (16 Wall.) 130 (1873)
Brown v. Maryland, 25 U.S. (12 Wheat.) 419 (1827)
Board of Education v. Illinois, 203 U.S. 553 (1906)
Cabell v. Chavez-Salido, 454 U.S. 432 (1982)
Calder v. Bull, 3 U.S. (3 Dall.) 386 (1798)
Calvin's Case (1608), 2 WHARTON'S STATE TRIALS 607–58
Campbell v. Morris, 3 H & McH. 535 (Md. 1797)
Canadian Northern Ry v. Eggen, 252 U.S. 553 (1920)
Chalker v. Birmingham & N.W. Ry. Co. 249 U.S. 522 (1919)
Chambers v. Baltimore & O.R. Co., 207 U.S. 142 (1907)
Chemung Canal Bank v. Lowery, 93 U.S. (3 Otto) 72 (1876)
Chicago, B. & Q. R. Co. v. Chicago, 166 U.S. 226 (1897)
Civil Rights Cases, 109 U.S. 3 (1883)
Colgate v. Harvey, 296 U.S. 404 (1935)
Commonwealth v. Aves, 35 Mass. (18 Pick.) 193 (1836)

Conner v. Elliot, 59 U.S. (18 How.) 591 (1856)
Cooley v. Board of Wardens, 53 U.S. (12 How.) 299 (1851)
Corfield v. Coryell, 6 F. Cas. 546 (Cir. Ct. E.D. Pa. 1823)
Cox v. Texas, 202 U.S. 446 (1906)
Crandall v. Nevada, 73 U.S. (6 Wall.) 35 (1867)
Crane v. Campbell, 245 U.S. 304 (1917)
Crowley v. Christensen, 137 U.S. 86 (1890)
Cruikshank, United States v., 92 U.S. 542 (1876)
Cumming v. Richmond County Board of Education, 175 U.S. 528 (1899)
Davidson v. New Orleans, 96 U.S. 97 (1878)
Douglas v. New York, N. H & H. R. Co., 279 U.S. 377 (1929)
Dred Scott v. Sandford, 60 U.S. (19 How.) 393 (1857)
Duncan v. Louisiana, 391 U.S. 145 (1968)
Edwards v. California, 314 U.S. 160 (1941)
Edwards v. Elliott, 88 U.S. (21 Wall.) 532 (1874)
Ferry v. Spokane, Portland & Seattle Ry., 258 U.S. 315 (1922)
Fletcher v. Peck, 10 U.S. (6 Cranch) 87 (1810)
Foley v. Connelie, 435 U.S. 291 (1978)
Gibbons v. Ogden, 22 U.S. (9 Wheat.) 1 (1824)
Giozza v. Tiernan, 148 U.S. 657 (1893)
Gitlow v. New York, 268 U.S. 652 (1925)
Guest, United States v., 383 U.S. 745 (1966)
Hague v. C.I.O., 307 U.S. 496 (1939)
Halter v. Nebraska, 205 U.S. 34 (1907)
Hamilton v. Regents of the University of California, 293 U.S. 245 (1934)
Harris, United States v., 106 U.S. 629 (1883)
Hemphill v. Orloff, 277 U.S. 537 (1928)
Henry L. Doherty and Co. v. Goodman, 294 U.S. 623 (1935)
Hicklin v. Orbeck, 437 U.S. 518 (1978)
Holden v. Hardy, 169 U.S. 366 (1898)
Hurtado v. California, 110 U.S. 516 (1884)
Iowa Central Ry. v. Iowa, 160 U.S. 389 (1896)
Kane v. New Jersey, 242 U.S. 160 (1916)
Kirtland v. Hotchkiss, 100 U.S. 491 (1880)
LaTourette v. McMaster, 248 U.S. 465 (1919)
Lemmon v. People, 20 N.Y. 562 (1860)
Lochner v. New York, 198 U.S. 45 (1905)
Lockwood, In re, 154 U.S. 116 (1894)
Logan v. United States, 144 U.S. 263 (1892)
Low v. Austin, 80 U.S. (13 Wall.) 29 (1871)
Lunding v. New York Tax Appeals Tribunal, 522 U.S. 287 (1998)
Madden v. Kentucky, 309 U.S. 83 (1940)
Martinez v. Bynum, 461 U.S. 321 (1983)
Maxwell v. Bugbee, 250 U.S. 525 (1919)
Maxwell v. Dow, 176 U.S. 581 (1900)
McCarthy v. Philadelphia Civil Service Commission, 424 U.S. 645 (1976)

McCready v. Virginia, 94 U.S. (4 Otto) 391 (1876)
McCulloch v. Maryland, 17 U.S. (4 Wheat.) 316 (1819)
Metropolitan Life Ins. Co. v. Ward, 470 U.S. 869 (1985)
Minor v. Happersett, 88 U.S. (21 Wall.) 162 (1874)
Missouri Pacific Ry. Co. v. Castle, 224 U.S. 541 (1912)
Mullaney v. Anderson, 342 U.S. 415 (1952)
Northeast Bancorp, Inc. v. Board of Governors of Federal Reserve System, 472 U.S. 159 (1985)
Omaechevarria v. Idaho, 246 U.S. 343 (1918)
O'Neil v. Vermont, 144 U.S. 323 (1892).
Orient Insurance Co. v. Daggs, 172 U.S. 557 (1899)
Orr v. Gilman, 183 U.S. 278 (1902)
Ownbey v. Morgan, 256 U.S. 94 (1921)
Passenger Cases, 48 U.S. (7 How.) 283 (1849)
Paul v. Virginia, 75 U.S. (8 Wall.) 168 (1868)
Pendleton v. State, 6 Ark. 509 (1846)
Plessy v. Ferguson, 163 U.S. 537 (1896)
Porter v. Wilson, 239 U.S. 170 (1915)
Presser v. Illinois, 116 U.S. 252 (1886)
Prudential Ins. Co. v. Cheek, 259 U.S. 530 (1922)
Quarles, In re, 158 U.S. 532 (1895)
Reese, United States v., 92 U.S. 214 (1876)
Reeves v. Stake, 447 U.S. 429 (1980)
Rosario v. Rockefeller, 410 U.S. 752 (1973)
Rosenthal v. New York, 226 U.S. 260 (1912)
Saenz v. Roe, 526 U.S. 489 (1999)
Selover, Bates & Co. v. Walsh, 226 U.S. 112 (1912)
Shaffer v. Carter, 252 U.S. 37 (1920)
Shapiro v. Thompson, 394 U.S. 618 (1969)
Slaughter-House Cases, 83 U.S. (16 Wall.) 36 (1873)
Sosna v. Iowa, 419 U.S. 393 (1975)
Spies v. Illinois, 123 U.S. 131 (1887)
Starns v. Malkerson, 401 U.S. 985 (1971)
State v. Claiborne, 19 Tenn. (Meigs) 331 (1838)
State v. Newsome, 27 N.C. 181 (1844)
Strauder v. Graham, 51 U.S. (10 How.) 82 (1851)
Strauder v. West Virginia, 100 U.S. 303 (1879)
Sturgis v. Washington , 414 U.S. 1057 (1973)
Sugarman v. Dougall, 413 U.S. 634 (1973)
Supreme Court of New Hampshire v. Piper, 470 U.S. 274 (1985)
Supreme Court of Virginia v. Friedman, 487 U.S. 59 (1988)
Toomer v. Witsell, 334 U.S. 385 (1948)
Travellers Ins. Co. v. Connecticut, 185 U.S. 364 (1902)
Travis v. Yale & Towne Mfg. Co., 252 U.S. 60 (1920)
Twining v. New Jersey, 211 U.S. 78 (1908)
Twitchell v. The Commonwealth, 74 U.S. (7 Wall.) 321 (1869)

Tyler Pipe Indus. v. Washington Department of Revenue, 483 U.S. 232 (1987)
United Bldg. and Constr. Trades Council of County of Camden and Vicinity v. Mayor and Council of City of Camden, 465 U.S. 208 (1984)
Waddell, United States v.,112 U.S. 76 (1884)
Walker v. Sauvinet, 92 U.S. 90 (1876)
Ward v. Maryland, 79 U.S. (12 Wall.) 418 (1870)
Ward v. Morris, 4 H. & McH. 330 (Md. 1799)
Washington v. Glucksberg, 521 U.S. 702 (1997)
Waugh v. Board of Trustees, 237 U.S. 589 (1915)
West v. Louisiana, 194 U.S. 258 (1904)
Western and Southern Life Ins. Co. v. State Bd. of Equalization of California, 451 U.S. 648 (1981)
Western Turf Ass'n v. Greenberg, 204 U.S. 359 (1907)
Western Union v. Commercial Milling Co., 218 U.S. 406 (1910)
Wheeler, United States v., 254 U.S. 281 (1920)
White v. Massachusetts Council of Construction Employers Inc., 460 U.S. 204 (1983)
Wiley v. Parmer, 14 Ala. 627 (1848)
Wiley v. Sinkler, 179 U.S. 58 (1900)
Williams v. Fears, 179 U.S. 270 (1900)
Wilmington Star Mining Co. v. Fulton, 205 U.S. 60 (1907)
Worcester v. Georgia, 31 U.S. (6 Pet.) 515 (1832)
Yarbrough, Ex parte, 110 U.S. 651 (1884)
Zobel v. Williams 457 U.S. 55 (1982)

Index

Abolition of slavery: 15, 31, 38–40, 43, 53

African-Americans: Articles of Confederation application to, 12; Constitutional Convention consideration of citizenship under Article IV, 18; denied citizen status in antebellum state courts, 28; denied citizen status in *Dred Scott*, 32–36, 51, 99; effect of Thirteenth Amendment on status as citizens, 39–41, 43; citizenship declaration in Civil Rights Act, 41, 43, 49; Fourteenth Amendment as establishing citizen status, 37, 38, 53; discrimination against, 39, 42, 53, 112, 125; privileges and immunities not a source of constitutional protection, 105

aliens: exclusion from rights of citizens 2, 3, 6, 22, 115, 118, 140; naturalization of, 6, 17, 32–34; equal protection rights, 75, 76; due process rights, 115, 118, 140

Amar, Akil: 37, 38

American Revolution: 1, 4, 10, 25

anti-slavery constitutionalists: 31

Aquinas, Thomas: 8

Articles of Confederation Article IV: adoption, 11–16; committee on effect comments on, 16; free inhabitants of each state entitled, 12; ingress and egress to and from states, 11, 14, 15, 19, 24, 99, 100, 134; paupers, vagabonds and fugitives from justice excepted, 12, 13, 19; privileges and immunities of free citizens, 11–13; privileges of trade and commerce, 11, 14, 15; property immunities of federal and state government, 11, 15, 16; property removal to state where owner resides, 11, 14, 15; purpose of Article, 13, 24; relationship to Article IV of Constitution, 12, 17–21, 70–73, 99, 100

Article IV, § 2, Cl. 3 of Constitution: Constitutional Convention discussion, 16–21; Articles of Confederation model for Pinckney proposal, 17, 18; draft of committee of detail, 17–19; impact on Pennsylvania's treatment of aliens, 19, 20; rejection of protection for property in slaves, 20–21; amendment of Mason on property removal not offered, 20; Federalist on, 17, 18, 21; relationship to Fourteenth Amendment: 38, 44–58, 101–103

attachment: of nonresident property within state, 21, 22, 27; by nonresident, 129

Attorney: residence requirement denies Article IV privilege to citizens of a state, 75; admission to bar not a Fourteenth Amendment privilege of citizens of the United States, 105

Berger, Raoul: 37

Bill of Rights: held inapplicable to the states in *Barron*, 27, 45, 107, 110; references to in debates on Fourteenth Amendment, 44–50; not privileges or immunities of citizens of the United States, 107–122; First Amendment freedom of religion, 39, 111; First Amendment freedom of speech and press, 35, 37, 39, 50, 108, 110, 111, 120, 121, 128; First Amendment right to peaceably assemble, 35, 37, 39, 111–113, 116, 121, 128; Second Amendment right to bear arms, 112, 113, 116, 119; Fourth Amendment protection against unreasonable search and seizure, 111; Fifth Amendment just compensation requirement for takings for public use, 114, 115, 117; Fifth Amendment grand jury indictment, 115, 120, 122, 140; Fifth Amendment privilege against self-incrimination, 119–122, 140; Sixth Amendment right to be informed of nature and cause of accusation, 110; Sixth Amendment right to confront witnesses, 120; Sixth Amendment right to trial by jury in criminal cases, 110, 117, 118, 122, 140; Seventh Amendment right to trial by jury in civil cases, 111, 113, 114, 119, 122, 140; Eighth Amendment rights against cruel and unusual punishment, 7, 116; most made applicable to states by due process clause of Fourteenth Amendment, 111, 117, 120–122

Bill of Rights of 1689: 7, 8

Bingham, Representative John: speeches as basis for argument on incorporation of Bill of Rights, 37, 38; opposition to Civil Rights Act on constitutional grounds, 42; belief that federal government lacked power to enforce fundamental rights, 42, 45; identification of privileges and immunities clause of Article IV with fundamental rights including Bill of Rights, 42, 44, 45; initial proposal for Fourteenth Amendment to empower Congress, 44–47; second proposal for Fourteenth Amendment, 47–49; voting not a privilege or immunity of Fourteenth Amendment, 49

Black, Justice Hugo: 108, 109, 121, 122, 132, 140

Blackmun, Justice Harry: 26, 78, 79, 90

Blackstone, William: 8, 9, 23, 139

bond: as condition of nonresident suit, 91, 92, 129; as condition for nonresident conducting business within state, 69, 72

Boyer, Representative Benjamin: 49

Bradley, Justice Joseph: 106, 107, 110–112, 114

Brandeis, Justice Louis: 131

Brewer, Justice David: 116, 119

Broomall, Representative John: 42, 49

Burchard, Representative Horatio: 54

Burke, Thomas: 14, 15

Calvin's Case: 2, 13

Campbell, Justice John A.: 101

Cardozo, Justice Nathan: 131

Carpenter, Senator Matthew: on congressional power to enforce privileges and immunities of Fourteenth Amendment, 55, 56, 105; argument in *Bradwell*, 105; Argument in *Slaughter-House Cases*, 105

Chafee, Zecharaiah: 18

charters of colonies: 1–5, 10, 11, 13, 14

Chase, Judge Jeremiah Townley: 22, 23, 25, 27, 29

Chase, Justice Samuel: 25

Chase, Chief Justice Salmon P.: 110

Cicero: 8

citizens: free African-Americans as, 12, 18, 28, 32–41, 43, 53; status determined by states prior to the Constitution, 17, 18; disagreement in *Dred Scott* on determination of native born persons

status as, 33–36; of a state determined by residence and United States citizenship under the Fourteenth Amendment, 50, 51; of the United States defined in Civil Rights Act of 1866, 41–43; of the United States defined in Fourteenth Amendment, 50, 51; of a state distinguished from residents, 86–88, 97, 98; dichotomy between citizens and residents under Article IV rejected, 86, 95
civil rights: of all persons, 23; inequality in as badge of servitude, 40, 41; contract as, 41; domicile as, 42; *habeas corpus* as, 42; legal capacity to sue and be sued as, 41, 42; personal security as, 41, 42; property acquisition and enjoyment as, 41, 42; speech as, 42; testimony as, 42; transit through states as, 42; political rights excluded from definition, 41, 42; not jury service, 41, 42; not school, 41, 42; phrase deleted from Civil Rights Act of 1866, 37, 42
Civil Rights Act of 1866: debate on, 39–43; constitutionality of, 39–44, 49; deletion of *civil rights and immunities*, 37, 42; fundamental rights compared with *Corfield*, 40; insertion of "as enjoyed by white citizens," 41; relationship to Fourteenth Amendment, 37, 39, 49–52
Civil Rights Bill of 1872: 56, 57, 102
Civil War: 21, 28, 31, 36, 38, 40, 44, 67, 70, 71, 112
Clifford, Justice Nathan: 112, 114
Coke, Edward: judge in *Calvin's Case*, 2; on Magna Carta and the ancient constitution in *Institutes*, 7, 8
commerce power: effect on Article IV, 18; importance for economic common market, 27; basis for abolitionists argument on abolition of slavery in territories, 31; dormant commerce clause doctrine, 28, 72–74, 81, 83, 84, 129, 131–133
common law: 3, 8, 10, 56, 70, 96, 113, 114, 120
Constitution of the United States: see Article IV, Bill of Rights, commerce power, due process, equal protection, privileges and immunities of state citizens, privileges and immunities of United States citizens, supremacy clause, Thirteenth Amendment, Fourteenth Amendment, and Fifteenth Amendment
Constitutional Convention: reasons for, 16; rival plans offered at, 17; committee on detail report, 17–19; committee on style, 20; discussion of privileges and immunities clause at, 19–21
Continental Congress: Articles of Confederation adoption by, 11–16; Declaration and Resolves of, 10
contract: rights in colonies, 4, 6; social, 8; constitutional prohibition against impairing obligation of, 26, 110; considered fundamental right, 40, 42, 44, 49, 50, 56, 68, 91; resident preference in state contracts, 83–85; fear of federal regulation of, 102; not privilege of citizens of United States, 105
Corfield: 21, 23–27, 40, 46, 49–51, 54, 70, 74, 77, 78, 99, 103, 107, 124, 138
corporation: as citizen under Article III, 71; not citizen for purposes of Article IV, 67, 70–74, 129; not citizen under Fourteenth Amendment, 129, 140
Cowan, Senator Edgar: 40
Currie, Brainerd: 96
Curtis, Justice Benjamin: 30, 33, 35
Curtis, Michael: 37, 107, 140

Daniel, Justice Peter: 33
Declaration of Independence: 6, 23, 31, 48
Delano, Representative Columbus: 42
discrimination: against aliens, 2, 3, 6, 11, 16, 19, 20, 22, 69, 75, 76, 128, 140; against nonresidents or citizens of other states, see privileges and immunities of citizens of a state; gender, 34, 74, 105, 124, 125; racial, 12, 18, 28, 33–36, 39–44, 48, 49, 52, 53, 55, 56, 99, 101, 105, 124, 125; religion, 5, 39, 111
Douglas, Justice William O.: 122, 132, 135

Dred Scott: 32–36, 40, 41, 51, 67, 70, 99, 123
due process: right in Magna Carta, 4, 7, 9; in Fifth Amendment 31, 36, 45, 46, 48; as privilege of citizens under Article IV, 44, 46; Fourteenth Amendment, 47, 100, 105, 126, 129, 131, 142; jurisdiction limit, 92, 93, 130; substantive, 36, 106, 131, 132, 138–40; as incorporating some of the Bill of Rights against state, 58, 107–122, 128, 140

elective office: residence requirement for in colonies, 6; restriction of federal offices to citizens of U.S., 19; may be restricted to state citizens, 75
Enforcement Act of 1870: 125
Enforcement Act of 1871 (Anti–Ku Klux Klan Act): 53–56, 102, 105
England: 1–11, 24, 110
equal protection: 44, 47, 48, 54, 55, 69, 72, 73, 75, 79, 80, 85, 88, 100, 102, 105, 106, 111, 126, 129–132, 134, 136, 138, 140, 142

Farnsworth, Representative John: 48, 54
federalism: 26, 31, 38, 51, 70, 74, 76, 82, 102
Federalist Papers, The: 5, 15, 17, 21, 71
Fessenden, Senator William: 49
Field, Justice Stephen J.: on corporations as citizens under Article IV in *Paul*, 69, 71; dissent in *Slaughter-House Cases* claiming fundamental rights were Fourteenth Amendment privileges, 104–106, 108, 110, 119; dissent in *Walker*, 114; dissent in *O'Neil* urging incorporation of cruel and unusual punishment, 116, 117, 119
Fifteenth Amendment: 104, 123–125
fisheries: 74, 77, 78
forum non conveniens: 97–99
Fourteenth Amendment: debates in Congress on, 36–53, 101; first proposal, 44–47; second proposal, 47–53; post-adoption discussion, 53–58; Section 5 enforcement power, 54–57, 102, 123; see also due process, equal protection, privileges and immunities
freedom of speech: as privilege of citizen of state, 35; denial reason for constitutional amendment, 37, 39, 50; not privilege of U.S. citizenship, 108; fundamental right, 110; secured against states by due process clause, 121, 128
fugitives: exception in Articles of Confederation for paupers, vagabonds, and fugitives, 12, 13, 19; fugitive slave clause of Constitution, 19, 30, 31, 45
fundamental rights: of citizens described by Blackstone, 8, 9; of citizens in Article IV described in *Corfield*, 22–27; violated by slavery, 30–31, 39; of citizens described by Taney in *Dred Scott*, 35; denied African-Americans, 38–41; as basis for Civil Rights Act of 1866, 39–43; as basis for privilege and immunities clause in Fourteenth Amendment, 37, 44–46, 49–51; distinguished from privileges and immunities of citizens of the United States, 58, 101–104, 108; "modern" sense for Article IV, 26, 78–80; see natural law, privileges, and immunities of state citizens

Gergen, Mark: 82, 83
Ginsburg, Justice Ruth Bader: 90

habeas corpus: in English law, 4, 9; as privilege of Article IV in *Corfield*, 24, 26, 27; denial by southern states as reason for constitutional amendments, 40, 42; fundamental right, 44, 50; as privilege of citizens of United States in *Slaughter-House Cases*, 104, 108, 118, 123
Hale, Representative Robert: 45, 46
Hamilton, Alexander: 5, 21
Harlan, Justice John Marshall (first): on Article IV, 91–92; support for incorporation of Bill of Rights by a fundamental rights theory, 107, 115–117, 119, 120

Harlan, Justice John Marshall (second): opposition to incorporation theory, 122
Henderson, Senator John: 51
Hendricks, Senator Thomas: 40, 51
Henkin, Louis: 141
Hobbes, Thomas: 8
Holmes, Justice Oliver Wendell: 98
Hotchkiss, Representative Giles: 46
Howard, Senator Jacob: 37, 49–52, 107, 118
Hughes, Chief Justice Charles Evans: 121

immunities: in Blackstone as residium of natural liberty, 8, 9; chosen instead of rights by Continental Congress in drafting Article IV of Articles of Confederation, 13, 14
incorporation of Bill of Rights: effect on aliens of choice of clause used to make Amendments applicable to states, 115, 118, 140; privileges and immunities clause of Fourteenth Amendment rejected as basis for, 107–122; due process clause of Fourteenth Amendment used for, 117, 120–122
inhabitant: class entitled to privileges and immunities under Articles of Confederation, 12–15, entitlement limited to free inhabitants, 12; replaced in Constitution by *citizens*, 17–18, 21; replaced in Civil Rights Act of 1866 by *citizens*, 41
international law: customary, 141, 142; customary human rights, 141, 142; treaties, 141
Iredell, Justice James: 25, 26

Jackson, Justice Robert: 132, 133
Johnson, President Andrew: 42, 43
Johnson, Senator Reverdy: 40, 51
jury: English principle, 7, 9; considered fundamental by Bingham, 44, 45; service on a political and not civil right, 41, 56; right to in criminal trials, 117, 118, 120, 122; no right in state civil trials, 111, 113, 114, 119, 122, 140
jurisdiction: diversity, 21, 29, 30, 32–34; obtaining by service of process, 76, 92, 93; difficulty in exercising over nonresident as justification for differences, 68, 82, 91, 93, 97; to tax, 76, 82, 87, 88, 90, 130
just compensation: 30, 115, 117

Kasson, Representative John: 39
Kay, Herma Hill: 96
Kennedy, Justice Anthony: 90
Kerr, Representative Michael: 42, 54
King: of England, 1–4, 7, 8, 10, 11, 17; James I, 2, 6; James II, 7; John I, 7; George III, 6; William & Mary, 7, 8
Ku Klux Klan: 53, 55, 102, 105, 116
Kurland, Philip: 139

Lawrence, Representative William: 43
Levin, Daniel: 139
Locke, John: 7–9

Madison, James: on Article IV improvement over Articles of Confederation in *The Federalist Papers*, 15, 17, 18, 21, 71; on state violations of Articles of Confederation in Preface to Debates, 16, 17, 73; on Pinckney's objections to clause, 20
Magna Carta: 4, 5, 7, 8, 11
Marshall, Chief Justice John: use of natural law in *Fletcher*, 26; decision that Bill of Rights do not apply to state in *Barron*, 27, 107
Marshall, Justice Thurgood: 90
Mason, George: 20
Matthews, Justice Stanley: 115
Miller, Justice Samuel: on privileges and immunities in *Slaughter-House Cases*, 55, 69, 101–105, 107–110, 118, 119, 123, 124, 129, 130, 136, 141; on right to travel in *Crandall*, 129, 130; rejection of incorporation in *Cruikshank* and *Walker*, 114; discussion of takings in *Davidson*, 114, 115; voting in federal election of eligible voter as privilege in *Yarbrough*, 125
Moody, Justice William H.: 119, 120

Morrill, Senator Lot: 56
Morrison, Stanley: 109
Morton, Senator Oliver: 56
Murphy, Justice Frank: 122, 132

natural law: as philosophical tradition, 8, 9; distinguished from matters of policy, 9; basis for American Revolution, 10, 11, 25; application to Articles of Confederation, 13; in Supreme Court opinions, 25–27, 30, 36, 70, 122; as privileges of citizens in *Corfield*, 25–27, 70, 79; in state courts, 28, 29; basis for opposition to slavery, 30, 31, 38, 39; rejected as basis for article IV fundamental rights, 26, 69, 70, 78, 79; objections to use in due process jurisprudence, 122; academic proposals for use in privileges and immunities of Fourteenth Amendment, 139, 142; see fundamental rights
natural liberty: 8–9, 26, 139
natural resources: power to prevent exportation under Articles of Confederation, 15; as property of citizens of state in *Corfield*, 25; state power to preserve, 77–82; preference in commercial access for citizens invalid, 77–80; preferences based on cost differentials for preservation of resource, 77–81; whether can be reproduced as grounds for preference, 82
natural rights: 7–10, 26, 28, 30, 39, 70, 78, 139
naturalization: colonial 6; power of states under Articles of Confederation, 18; power in Congress under Constitution, 17, 18, 71; inapplicable to native-born persons, 33; included in definition of citizen in Fourteenth Amendment, 50, 67

O'Connor, Justice Sandra Day: 90, 99, 100

Parliament: power of, 2, 6, 8; not limited by colonial charters, 7; privileges of, 3, 7; source of rights, 7; colonists' rejection of authority for lack of representation in, 10
Paterson, William: 17
paupers: prevented from moving into local colonial communities, 5; colonial laws to prevent immigration invalidated, 6; and vagabonds excluded from privileges under Articles of Confederation, 12, 13; not excluded from privileges of Constitution, 19; exclusion by states held unwarranted, 132
Peckham, Justice Rufus: 118, 119
Petition of Right of 1628: 7
Pinckney, Charles: 18, 20
Pinckney, Charles Cotesworth: 20
Poland, Senator Luke: 51, 54
police power: 14, 28, 101, 132, 133
political rights: not defined as privilege or immunity under colonial charters, 4; colonial residence requirements for, 6; not privilege under Articles of Confederation, 13, 14; not a privilege or immunity of Article IV, 21, 22, 74–76; as privilege in *Corfield*, 22, 74; Bingham fear might be considered civil right, 42; not protected by Civil Rights Act of 1866, 41, 43; not included in congressional debate on Fourteenth Amendment as privilege or immunity of citizens of United States, 50–52; not exercised by nondiscretionary civil service employees or notaries, 74; exercised by police, probation officers, and public school teachers, 75; see aliens, attorneys, electoral office, voting
poor law: 5, 6, 9, 132
privileges: definitions, 2–4, 9, 13,14; equal, 5; of Parliament, 3, 7; against self-incrimination, 3; of trade and commerce in Articles of Confederation, 14, 15
privileges and immunities: Blackstone's discussion of, 8, 9; colonial, 1–5, 10, 11; of Romans, 3; see Articles of Confederation Article IV, privileges and immunities

of American colonists, of citizens, of citizens of a state, and of citizens of the United States, of Englishmen

privileges and immunities of American colonists: measured in charters by rights of Englishmen, 1, 2; to inherit and own property in areas subject to the English King, 2; to rights in England, 2–4; to rights of Englishman in colony, 3–4; travel, 4–6; taken abstractly as right not to be taxed without representation, 10, 11

privileges and immunities of citizens: described in *Corfield*, 22–26; protection of government, 23, 26, 41; enjoyment of life and liberty, 23, 26; habeas corpus, 24, 26; acquire and possess real and personal property, 22, 23, 24, 26, 43, 78; pursue happiness and safety, 23, 26, 43; institute and maintain actions in court, 24, 41, 78; equality in taxation or other impositions 22, 24, 26; domicil, 24, 41; transit, 24, 35, 41; subject to regulation for the general good, 24, 27, 52; inferred from Taney in *Dred Scott*, 35; right to bear arms, 35; speech, 35, 41; due process, 44; give evidence, 41; contract, 41; petition, 41; intent of framers of Fourteenth Amendment to secure, 37, 44–53; see fundamental rights, natural law, privileges and immunities of citizens of a state, travel, voting

privileges and immunities of citizens of a state (Article IV, §2, Cl. 1): limited to those that are fundamental, 22–24; political rights excluded, 21, 22, 74–76; undefined except as applied in particular cases, 30; modern sense as those bearing on vitality of nation as single entity, 26, 78–80; right limited to nondiscrimination on the basis of citizenship, 68–70; federal inability to authorize state abridgement, 74; municipal ordinances favoring city residents subject to, 84; distinctions permitted where noncitizen of "peculiar source of the evil aimed at," 77–85; recreational hunting not privilege, 78–80; public funding not privilege, 80–83; state as employer requires less justification for preference, 83–85; bases for distinctions between citizens and nonresidents, 86–99; comity concerns for other states, 93–95; difficulty in regulatory supervision, 97; forum shopping avoidance, 93–95, 98, 99; jurisdiction for service of process difficult, 91–93; jurisdiction to tax less than for residents, 86–91; marital relationship situs problems, 86, 95, 96; proprietary interests in state-owned resources, 25, 77–84

privileges or immunities of citizens of the United States (Fourteenth Amendment): discussed prior to adoption of Amendment, 31, 42–53, 100, 101; discussed in Congress after enactment, 53–58, 105; distinguished from privileges and immunities of citizens of a state in *Slaughter-House Cases*, 101–104, 107; rejected as source for applying Bill of Rights to states, 107–22; include laws, treaties and other express sources of federal rights, 123, 124; protection of federal government on high seas or in foreign jurisdiction as, 126, 141; inferred from functioning of the federal government to include voting of eligible voters in federal election, 124–126; occupation of land obtained by federal law, 124, 126; security in federal custody, 124, 126, 127; right to inform federal official of violation of law, 124, 127; right to discuss issues of federal law, 112, 113, 116, 121, 124, 127, 128; rights to travel, 128–38; federal government unable to authorize abridgement, 137; theories for future interpretation, 138–142; as customary international human rights, 141, 142

privileges and immunities of Englishmen: Magna Carta, 4, 5, 7, 8, 11; parliamentary consent to taxation, 7, 10; property, 2; trade, 4; travel, 4, 6; trial by jury, 7,9

property: passim; see Articles of Confederation Article IV, Bill of Rights, civil rights, due process, fundamental rights, privileges and immunities of citizens
public goods: 25, 74, 81, 82

racial discrimination: see African-Americans, discrimination, slavery
Randall, Representative Samuel: 49
Raymond, Representative Henry: 49
Reed, Justice Stanley: 132
Rehnquist, Justice William: 90, 137
residence: as part of definition of state citizenship in Fourteenth Amendment, 50, 51; distinguished from citizenship, 86–88, 97, 98; citizenship dichotomy rejected as basis for permitting discrimination, 86, 95; durational requirements, 6, 135–138, 141
Roberts, Justice Owen: 121, 128
Rogers, Representative Andrew: 46, 49
Roman Law: 3
Rutledge, Justice Wiley: 122

Shaw, Lemuel: 28
Slaughter-House Cases: arguments of counsel in, 101; effect of Article IV limited to non-discrimination in, 69, 70; distinction between privileges and immunities of citizens of a state and of United States, 101, 102, 119, 121; rejection of fundamental rights interpretation of privileges and immunities in, 58, 102, 105; listing of privileges or immunities of citizens of United States in, 103, 104, 123, 124; right to travel in, 103, 130; right to migrate in, 136; right to protection abroad in, 103, 141; relevance to incorporation debate of, 104, 107–112, 114, 118; dissents in, 104, 107, 110, 111
slavery: in Roman law, 3; contrasted with citizenship, 12, 18, 31, 40, 41, 43; as property, 15, 20, 28, 30, 31; abolition of, 15, 31, 38–40, 43, 53; as violation of natural law, 28, 30, 31, 38, 39; slave trade, 31
Shellabarger, Representative Samuel: 54
Smith, Representative Green: 39
Souter, Justice David: 139, 140
Stamp Act: 10
state action: necessary to find violation of the Fourteenth Amendment, 54, 56, 125, 126, 133, 134
state participation in market: 83–86
state sovereignty: concern for in Articles of Confederation, 16, 21, 70; ambivalence over of framers of Fourteenth Amendment, 38, 52, 53; as limit in interpreting Fourteenth Amendment, 55, 103
statute of limitations: 93, 94
Stevens, Justice John Paul: 128, 129, 134, 136
Stevens, Senator Thaddeus: 48
Stewart, Justice Potter: 133
Stewart, Senator William: 47
Stone, Justice Harlan Fiske: 121, 131
Sumner, Senator Charles: 56, 102
supremacy clause (Article VI, section 2): 47, 105, 123, 124, 129
Swayne, Justice Noah: 106, 107, 110–112

Taney, Chief Justice Roger: opinion in *Bank of Augusta* that corporations not citizens under Article IV, 29, 30, 70; opinion in *Dred Scott* stating African-Americans not citizens, 32–36, 40, 41, 51, 99, 123; dissent in *Passenger Cases* affirming right to travel, 34, 130
taxation: consent to by legislative bodies, 7, 10; equal treatment of nonresidents, 22, 24, 26, 68, 69, 96; immunity of government from in Articles of Confederation, 16; as justification for restricting subsidies and public goods to residents, 76, 77, 80–82; effect on equality of differences in amenability to, 86–91; on interstate travel, 129; on activity of citizens in other states when activity not taxed within state, 130–132
territories: privileges and immunities of Article IV applicable by statute to, 75, 78

Thirteenth Amendment: abolished slavery, 36, 53; relevance to interpretation of Fourteenth Amendment, 38; debate on, 39; as basis for Civil Rights Act of 1866, 39, 40, 43, 44, 54, 55; as privilege of citizens of the United States, 104, 123; as basis for laws against racially based violence, 126
Thomas, Justice Clarence: joining in Rehnquist dissent in *Saenz*, 137; call for re-examination of privileges and immunities clause in *Saenz* dissent, 138, 142; support for natural rights, 139
Thurman, Senator Allen: 56, 57
travel: colonial, 5–7; right in Article IV of Articles of Confederation, 12, 14, 99; as right of citizen in Article IV of Constitution, 24, 26, 34, 35, 69, 99, 100, 128, 129; in debates after Civil War, 42, 49; right implied from relationship to national government in *Crandall*, 129, 130; Justice Stevens distinction of separate rights, 128; to be treated as a welcome visitor, 128, 129; to enter and leave another state, 129–135; refusal of court to identify source, 133, 134; interference with by private individuals impairs privilege of citizenship, 133, 134; right of migration as privilege of citizens of United States, 135–138
Tribe, Lawrence: 139
Trumbull, Senator Lyman: sponsor of Civil Rights Act of 1866, 39, 40, 43, 49; contention that Fourteenth Amendment did not affect privileges of citizens, 55, 58, 105; as counsel in *Presser*, 116

Van Winkle, Senator Peter: 40
Varat, Jonathan: 82, 83
Vinson, Chief Justice Fred: 77
voting: colonial residence requirements, 6; not privilege in Articles of Confederation Article IV, 12–14; not privilege in Constitution Article IV, 22, 24, 25, 75; by free African-Americans, 33; whether civil right in discussion of Civil Rights Act of 1866, 49; not protected by privileges and immunities of Fourteenth Amendment, 50–52, 124–126; exclusion of women, 124, 125; privilege of citizens of United States against race discrimination in, 125; privilege of citizens of United States for eligible voter in federal election, 125, 126

Waite, Chief Justice Morrison: 112–114, 125
Washington, Justice Bushrod: 23–27, 29, 43, 46, 49–52, 54, 74, 77–79, 99, 107, 138
Wayne, Justice James: 28, 33
welfare: poor laws, 5, 6, 9, 132; limitation to residents constitutional, 80–82, 85; durational residence requirements, 135–137
wildlife: state interest in preservation of, 77; cannot favor residents in commercial use, 77, 78; resident preference upheld for recreational purposes where justified by tax subsidy costs, 78–80; academic theories on permissible preferences for residents, 81–83
Wilson, Senator Henry: 39
Wilson, James: 19, 20
Wilson, Representative James: 41, 42, 49

ABOUT THE AUTHOR

DAVID SKILLEN BOGEN is Professor of Law at the University of Maryland School of Law. He is the author of *Bulwark of Liberty: The Court and the First Amendment* (1984).